# The Poems
# of Robert Frost

*an explication*

# The Poems
# of Robert Frost

*an explication*

MORDECAI MARCUS

G.K. HALL &CO.

70 LINCOLN STREET, BOSTON, MASS.

Quotations from the following books are made with the kind permission
of Henry Holt & Co. of New York: *The Poetry of Robert Frost,* ed. Edward
Connery Lathem (Holt, Rinehart and Winston, 1969); *The Selected Prose
of Robert Frost,* ed. Hyde Cox and Edward Connery Lathem (Holt, Rinehart
and Winston, 1966); *Selected Letters of Robert Frost,* ed. Lawrance
Thompson (Holt, Rinehart and Winston, 1964); *Interviews with Robert Frost,*
ed. Edward Connery Lathem (Holt, Rinehart and Winston, 1963); *Robert
Frost on Writing,* edited by Elaine Barry (Rutgers University Press, 1973).

First published 1991
by G.K. Hall & Co.
70 Lincoln Street
Boston, Massachusetts 02111

10 9 8 7 6 5 4 3 2 1

**Library of Congress Cataloging-in-Publication Data**

Marcus, Mordecai.
    The poems of Robert Frost : an explication / Mordecai Marcus.
       p.  cm.
    Includes bibliographical references and index.
    ISBN 0-8161-7267-6
    1. Frost, Robert. 1874-1963 – Criticism and interpretation.
  I. Title.
  PS3511.R94Z785  1991
  811'.52 – dc20

                                        90-46594
                                        CIP

# Contents

# Acknowledgments

I owe many debts of gratitude for help in the writing of this book. The department of English at the University of Nebraska-Lincoln gave me a faculty development fellowship, which relieved me of teaching duties for a semester, during which much of my first version was written. My colleague Greg Kuzma made me the invaluable gift of a large file of articles about Frost. The librarians at the interlibrary loan service of Love Library helped me secure materials about Frost from places as far-flung as Europe, South Africa, and Asia. Individual chapters, at various stages, have been read and criticized by my colleagues Linda Pratt, Robert Knoll, Greg Kuzma, Robert Narveson, James L. Roberts, Stephen Behrendt, and Melvin Lyon, the last two having been especially generous in the scope and detail of their comments. Colleagues in the departments of anthropology, classics, life sciences, modern languages, and physics and astronomy provided helpful information. My wife, Erin Jenean Marcus, assisted me with her broad-ranging knowledge, her large fund of common sense, and her skill at interpretation. Linda D. Rossiter, with unfailing patience, taught me to write on an IBM word processor. The editorial staff at G.K. Hall did much to increase the precision and readability of my writing.

# CHAPTER 1

## Introduction

A book as long as this one deserves a short introduction. In writing this book, my intention is to fill a need not met by any of the excellent critical books and collections of essays about Robert Frost's poems. A few of these books provide analysis of up to 50 or 60 of Frost's poems. But none offers, as this work does, a basic commonsensical explication of all 355 poems in *The Poetry of Robert Frost* (1969), edited by Edward Connery Lathem, now the standard collection of Frost's poems. I introduce this material with concise summaries of Frost's life, theories, techniques, and themes as a review for the initiate and as important background for the newcomer. Many of my comments are guided by an awareness of the difficulties in reading Frost experienced by the hundreds of students with whom I have discussed his work, especially at the University of Nebraska–Lincoln, and also sometimes shown in what seem to me patent misreadings by published critics. I provide basic factual information about history, geography, literary allusions, and obscure words as they appear in the poems, and especially about grammatical structures that look tricky at first view. I make sparing reference to Frost's life as background to these poems (which might provide material for another book) so that I can concentrate on the poems themselves.

The book can be read continuously, for which purpose I provide transitions between and cross-references among poems, and it can also be read in part or used for ready reference. I omit comment on Frost's position among poets of America and of the English language, and on the various qualities of his superb accomplishments, except to remark that I think many of his neglected poems will prove enormously rewarding for the devoted reader and to acknowledge that a few of his poems are too trivial to have deserved publication but are nevertheless discussed here. In the first paragraphs of the analytic chapters, however, I do briefly point out which poems have achieved the most popularity and the highest praise.

Finding space to explicate such a large body of work forbids discussion of the poems' comparative merits. The need for basic clarification often leads to the devotion of more discussion to inferior poems than to some masterpieces. Also, with occasional exception, I do not comment on the poems' techniques. In addition to explication of Frost's poems throughout books about him, more of such material abounds in periodical articles and in chapters of books. Much of this large body of commentary has helped me, though my explications have more often been confirmed than established by it; in fact, in this book I comment on perhaps as many as 200 poems that have gone virtually undiscussed until now. I do, however, refer to other critics occasionally – mostly when they have distinctive or controversial but valuable points to make. I do not cite eccentric views, which abound and which might provide material for an essay. Explications as brief as mine can make no claim to definitiveness. I hope they will lead to profounder understanding than I can offer and to the kind of loving appreciation I have been barely able to suggest.

Except in this introduction, I write this book in the third person to help maintain an even-handed stance toward variant interpretations – both those that seem reasonable to me and those that seem worth citing even though I find them doubtful. Inspecting much of this criticism has increased my awareness of the subjective nature of much interpretation, and I make limited claims for the objectivity of my own. Still, I try hard to place common sense at the core of my interpretations and remoter implications at the fringes. Frost's poems present structures of both experience and ideas, and I strive to keep the experiences from getting lost in overelaborations of ideas. One result is that much of Frost's subtlety must go neglected; an attempt at full exploration of it would require a voluminous unwieldy book. The subtleties of technique and implications of idea and feeling in a first-rate poet can be inexhaustible. My explications are intended to provide a basis for such readings rather than to form the substance of them.

This book is best read with the accompaniment of the 1969 edition of *The Poetry of Robert Frost,* though the 1949 *Complete Poems*, supplemented by *In the Clearing,* will do as well, or – except for the original text of *In the Clearing* – even better. The text of the 1969 Lathem edition seems distinctly inferior to that of the 1949 edition, but it is now the accepted text and occupies more shelves than any other collection. I argue with its emendations or choices among Frost's texts only a few times. Readers with only the 1963 *Selected Poems* or one of Louis Untermeyer's various selected editions will have a generous number of Frost's better poems on hand and may, I hope, also take benefit and joy from this guide.

Reference to comments by other critics is effected by the numbers of bibliographic citations in parentheses followed by page numbers when these are useful.

# CHAPTER 2

## Biography

Robert Lee Frost, twentieth-century New England's most famous poet, was born in San Francisco on 26 March 1874 and named by his father for the Confederate general. For many years Frost's birth year was incorrectly given as 1875, but its true date of 1874 was established by the poet's designated biographer, Lawrance Thompson, and then authenticated by Frost himself (12:xlvii-xlviii).

The poet's father, William Prescott Frost, Jr. (1850-85), a native of New Hampshire and graduate of Harvard University, met the poet's mother, Isabelle Moodie Frost (1844-1900), when the two taught at Lewistown Academy in Pennsylvania. Married in 1873, the couple soon moved to San Francisco, where the senior Frost worked intermittently as a journalist and dabbled in Democratic politics. Mr. Frost lived so dissolutely, however, that his wife returned for a while to her family in New England, where the poet's only sibling, his sister Jeanie (1876-1929), was born. Mrs. Frost soon dutifully went back to San Francisco, where Robert lived for his first eleven years. Educated at home, Frost roamed the streets and waterfront retaining memories that appear occasionally in such poems as, "A Peck of Gold," "Once by the Pacific," and "At Woodward's Gardens."

After Frost's father died of tuberculosis in 1885, Mrs. Frost took her two children to her husband's parents in New England. Later, after living in several communities, the family settled in Lawrence, Massachusetts, where Mrs. Frost eked out a living teaching in private and public schools. Isabelle Frost, who had been brought to America from her native Scotland at the age of nine, was a conventional, refined, and cultivated lady, committed to the visionary ways of the Swedenborgian church, whose doctrines she tried to impress (with only small success) on her children. Robert graduated from Lawrence High School in 1892, where he was covaledictorian with his future wife, Elinor Miriam White (1873-1938). He excelled in most of his studies, including Latin, and published several poems in his high-school magazine.

In 1892 Frost began a few months of study at Dartmouth College, which he left early in 1893. In the fall of 1897, already married, he enrolled at Harvard as a special student, hoping to qualify as a teacher, but withdrew during the spring of 1899. In the intervening years he had worked as a light trimmer and gatekeeper at a textile mill in Lawrence, taught briefly at a district school and then at his mother's private school, and also put in short stints writing for two newspapers. In 1894 he had printed two copies of a poetry pamphlet – one for himself and one for Elinor White, who was then studying at St. Lawrence University in Canton, New York, and was determined not to marry until she finished college. Frost, feeling rebuffed after visiting Elinor to present the pamphlet and to press his suit, embarked on a four-week jaunt to the Dismal Swamp in Virginia and the Outer Banks of North Carolina. Elinor did become his willing bride in December 1895, after she had graduated from college.

A succession of children followed: Elliott (1896-1900), daughter Lesley (1899-1983), son Carol (1902-40), Irma (1903-?), Marjorie (1905-34), and Elinor Bettina (1907). (Elinor Frost also had a miscarriage in 1925, when she was past the age of 50.) Elliott succumbed to infantile cholera; Carol, despite having a devoted wife and son, killed himself in a despair born of aimlessness and disappointed ambitions; Irma, after an unsuccessful marriage, was institutionalized for severe mental disturbance, as had been Frost's sister Jeanie; Marjorie, the most-loved child, died of childbed fever less than a year after her marriage; and Elinor Bettina died two days after her birth. Lesley's two marriages were unsuccessful. Frost left behind four grandchildren, one of whom perpetuates his memory through Frost scholarship.

In 1899 Frost and his wife lived briefly on a farm near Lawrence. In 1900, shortly before the death of his mother from cancer, they moved to a farm near Derry, New Hampshire, purchased for his use by his paternal grandfather, who left him both the farm and an annuity when he died in 1901. During his Derry years, Frost developed his poetic gift, farmed in a desultory way, cultivated the friendship of farmers and agricultural workers, had a minor involvement in agricultural journalism, and placed a few poems in magazines. He also began what was to be an almost lifelong career as a part-time teacher, first in neighboring Pinkerton Academy and later at New Hampshire State Normal School at Plymouth, where he moved his family in 1911. He was, however, determined to become an important poet and during these years he composed a large number of the poems that filled his first three or four volumes (though many of these were much revised before publication). His notebooks from this period probably contained the germ for much of his later work.

Frost's most significant literary friendship had been with Susan Ward Hayes, coeditor of The *Independent,* the New York magazine that had published his first accomplished poems. In 1912, yearning for broader perspectives, richer literary companionship, concentration on his poems, and book publication, Frost took the proceeds from selling the Derry farm and moved with his wife and four children to England, where he had no personal contacts. They lived in Beaconsfield, Buckinghamshire (fairly close to London) for a year and a half, and then in 1914 moved to a country house in Gloucestershire, where they remained for nine months. Visiting Harold Monro's Poetry Bookshop in London, Frost began to make a wide range of literary acquaintances and friends, the most important of whom were Ezra Pound (1885-1972) and Edward Thomas (1878-1917). By the time he had met Pound, Frost had already placed *A Boy's Will* with the London firm of David Nutt, but Pound was among the first to celebrate this and Frost's second book in reviews. Pound also gave Frost further literary encouragement, criticism, and contacts, though friendship never flowered between them. Edward Thomas, near whom Frost lived during his stay at Gloucestershire, became the best friend of his life, and Frost was the key figure in Thomas's turning from journalistic hack work to the poems that distinguished his last three years before his death in World War I. Frost also numbered many minor poets and critics among his English friends. He came slowly to recognize their limitations, but still he visited the survivors when he returned to England briefly in 1928 and 1957.

With his first two books published in England and America, Frost returned to the United States in 1915 and began a long career during which he alternated between residences at various farms in New Hampshire and Vermont, many stints as a teacher and poet-in-residence at various colleges and universities, and a large number of public readings and talks. He was able to purchase the farms he lived on, but the small amount of farm work performed on them was done mostly by hired help. In the 1930s he established a winter home in Florida, where Elinor was to die in 1938. At the time of the publication of *North of Boston* (1914), he was the author of many of the century's best and most famous poems, but he had just emerged from an obscurity of almost twenty years. This fact and brute necessity made him jockey for adequate payment for magazine and book publications of his work and fueled his struggles for renewal of teaching contracts with conditions that would give him adequate income and time to write. His chief teaching positions were at the University of Michigan, Dartmouth College, Amherst College, and Harvard, but the longest and most rewarding stints were at Amherst. Most of his teaching assignments involved a small number of classroom hours, provided him wide leeway in subject matter, and allowed him to travel almost at will. Frost was a contentious colleague and a startlingly unconventional, occasionally negligent, but persistently stimulating teacher. He was a repository of independent-minded learning and, reportedly, an excellent talker on a large number of topics. As a teacher he was informal, discursive, and usually accessible and warm. He showed little interest in systematic analysis of literature but was receptive to the kind of speculative generalizations and epigrammatic perceptions  at which he excelled. A prolific letter writer and an occasional and pithy lecturer and writer of essays, Frost never tried to emulate the commitments to criticism and social commentary of such poet-critics as Matthew Arnold and T. S. Eliot and would probably not have been equipped to do so.

Despite his literary successes, college appointments, and esteem, he continued to be a restive spirit. Beneath his guise of cracker-barrel philosopher, which far too many people took to be his true nature, he remained a profoundly speculative man and a deeply troubled soul – in his concern and struggles with his poetic art, in his relationships with colleagues, friends, and family, and in his feelings about society, the nature of whatever creator there might be, the destiny of the human race, the salvation of his own spirit, and the proper use of his gifts. Despite a profound and mutual devotion, Frost and Elinor suffered from a disparity in temperament and argued about religious, intellectual, personal, and family matters – tensions that are probably reflected in some of his poems about human isolation, though Elinor is usually an object of admiration and devotion in his work. He suffered deeply over the failings and troubles of his children, with whom he may sometimes have been too competitive and authoritarian.

Frost also had major fallings out with some of his friends and showed some bigotry about people's sexual orientations, choices in marriage partners, and political and literary commitments (despite his  close friendships with many whose politics were to the left of his). He issued a slow but steady stream of books that won him a secure place in contemporary letters, but he was deeply jealous of the reputations of competing poets, many of whom were indeed unjustly rated as his equals or superiors. He stood in opposition to the New Deal and to the growth of left-wing politics in his country and among its leading intellectuals but wittily denied that he was conservative. Although widely read in science and history, Frost was dubious about modern theories of psychology and evolution and remained skeptical of much literary innovation, though he was intelligent and diligent enough to give it close attention. Eventually he accumulated many honorary college degrees, four Pulitzer Prizes, and other honors, but these did not seem to satisfy his need for a recognition that would make up for two early decades of neglect, and he was bitter at not receiving the Nobel Prize for literature. After the death of W. B. Yeats, he shared with T. S. Eliot the reputation of being the best living poet in the language.

Family tragedies continued to occur, culminating in the death of his daughter Marjorie in 1934, the death of his wife in 1938 after a heart attack, and his son Carol's suicide. But Frost persisted in writing and teaching and seemed capable of living alone. After Elinor's death, Kathleen Morrison, wife of the poet-professor Theodore Morrison, became his secretary, and there are indications that he tried to persuade her to abandon her husband and marry him. Their friendship, however, survived.

After World War II Frost was asked to serve as a cultural emissary to Brazil; in 1957 he made a triumphant tour of England and Ireland, receiving honorary degrees from three major universities. A year before his death he made a much-documented tour of the Soviet Union, where he succeeded in gaining an interview with Premier Krushchev, whom he seems not to have persuaded to diminish the cold war.

During all this time his reputation as sage and poet rose steadily. Long regarded as somehow inferior to such modernists as T. S. Eliot, Frost lived long enough to see a decided change in attitude toward his work on the part of professors and critics who were devoted to modernism. Frost eventually had the pleasure of receiving great praise from his old rival Eliot, although after 1942 his literary productivity descended to a trickle and his reputation rested largely on his past accomplishments and his public presence. His closest friend among well-known writers was the poet-anthologist Louis Untermeyer, with whom he conducted a long correspondence. He continued friendships with companions of his younger years and was well acquainted with many of the country's best-known writers, though he had serious breaches with some of them. Frost also sponsored and assisted in the work on biographical projects, including Lawrance Thompson's authorized biography. When its three volumes appeared in the years after Frost's death, some critics praised it for its thoroughness and accuracy, while others denounced it for its portrayal of Frost as a monster of jealousy and cruelty. Thompson's critical view, whose harshness may be more incidental than central, has been countered since Frost's death in many articles and at least two books.

Frost, who had been subject all his life to severe colds and bouts with pneumonia (some of which were perhaps induced by emotional distress), forged on in his lonely way, weakening slowly in his last years. He continued to give popular readings and to write poems, though his last productions were judged to be comparatively slight, and his friends had to protect him from the knowledge of harsher judgments of his later publications. Frost's last residence was an apartment in Cambridge, Massachusetts, from which he occasionally ventured forth to give readings. After an operation in December 1962, his heart finally gave way, and he died on 29 January 1963.

# CHAPTER 3

## Frost's Theories, Practices, and Themes

Most of Frost's comments about his poetry and the art of poetry were casual and unsystematic. They appear in a small number of essays and reviews, in scattered comments throughout his letters, and in recorded conversations. The most important prose writings are gathered in the short *Selected Prose of Robert Frost* (13) and in the more comprehensive *Robert Frost on Writing* (11). In these books, Frost's fundamental views on various aspects of poetry and on writing in general tend to be repeated in slightly altered phrasing and in a curiously pithy, meditative, and metaphorical style, as if he were groping for things deeply felt but hard to express. Most of his more important statements came late in his career, often in reaction to the contemporary literary situation. He was particularly critical of the experiments in modernism that flourished all around him; to his thinking, they often misled the young and diverted attention from his own sturdy accomplishments and struggle for individuality.

Regarding meter, Frost's most famous statement is the oft-repeated one that he would as soon write free verse as play tennis with the net down; this remark was probably inspired by his competition with the easy popularity of Carl Sandburg. Almost equally well known is Frost's claim that there are only two meters in English, "strict iambic and loose iambic" (13:18), which he modified with numerous comments on the function of variety, centrally praising the endless "possibility for the tune from the dramatic tones of meaning struck across the rigidity of a limited meter" (13:17). Elsewhere Frost speaks of words "breaking . . . with all their irregularity of accent across the regular beat of the metre [*sic*]" (12:80). In these formulas Frost recognizes the necessity of an interplay between metrical boundaries and rhythmic boundaries (or rhythmic phrasing) in traditional poetry. This function, noted by many critics and readers to be the effect of specific variations within regularity, has been the subject of sophisticated study in which it is characterized as including continuing effects of syntax, diction, meter, and other sound effects. As for word choice, Frost denounced poetic diction, opted for ordinary words, and spoke disparagingly of the archaic words he had allowed into some of his early poems (15:27, 172).

Frost's most famous claim to originality was his belief that he was the first writer to discover and to capture "the sound of sense" by developing an ear for "sentence sounds" and transforming them into poetry. Sentence sounds are Frost's equivalent for the way in which diction and syntax capture emotional tone. He seemed to think that such sounds function only when the language of poetry blends essential qualities of speech with the formal heightening contributed by meter and expressive concentration. Thus, though he never quite said so, he seemed to believe that his poems gain their special effects from a combination of speech informality and the formality of meter, metrical variation, varied sentence patterns, figurative heightening, and the rise and fall of emotion. "Everything written is as good as it is dramatic," he insisted (13:13), clearly having in mind the voices of lyric speakers as well as the effects of dialogue and narrative. Presumably he meant that lyric speakers act out their emotions through changes of stance and tone. Still, the overall notion of the sound of sense remains mystical and elusive, despite Frost's attempt to illustrate it with the claim that hearing speech through a door when we cannot make out the words communicates to us emotional tones like those captured in successful poetry – an idea that attempts to draw an equivalence between what the voice box does in producing and shaping sounds and how the relationships among words in sentences create meaning and emotion.

Allied to Frost's theory of the sound of sense is his claim that "the object in writing poetry is to make all poems sound as different as possible from each other" through the resources of "vowels, consonants, punctuation, syntax, words, sentences," reinforced by the all-important addition of meaning (13:17). Here Frost's ideas about form fuse with his concern for content or meaning, an emphasis that originated in his frustration with modern experimentalism that stresses sound effects, association, loose rhythms, pure description, and random closure as if these elements create good poems. Frost connected his ideas about form to all composition by remarking that "we bring up as aberrationists, giving away to undirected associations. . . . Theme alone can steady us down" (13:18).

Thus Frost closely associated form with meaning and with the process of discovery, an idea encapsulated in his famous formula about "The Figure a Poem Makes": "The figure is the same as for love. . . . It begins in delight, it inclines to the impulse, it assumes direction with the first line laid down, it runs a course of lucky events, and ends in a clarification of life – not necessarily a great clarification, such as sects and cults are founded on, but in a momentary stay against confusion" (13:20). The last five words here are Frost's most famous statement about poetry, forming both a description and a defense of the tentative and probing quality of his vision–but the entire statement is important, especially in terms of the parallel Frost draws between the evolution of a poem and the course of love. Frost saw poems as originating in an emotional impulse–a delight in a person or an experience–and, through the poet's acceptance of that impulse, resulting in a wise apprehension of the love object or the experience, no matter how temporary. The same perspective is expressed differently in his statement that "Every poem is an epitome of the great predicament; a figure of the will braving alien entanglements" (13:25), though here Frost reveals more of his conflicts and defenses. "Alien entanglements" suggests everything outside the self and thereby reveals that poems seek to make sense of both that which one loves and that which one must resist (presumably, the two are often fused).

This desire for momentary stays against confusion, for resistance to and embracing of alien entanglements, for the transformation of the delight of love into the wisdom of cherished possession, connects to Frost's belief in and use of metaphor. Poetry, he believed, was above all metaphor: "saying one thing and meaning another, saying one thing in terms of another, the pleasure of ulteriority. Poetry is simply made of metaphor" (13:24). The power of metaphor enabled him to approach the alien entanglement, the tentativeness of love, the immediate chaos of experience, and to give it that form which enabled him to live, to believe in life, and to resist dissolution. By way of metaphor, Frost sought "the one permissible way of saying one thing and meaning another," for "we like to talk in parables and in hints and indirections–whether from diffidence or some other instinct" (13:36-37). In his own case the diffidence reflected his tendency toward reclusiveness, while the other instinct was his combined quest for form and a universalization that would teach him how his struggles and resolutions were common to the human lot. Again, Frost's theories of expression lead directly into his philosophical quests, as can be seen in his description of "the height of poetic thinking" as "that attempt to say matter in terms of spirit and spirit in terms of matter" (13:41). This reveals that what he had called a matter of "diffidence or some other instinct" is really an imaginative means to a pursuit not otherwise achievable. Frost admits the personal nature of his quest when he declares that "anyone who has achieved the least form to be sure of it, is lost to the larger excruciations" (13:106) and by his description of "the background in hugeness and confusion shading away from where we stand into black and utter chaos; and against the background any small man-made figure of order and concentration" (13:107).

Frost attempted more technical description of metaphor when he told Louis Untermeyer, "If I must be classified as a poet, I might be called a

Synecdochist, for I prefer the synecdoche in poetry – that figure of speech in which we use a part for the whole" (12:485). Although critics have distinguished various uses of figurative language in Frost, he was impatient with such distinctions. He once declared, "After all these years I'm sorry when I'm caught unready for somebody's figure of speech – somebody's metaphor. The symbol will do for it all. But metaphor, parable, allegory, synecdoche – all the same thing" (10:42). Perhaps the greatest curiosity of Frost's lifework is that while it created his popular reputation as a plain speaker who presents radiantly clear scenes and actions, Frost himself stressed its metaphorical indirectness. The truth is that he combines directness with metaphorical or analogical suggestions in such a subtle fashion that the indirections can be overlooked by some readers yet interpreted by others as a sign that nothing of what he says can be taken at face value. The idea that Frost says one thing and means another proves to be somewhat misleading, as he might have realized if he had paid more attention to the relation between his own statement and some of the overinterpretation of his work that annoyed him.

It is easy to see that in practice Frost's prosody is quite traditional on the surface. Iambics are indeed the norm in his poetry and, like most traditional poets, he uses the five-foot line, or pentameter, more than any other. Some of his poems, however, consist of lines with two to four iambic feet; some are close to strictly iambic and others contain so much variation that they sound almost anapestic. Two facing pages in the 1969 edition of *The Poetry of Robert Frost* show in two sonnets, "A Dream Pang" and "Mowing," a variation from a regular iambic rhythm to a loose one full of anapestic substitutions, which give the second poem the feeling of conversation. Comparison of "Happiness Makes up in Height for What It Lacks in Length" with "The Subverted Flower" shows how three-foot lines can vary. In the first poem, they have a rapid regularity, an arrowlike momentum speeded up by frequently run-over rhymed lines; in the second, frequent reversals of accent, combined with an irregular rhyme pattern, created a sense of inner and outer struggle. A wide variety of manipulations of sentences and of interactions between sentence units and lines that end with strong rhymes show Frost playing natural speech off of poetic formality. This can be seen by comparing "Once by the Pacific" with "The Onset": the couplets of the first poem create a sense of granite units, whereas those of the other poem suggest a laboring, forward thrust against difficulties. Various degrees of casualness are achieved with the addition of extra syllables in some of Frost's poems including "The Lockless Door" and "Gathering Leaves." In contrast, such poems as the strikingly different "Stopping by Woods on a Snowy Evening" and "All Revelation" are notable for their relentless, but far from mechanical, regularity.

Frost is also a master of blank verse; most of his narrative poems are composed in it. In such poems as "An Old Man's Winter Night," "The Wood-Pile," and "Two Look at Two" he almost invents a new form: concise narratives of a briefly seen stasis or activity of one or two people possess lyric intensity, with verbal effects ranging from the haunting vowels of "An Old Man's Winter Night" to the subdued conversational plainness of "The Wood-Pile," in which the word choices reflects the drab surroundings and the speaker's groping bewilderment. In general, however, the blank verse of Frost is unlike that of Wordsworth, Tennyson, and Wallace Stevens, for it refuses to sing. It reflects the plainness of his characters' lives and it surges with the combination of their drivenness and their reflective hesitancies. Counting irregularities in it is easy enough but these will be found less to have local effects of quickly changing emotions or bursts of poignancy, as in Wordsworth and Tennyson, than to surge in various directions for long sweeps. When there is dialogue, Frost maintains the sense of distinctly different speaking voices without making use of local dialect. He boasted that his speakers could be identified by their tones alone, and this is true, except in a few cases.

The effects of prosody, of course, interact constantly with those of diction. W. H. Auden described Frost's style as "Good Drab," borrowing the term from C. S. Lewis's distinction between the plain and aureate styles of late-sixteenth-century poetry (60:340). Frost's plain style is also related to his concentration on the factual, his notion that his brand of realism presents the potato with the dirt brushed off (12:485). His is a style rich in detail, determined to stay with the exact but down-to-earth word, and bent on avoiding exaggeration. Thus Frost's language is loaded with a kind of understatement that goes along with his sly discovery of significance in ordinary places and his shy manner of pointing it out. Understatement is most obvious in such phrases as "Someone had better be prepared for rage" and "There would be more than ocean water broken" in "Once by the Pacific" and in the repeated first line of "Acquainted with the Night," but it is also present in the pretended groping of "I must go measuring stone walls, perch on perch," culminating in the explicit self-denigration of "the one world complete in any size / That I am like to compass, fool or wise" in "A Star in a Stone Boat." Late in his career, Frost still plays variations on understatement, as when he refers quietly to "the absolute flight and rest / The universal blue / And local green suggest" in "The Middleness of the Road," a poem whose title itself shows Frost's unwillingness to grasp at absolutes. Frost also varies his voice, from the gruff growl of "Provide, Provide" to the passionate flight of "The Master Speed" to the near-aureate combination of glory and gloom in the first lines of "Acceptance." But Frost's most representative understatement is an intensely observant quietness about matters of great significance – a quiet that sometimes makes the substance of scenes hard to recognize on first reading, as in the description of a field about to become a place of wartime slaughter in "Range Finding."

Frost's insistence that poetry says one thing and means another has doubtless contributed to the overreading and allegorizing of many of his poems. What he was chiefly after was the idea that his everyday scenes communicate general ideas about life or radiate out from commonplaces of scene toward heart-rending fixities and changes in human relationships. Thus he repeatedly uses the cycle of the seasons to reflect the ups and downs of human emotion, the borders between life and death, the stultifications and flowerings of human love, the arrest and rebirth of the human spirit. This is done rather obviously when such changes are directly associated with human feeling, as in "The Onset" and "Desert Places." It becomes more subtle in "After Apple-Picking," in which the images are archetypally natural yet contain hints of religion and of the life cycle; thus, the poem may be interpreted either as referring only to earthly concerns or as relating them to spiritual concerns beyond the earth. Frost treats love metaphorically in "Hyla Brook" and in "Putting in the Seed." The first poem merely implies its analogies to human life and then generalizes about both nature and people through its concluding "We love the things we love for what they are." The second poem, which relates planting seeds to the commitments and inseminations of human love, also features people who are so enthralled by witnessing this process in nature that they act out within the poem an awareness of analogies dramatized by the pervasive metaphors.

In all these representative poems, metaphors function structurally. They use synecdoche insofar as the scene is partial; that is, the scene is one occurrence of a phenomenon that extends to all of human life. Frost, of course, also uses a large number of supporting metaphors and sunken metaphors. In "Hyla Brook" the brook's "bed is left a faded paper sheet;" the sunken metaphor runs into a more distinctive metaphor. In "Range Finding" a cobweb is "diamond-strung" and later appears as a "wheel of thread / And straining cables," showing first beauty and then tension, which variously resist the incipient violence of war.

A brief listing of Frost's most famous scenic images also provides a compendium of synecdochic metaphors: snow, running water, pools, woods, roadways, houses, walls, stars, birds, flowers, insects. Each of these creates fully convincing scenes, sometimes with biblical overtones (often concerning Eden and expulsion from it). We are convinced the speaker is making his way across a field or road, standing at the edge of or penetrating a wood, listening to birds, fleeing from snow, gazing up at the stars, contemplating the fate of insects, gathering flowers, looking at or recalling fallen houses. And as we watch these experiences we feel an aura of the mysterious about them – something precious, regretful, aspired toward, resisted – the eternally problematic goal of life within them. Thus Frost puts a beautifully quiet numinosity onto the phenomenal glow of things.

Frost's metaphors are varied in structure. Usually a scene achieves coherence through its realistic descriptions, and thus a structure of scene and activity suggests a structure of experience, but sometimes one thing is systematically compared to another so that the scene dissolves into the metaphorical base. This happens in "The Silken Tent," which describes not a tent but a woman, who is systematically analogized to a tent swaying in the breeze. Another, rarer metaphorical structure appears in "To Earthward": what at first looks like a series of scenes relating the speaker to his physical environment turns out to be a series of analogies for his relationship to objects of love and to life in general. Stars may shine specifically in the heavens or may occasionally come down in the form of meteorites, as in "A Star in a Stone Boat," or as embodiments of the dog star, Sirius, in the wandering earthly dog of "One More Brevity." Houses may stand decayed at the edge of a burned-over scene, as in "The Need of Being Versed in Country Things," or seem to be projected from an experience into a haunt of the imagination, as in "Ghost House," or appear as imaginary embodiments of the past, as in "Directive." Seemingly real birds can hint at having a degree of human feeling and then reveal that they lack it, as in "The Need of Being Versed in Country Things," or reverse this process, unobtrusively turning from the purely phenomenal into voices for human feelings, as in "Acceptance," or start as richly natural phenomena transformed by the speaker's imagination into representatives of his own poetic urges, as in "Our Singing Strength." Frost's speaker's are notorious for their refusal to enter woods, but in "The Wood-Pile" and "An Encounter" they do indeed enter and penetrate as far as they can, only to find severe limits. Travelers gaze out of railroad trains at passing landscapes and people, weaving a variety of fancies about what they see. A man can drive along the middle of a road and be forced to recognize the limits of his vision and the pure guesswork of determining his final destination. Although Frost was impatient with detailed analysis of his poems, his occasional willingness to grant primacy to the analogies they suggest has provided justification for readers who, wishing to discard the scenes and perceive only ideas, elaborate on the ideas in almost any direction they please.

Insofar as many of these poems insist on limits or the importance of persistence in the face of limits, they resemble parables. But Frost can be more specifically parabolic, as when he tells little stories about the differences and similarities between bears and humans, or between monkeys and humans, and between ants and humans, and ends up with generalizations about what we can learn from these comparisons. Or he narrates everyday incidents, such as the vain effort to balance an excessively large load of packages in one's arms or the vain attempt to find one's way from room to room in the dark, and suggests such a heightening in the everyday experience that we guess what comment on human affairs is intended. In "On the Heart's Beginning to Cloud the Mind" he amuses himself with contrasting interpretations of isolated human dwellings seen at a distance at night from a railroad train, implying how our fancies make us optimistic or pessimistic about the alienation or bonding of couples and groups. But in a conversation years after writing that poem, he declares that he was thinking about the New Deal (15:133), implying that pessimism about human isolation is a trait of social engineers and that optimism is a trait of his own more conservative faith. However, these look like ideas about the poem unlikely to occur independently to most readers: possibly the author read them into the poem years later.

Mainly in the poems of his late career, Frost seizes intellectual subjects directly and writes sarcastic poems about science or about people who hope to control atomic weapons or about political radicals. In his satirical poems about social and political views, he places exchanges about such views into dialogues that more than hint where his own sympathies lie. He thereby abandons his power to create numinous scenes and gently haunting ambiguities but surely enjoys taking shots at those who think easy solutions to social problems are just around the corner or who revel in the prospect of the destruction of humanity because no one has listened to their sage advice.

This survey has suggested how Frost's poems may be classified by type. The more personal poems are usually first-person lyrics, though some are short narratives or meditations such as "Birches" and "The Wood-Pile." Frost's narratives play off human types against one another to suggest the superiority of one attitude over another, or the difficulty of seeing which attitude is better than another, or more often perhaps to simply show the desperate situations people get themselves into by going their own ways without an empathic understanding of the needs of those around them. These narratives usually present scenes sketchily and rarely include physical descriptions of the characters. Their dialogues seem natural and yet are cut down to the bare bones of confrontation, or occasionally accommodation. Sometimes they contain summary philosophical views, usually played off against one another rather than presented definitively. Often Frost's characters are at the end of a cul-de-sac, as in "A Servant to Servants" or "The Witch of Coös" or "An Old Man's Winter Night," and all they have left is the strength to face their tragedy and some hold on the residue of their dignity. At other times they forge on into the future, having learned something of value, such as the unstated balance of attitudes in "The Death of the Hired Man" or the limited preciousness of triumphant memories in "The Pauper Witch of Grafton." Although they are not the last poems he wrote, Frost seemd to consider his career concluded with two closet dramas, "A Masque of Reason" and "A Masque of Mercy." The protagonist of the first jokes about his inability to solve the problem of evil, and that of the second seeks to justify his personal and poetic efforts to maintain a provisional and informal faith.

Frost's views of the poem as "a momentary stay against confusion" and of poetry as showing "the will braving alien entanglements" do much to explain his core themes. His central theme might be summarized as the way in which humans relate to each other and try to maintain simultaneously a fruitful affection and dependence and also a self-respecting and self-reliant independence. The main accompanying theme is the desire to understand humanity's relationship to the cosmos or to the source of ultimate values. These themes might be simply defined first as love, friendship, family, and social relationship, and second as finding sufficient faith in the self, nature, and the cosmos to fuel persistence amid suffering and chaos. Frost sees people as essentially lonely and yet constantly dependent on the affection and support of others. This love and support, however, must not be bought or given at the price of the giver's or taker's individuality. Frost tends to show the struggle for survival and individuality in portraying people who face existence alone as they walk through field and wood, keep house alone, face the fact of abandonment by those closest to them, gaze into the sky or across threatening landscapes, and struggle to maintain their values and codes in opposition to others. Their achievements are marked by symbolic assertions of, or abandonments of, self-reliance. When humans are together, they join forces for mutual fruition or they struggle to adjust differing character traits and values, and often they remain in a state of struggle. Thus people are eternally alone with their weaknesses and strengths yet are also partly dependent on those around them. Frost alternates between praise of barriers and awareness that they must be bridged. Barriers preserve individuality but leave one isolated. Lovers conflict with each other but also enter into profound communion through mutual passion and attachment to the earth and its processes. If they see things differently, they usually find events or symbols that bring them together. They draw apart for self-renewal, but even then communicate across their separateness until they come together again.

The natural scene and the simple social arrangements of rural life provide the great backdrop for Frost's struggles with human bonds and with the cosmos. Scenes of emptiness and of simple struggles for loyalty provide for the dramatization of inner assertions and lead people to reach across the emptinesses to one another. The stars in the sky suggest cosmic that which are either meaningless or representative of the ideals toward which we strive. Singing birds take their meaning from our inmost intuitions but perhaps also represent forces outside ourselves that correspond to our richest values. The cycle of the year provides a model for our fears and hopes, losses and gains, despairs and assertions. The bounty of nature provides for our sustenance, but our depredations demand restraint if we are to survive. Nations war with one another but if they let barriers down excessively, humans lose their productive distinctiveness and sink from self-respect into sentimental and weak disregard of their rights and the fruits of their own efforts.

Although ideals are best realized in the present, humans need an aspiration toward absolute values if they are to maintain hope for some kind of permanent meaning and for achievement in return for their efforts. In swinging back and forth between the real and the ideal, humans test their capacities and extend their aspirations. They must accept their limitations and yet somehow strive for the infinite or at least for brief manifestations of it. Chaos exists all around them, but they must cooperate with whatever holds it back. Frost finds no final answers but never yields his posture of quest and affirmation except to make backward steps for the sake of retrenchment and renewal. He may lose sight of charity but he tries to demand as much of himself as of others. He may refuse to make final declarations about anything, but he insists on remaining a pursuer of the real and the ideal.

For Frost, people and the individual persist through inner strength and defiance. His view of human nature, then, is Emersonian, but his view of nature is more skeptical. Nature provides many emblems for the human spirit and for forces that assault that spirit, but it may or may not reveal those values and processes that humans have internalized. God, for Frost, appears to be the ideal whose sources, nature, and intentions are hard to be sure of but that can be known as it manifests itself in the human spirit and possesses a permanence toward which we aspire. Like William James, he believes that faith is tested by what it accomplishes, that as we create our values we tend to prove that they are real, no matter what their source. The poems say much about the diminishments of faith in the twentieth century, but Frost is curiously ambivalent about the persistence of faith in old-fashioned forms. He will not grant that our times are worse than others, and he still thinks that we can find adequate sources inside ourselves and save both the integrity and future of our country and of the human race.

# CHAPTER 4

## *A Boy's Will*
## (1913)

Frost's first book of poetry, *A Boy's Will*, was published in London by David Nutt in 1913 and in America by Henry Holt the next year. Although Ezra Pound claimed credit for discovering Frost, Frost himself had taken the manuscript to Nutt, and achieved publication on his own. The book was reviewed by Pound and by many well-known British critics and was widely praised as a fresh voice from America, though some of the reviews were casual and patronizing. Frost had brought most of these poems, and many later published in *North of Boston*, with him from America; several had been among his first magazine publications years earlier. For *A Boy's Will* Frost chose poems mostly lyrical and autobiographical, reserving substantially narrative poems for his second volume. The original table of contents divided the poems into three numbered sections and also included a gloss for all but two of the poems. From Frost's 1930 *Collected Poems* onward, in his collected and selected editions, three of the poems were omitted, one ("In Hardwood Groves") was added, and the gloss was dropped. In the following discussions, after all relevant titles, each item from the gloss is italicized, as in the original, and then bracketed.

The volume takes its title from part of the refrain to Longfellow's poem "My Lost Youth," in which it is enclosed in quotation marks: "'A boy's will is the wind's will, / And the thoughts of youth are long, long thoughts.'" Longfellow's 90-line poem reminisces lovingly about his boyhood in Portland, Maine, rehearses his dreams of the future, and at last becomes reconciled to his loss, a stance resembling that in many of Frost's early lyrics. Frost considered "Mowing," in which he claimed to have discovered his method of writing according to "the sound of sense," the best poem in the collection, and many critics agree. Other poems favored by critics and anthologists include

"My November Guest," "Storm Fear," "The Tuft of Flowers," and "Reluctance." Although it is not rated high, "The Trial by Existence" continues to interest critics because of its relation to Frost's formulas about his life and the recurrence of its themes and phrases in works as late as his two dramas, *A Masque of Reason* and *A Masque of Mercy.*.

## Epigraph to *A Boy's Will*

Frost's eight-line invitational pastoral "The Pasture" originally appeared as the introductory poem to *North of Boston,* but starting with his 1930 *Collected Poems,* it was made the overall introductory poem for all such editions, and Frost placed it first among the selections from *A Boy's Will* in his 1963 *Selected Poems*. It makes a more suitable introduction for his whole body of work than for the rather harsh poems of *North of Boston*. The poem seems to be addressed to the reader, though originally it may have been addressed to Frost's wife Elinor as an apology for friction between them; it has often been admired as a love poem novel in its combination of simplicity and intensity. The speaker is going forth in early spring to clear a spring of water in preparation for the growing season. He insists that his work will be fairly brief, and though he promises a quick return, he bids the person addressed to come with him. Thus he presents a conflict between departure, return, and accompaniment, with the hoped-for clearing of the water implying that things will now flow better and allow for clearer vision and/or reflections. In the second stanza, the subject switches from the spring to a little calf, whose recent birth also reinforces the seasonal self and presents the speaker as a caretaker of growing things, while the calf's future promises that it will stand by itself.

Many critics have found elaborate symbolism in this lucid lyric. John Lynen declares that the person invited stands for the average person who needs a guide to see the beauty in such a natural scene and that the poet's invitation is to a kind of vision different from everyday reality (38:22). Frank Lentricchia relates the poem to Frost's overall vision by proposing that the poet-farmer performs the acts first of cleansing and then of fetching, which tend to merge with the poetic acts of "making form out of chaos," which in turn relates to Frost's pattern of venturing out and then returning to enclosures as protection from threats to the self (37:24-25). Without disagreeing with such ideas, William Freedman proposes that the poem is chiefly an invitation to the sources of Frost's poetic art, with emphasis on stripping away a stale poetic inheritance, symbolized by dead leaves, and returning with revitalized poems, represented by the growing calf (232).

## Part I of *A Boy's Will*

*A Boy's Will* opens with a poem in which the speaker flees from the world but subtly bids those he leaves behind to follow him. "Into My Own" [*The youth is persuaded that he will be rather more than less himself for having forsworn the world*] is a sonnet in couplets. The phrase "the edge of doom" from Shakespeare's sonnet 116, "Let me not to the marriage of true minds," a figure for love's persistence before all obstacles, makes a slightly ironic comment on this poem's movement from dear people toward self-assertion. During Frost's youth a highway was any road traversing the countryside; in this case the road is an unpaved one whose sand retards wagon wheels. The scene is a real landscape, but its sparseness and metaphorical heightening help it also represent the speaker's state of mind. If the dark trees border a challenging realm, his prospective flight will carry him away from the shallowness of everyday commitments. His thrust toward independence becomes a mildly vindictive challenge to those he would leave behind, and he thinks of testing their love by fleeing and seeing if they will pursue. But if they should find him out, it will confirm not his affection but his truth to himself. His exaggerations suggest his awareness that he is showing off. The combination of his concealed longing for those he would flee and his emphasis on his unchangeability suggests that he cares more than he will admit for those he is fleeing. Donald T. Haymes argues that the youth neither enters the woods nor leaves anyone behind and that the woods do not stretch away into infinity. If so, there is no certainty that he will be as unchanging as he asserts, displaying an adolescent boastfulness of which the writer seems aware (92:454-55).

In "Ghost House" [*He is happy in society of his choosing*] the speaker also projects himself into a distant scene, either created by imagination or retrieved by memory, as he goes back to a ruined house with its own graveyard. Evanescence, combined with fertility, permeates the scene. The healing of wood and path predict the healing of human conflicts that are soon hinted at. Remembered toads and the bat and whippoorwill that haunt the deserted scene combine grief with an eerie nostalgic relaxation – preparation for the subtle recovery of the last two stanzas in which the speaker summons back departed figures from life and imagination. The summer star recalls the time when the ghost house flourished, and the mute folk seem as puzzled as the speaker. They are probably the dead whose names appear on the gravestones but also seem to be apparitions from the speaker's past. The lass and lad may represent the speaker and his lover as they were not very long ago, before experience brought friction. They are tireless because their memories live in his imagination, and they are sweet companions in view of time's disillusionments. As in "Into My Own," human relationships are tentative. There, Frost's challenge reveals shadowy tensions. Here, he longs for a past diminished by present tensions. Both poems show longing for an elusive ideal.

The speaker of "My November Guest" [*He is in love with being misunderstood*] is another lonely figure in a landscape even more internalized, and with a companion who blends with the scene, the season, and his inner life. In the central metaphor, autumn is a woman whose garments are the seasonal scene and its changes. She strides across the landscape, talking to the speaker yet unaware of his presence, and also so dear to and intimate with him that she is within him, thus combining detachment and closeness. The sparse details emphasize the transformation from summer and the imminence of another departure. Treading foot, rain-shedding skin, and thoughtful eye broaden physical involvement. "Stay" (in "Her pleasure will not let me stay") means to stop or stay in one place; "fain" (for glad) and "list" (for listen) are also archaic. The season's pleasure in itself – its indulgence in nostalgia and grief – compels the speaker to participate. But the third stanza reemphasizes the separation between him and his companion. Her wish for an explanation vexes him because he doesn't fully understand his own feelings, and the last stanza suggests why. He has loved such days in the past, aware that they are recurring reminders of renewal and mortality (as if to say, I have known such beautiful grief before – haven't we all?) The seasons's secretiveness represents the mysteries of natural process and resembles the inward-dwelling mood of "Into My Own" and "Ghost House." The speaker continues struggling for value in conflict, and he enjoys his combined intimacy with and distance from his grief and its embodiment in the season.

"Love and a Question" [*He is in doubt whether to admit real trouble to a place beside the hearth with love*] tells a pithy story in a balladlike manner. The scene and action are vivid and stark, yet the communication between the speaker and the pauper-stranger, and then between the speaker and his bride, are shown through action and imagery rather than through statement. The capitalization of "Stranger" makes him larger than life and may associate him with deities. An inverted phrase saying that all he carries is care shows his poverty and woe, and his plea for shelter is almost wordless. As the bridegroom tries to judge whether he should offer shelter and discovers that his needs are different but greater than the stranger's, he probably resolves not to allow himself to yield to them; the bride seems present behind his shoulders, a reminder of young lover's need for privacy and for freedom from the sorrow and decay they hope will never overtake them. This may be their wedding night, and the bride seems to feel sufficiently protected. As the poem ends, the bridegroom's anger shows through in his mildly sardonic disgust at his own emotional gestures – easy gifts and sayings that deny what is most needed – but this disgust isn't sufficient to make him admit the stranger with his gloomy aura. The bridegroom's indecision emphasizes his dilemma and the depth of his contemplation, and the final phrase, "The bridegroom wished he knew," is also slightly sardonic, implying that no one knows how to solve such a dilemma. The speaker here, unlike the detached ones of the preceding three poems, has drawn close to one person, delights in companionship amid solitude, and feels threatened from the outside. Critics have found here an early expression of Frost's conflicts between personal and social commitments.

"A Late Walk" [*He courts the autumnal mood*] engages the desolation of autumn with less loneliness than does "My November Guest" and less threat than does "Love and a Question." The first two stanzas show order created by the stubblefields and the harvest. The half-closed garden path promises healing, like the footpath of "Ghost House." The sustenance-deprived birds and almost-leafbare tree parallel the speaker's desolation, so that he fancies that his thoughts affect the scene. But the conclusion closes up a circle of grief and then leads out of it: the speaker returns to a beloved person, and his giving her a flower joins them in awareness of the season's sadness and affirms their bond, overcoming the sense of desolation. His carrying the flower to her "again" makes both the seasonal and the personal gesture a lasting ritual between them.

Desolation persists in "Stars" [*There is no oversight of human affairs*], a grammatically difficult and verbally old-fashioned poem. Images of stars and snow create the feeling of isolation in a puzzling universe, as they will with more elaboration and sense of threat in many later poems. The thick cluster of stars and heavy drifts of snow parallel arenas of human struggle. Their "keenness" for our fate suggests both that they are aware of our difficulties and that they want to see us suffer. Stars and snow beckon us toward death as a state of rest and peace. But the last stanza denies all this. This elliptical passage can be completed by placing *are* between "stars" and "like." Frost states that the stars (and by implication the snow they resemble) have no feelings about people and also no knowledge or insight. They resemble a statue of Minerva, the goddess of wisdom, but possess a blankness like that of a statue's marble eyes, which denies the goddess's wisdom. The condensed wording creates some obscurity, and the concluding lines show an icily esthetic wonder notably different from Frost's later stoical, and sometimes whimsical, detachment.

In "Storm Fear" [*He is afraid of his own isolation*] the winter of "Stars" has come close to home: into the speaker's dwelling place and his inner spirit. The title encapsulates the opposition: storm outside and fear within, an opposition reinforced by the personification of the wind as an animal. The wind "works" and "pelts" the window with snow, showing its angry wish to destroy—a wish stifled by its self-created surroundings and, psychologically, by man's clever opposition to the beast's rising anger. The beast issues a challenge to confront it, even to yield to its hypnotic power. The human strength within the house seems slight. If there are only two adults and a child within, and the speaker singles out "those of us not asleep," possibly it is both his wife and child who are asleep and therefore safer than him. He may be the only one aware of dying fire and rising snow and, mostly, their (centrally his) powerlessness. The unplowed dooryard and road are a threatening level across which access to the barn's supplies now seems impossible. "Owns" means both possesses and admits, showing the speaker's reluctance to accept his situation. The rhyme of "doubt" has been delayed from ten lines back, emphasizing his struggle. The conclusion looks forward to a long night and anticipates that the family's isolation may be too much to bear, yet it makes only a muted cry for help. The concluding lament seems more a description of a typical extreme situation than an expression of self-pity. The irregular lines and rhyme scheme reinforce the sense of muscular attack and cramped resistance.

In "Wind and Window Flower" [*Out of the winter things he fashions a story of modern love*] the personification of both the flower and the winter wind results in *A Boy's Will*'s first comprehensively allegorical poem. Addressed to lovers and referring to some dwellers in the house as awake that night, this poem suggests possible analogies between its allegory and the lives of the men and women elsewhere in this volume. The interior of the house offers security and domestic comforts: a canary sings over the protected window flower. The winter breeze notices the sheltered flower but goes about the outdoor winter business he really loves. He passes her by and comes again at dark, presumably to give her more serious attention than earlier. The wind is divided between his outdoor concerns and the attractions of the flower and her world; his attraction and her response are symbolized by the way winter wind shakes a window. The personifications intensify in the last two stanzas, in which both wind and flower may "perchance" be revealing feelings: he tries to woo her from her comforting world to his wild and raw one and she declines his advances with shy gestures. The wind seems happy in the flight that takes him far away. The flower retains her comfort and the wind his freedom. This allegory seems a variation on portrayals of detachment and commitment elsewhere in these poems, and its contrast of threatening wind and comforting interior make, for a light-hearted variation on the conflict in the poems just before and after it.

"To the Thawing Wind" [*He calls on change through the violence of the elements*] signals an exuberant change from winter to spring. Its speaker stands alone, addressing a prayer to a force that is already at work and, through one of Frost's rare identifications of himself as a poet, stressing the imaginative and creative potential released by natural forces. As an imminent thaw predicts the earth's renewal, the plea that the speaker's window may melt moves from realism into mild fantasy. The image of window sticks arranged like a hermit's crucifix around a narrow enclosing room (like a monk's cell) shows that winter has reinforced the speaker's tendency toward isolation and spiritual stasis (though the religious imagery may also have positive connotations). The wall picture and the book that he wants to see in disarray suggest overdependence on the forms of art and thought. The scattering of his poems implies that they need more of the wildness and self-release he may achieve by being thrust out into the world of spring.

"To the Thawing Wind" addresses a power in both nature and the speaker. "A Prayer in Spring" [*He discovers that the greatness of love lies not in forward-looking thoughts*] moves subtly toward a more conventional prayer. No pantheist, Frost finds in nature forces like those within the human spirit, stemming from a realm or power he can never quite identify or explain. Frustrated by his limited vision, he yet tries to take joy in its puzzling promise. The poem celebrates an immediate fullness made poignant by limitations that create a framework: the poem's opening contrasts the present fullness of spring to its uncertain results, and its conclusion contrasts the meaning of spring's fullness to any ultimate significance and permanence God may give it. The two middle stanzas show motion and change but also imply a striking state of arrest, or at least the speaker's sense that these moments are somehow timeless.

The orchard's white flowers are incomparably beautiful by day, but by night their ghostlike contrast to the darkness must shine like a happy haunting. The bees' dilation suggests a spiritual opening out. The darting bird is a hummingbird, whose famous whirling wings and ability to hover in flight focus the poem's combination of motion and arrest and offer a single figure in contrast to the bees' social swarm. The "this" of "For this is love" refers specifically to flowers, bees, and bird, but also generally to the whole scene and to the speaker's response. "Nothing else is love" rather than excluding human love, stresses that the scene and the human response to it are sufficient illustration of the power and impulse toward love. The last three lines suggest that humans can't see the ultimate meaning of the love force and that if God doesn't make plain its meaning, we must accept and persist in living out love for its sake as well as our own.

That presence of a beloved only hinted at in "A Prayer in Spring" becomes the focus of "Flower-Gathering" [*nor yet in any spur it may be to ambition*] (the gloss here continues from that for the preceding poem). In full spring or summer the speaker has been absent from the woman for a day, and he returns in the evening with a treasure of flowers, a counterpart to the autumn scene of "A Late Walk." The woman had walked part of the way with him when he left in the morning in order to show her loving reluctance to part with him, however briefly. Morning and evening have special auras – morning a sharp glow, evening the dissolving light of dusk. Worn and soiled by his travels, the speaker wonders exaggeratedly if she still recognizes him, and he feels changed by his lonely concerns. Thus he asks if she remains silent because she no longer recognizes him or because she sees that he is changed and may be more separate from her. Still, his surprise that her puzzled attention is for him rather than for the flowers that separated them shows his awareness that she really knows him. He has exaggerated her look of sympathetic wonder into a division, but her (and his) continued response shows him to be confident of her love and delighted to be back. What he has gathered becomes his tribute to her; he bids her find and treasure in the flowers the scope of his devotion, which measures the intensity of his separation from her. What had seemed like ages can again be seen as a brief time because they are now together, and the flowers he has brought back are a concentrate of his time away and of his feelings for her.

In "Rose Pogonias" [*He is no dissenter from the ritualism of nature*] (this sentence is continued in the gloss for "Asking for Roses," which Frost omitted from subsequent editions) the lovers of the preceding two poems stand together, mutually aware of themselves and the scene. The ritual here is more self-conscious than in "A Prayer in Spring" and less one-sided than in "Flower-Gathering." The meadow they stand in is enclosed by trees and shaped like the sun, to which it forms a temple, and so perfect in its flowering appearance that it can be inspected as though it were a jewel (it must be many thousands of times larger than a jewel). The inundation of odors and heat blends its oppressiveness into a sacramental richness. The temple it creates provides a world for them, protected from everything outside. They bow to the sun in a form resembling, yet strikingly different from, ancient sun worship, for the object of their gesture is not the sun but the beautiful orchids they gather ("pogonia" and "orchis" are interchangeable terms for a kind of purple or white orchid). They felt free to pick the flowers because no one would miss them from this isolated spot, which seems to belong particularly to them.

The grass is (or seems to be) scattered because the meadow is drenched with water, but there appear to be as many flowers as spears of grass, and their winglike petals blend into the atmosphere. As a second act of worship, the lovers ask that the spot be spared any further predations. The general mowing would be a harvesting of the grass, resembling their own taking of flowers but differing from it because they gather as a gesture of love, not out of careless disregard. Or if chance will not have it so, they want the place undisturbed – that is, until something of its present holiness is diminished. Thus this couple pays homage to the unity of this scene by first gathering its orchids and then praying that the place be left undisturbed except for them. The poem trembles between awe for a beauty that is sufficient to itself and a mild criticism of those who would not tread here with the right respect for its mystery. Donald T. Haymes argues that the flowers and flower-gathering in "Flower-Gathering" and "Rose Pogonias" symbolize the esthetic way of life and the production of poems that set the speaker apart from the surrounding community, and he thinks that only such a view explains the combined gloss for "A Prayer in Spring" and "Flower-Gathering" (92:458).

In "Waiting" [*He arrives at the turn of the year*], the only blank-verse poem in *A Boy's Will*, the speaker contemplates a natural scene in isolation and then thinks of his absent lover, with whom he hopes to communicate by the poem's summation of what he felt while absent from her. The scene is a mown harvest field. The speaker enjoys his isolation and the occasion for dreams. In this faint light he would look like a specter, but that word chiefly connotes his dreaminess. Senses of sound and light blend as he calls the opposition of the sun's dying rays and the moon's rising light an antiphony; this reference to sound emphasizes the silence of the scene, which will soon be broken. He loses the sense of his location, fixed thoughts, and identity among haycocks all alike.

The opposing lights are the last of sun and first of moon, which keep shadows from forming until the moon's rays can dominate. The speaker dreams not about but "upon" these lights and then on a variety of creatures – birds, bats, and insects – perhaps more at home than he, for they may be close to mysteries that he can not grasp. He is hiding from everyone as represented by two kinds of birds, the hunter-minded bat, and then small creatures such as crickets which gather in harvest piles, where they silence themselves for protection and make their rasping or chirping noises to test for alien presences. Those who would seek him also evade him, this parallels his own inner divisions. He also dreams of the book of poems he carries: Frances Palgrave's *Golden Treasury*, alluded to in a series coordinate with references to nature to show how its relevance has been subdued in this atmosphere of pure dream (though perhaps he is contrasting its world of imagination to the withering sweetness of autumn, symbolizing the opposition of the permanence of imagination to the natural fullness and decay in the scene, whose ambiguities entrance him). The elliptical next-to-last line declares that he dreams most on the absent beloved, for she could fulfill or at least share the dreams in which he indulges in her absence. The last two lines imply an apology for his absence, as if his aloneness has been a necessary but concealed gesture.

"In a Vale" [*Out of old longings he fashions a story*] is an allegorical fantasy, reminiscent of poems by Poe and of "Wind and Window Flower." In this poem, however, the relationship is between the speaker and a world of flowers that he imagines have taken the shape of maidens who hovered at his windows during the nights in response to his loneliness, bringing him visions of the creation's source. The inverted phrase "the maidens pale / I knew so well" means he knew the flowers, under circumstances that made them appear like maidens. The different flowers came to his window, each with her own distinct face and voice. They knew ("wist") such a lonely person was glad ("fain") to hear them. Their haunting gave him a feeling for the mysterious unity, source, and meaning of everything in nature. But though he boasts of his knowledge, he does not reveal it. This both undercuts his claim and playfully implies that its dreamlike source is inexpressible.

"A Dream Pang" [*He is shown by a dream how really well it is with him*], a hybrid sonnet, presents a more convincing dream, its material reminiscent of man-woman conflicts in other poems. In his dream the speaker has withdrawn from his lover and is pursued. The suggestion that he has done wrong echoes the implied disillusionments of "Ghost House," and the tension between the couple looks forward to such poems as "The Thatch." The reference to song swallowed in leaves connects to communication with his lover through flowers and poetry in other poems. The speaker's shadowy and hidden stance suggests his retreat from human contact, his elusive character, and his lover's reluctance to find him. She stands at the edge of the forest (as Frost's masculine speakers often do), resists the urge to pursue him, and waits for his apologetic emergence. In the sestet, he claims that he was not trying to evade her, for he was close by, apparently obscured by trees at the rim of the wood, yearning but unable to call out to her.

This is the strongest emotion he recalls from the dream – a "sweet pang" that lasts. Presumably his refusal to call was a partial denial of his guilt, and both denial and guilt help him take a secret pleasure in her pursuit of him. This shows that his claim that he did not dwell aloof is not wholly true. He offers only a partial proof – that the wood wakes – that is, that the realm of his dream has become a reality they share and that she is present to prove this as well as the strength of their bond. Thus the separation and ritualistic pursuit he has dreamed present a more complicated reality than his concluding statement admits. He has actually confessed his aloofness, the satisfaction he derives from combating and denying it, and a feeling that these rituals cement their relationship and return him to reality.

The couple of "In Neglect" [*He is scornful of folk his scorn cannot reach*] oppose not each other but people who are disappointed in them. Having chosen an independent path, they ignore conventional ambitions and provoke looks of disapproval and disregard. They respond sometimes by looking "mischievous," vagrant, [and] seraphic," a strange combination. The mischievousness is delight in their impropriety, the vagrance is admission that they have no direction and yet are pleased with their freedom, and the seraphic (angelic) quality is the delight in their happiness and a sort of eye-rolling, self-mocking despair at not being understood by busybodies. They must try to feel forsaken because they have no real cause for such feeling – they are glad to be disregarded – but have a duty not to disappoint those who seem to enjoy disapproving of them. The poem may have originated in Frost's casual approach to farming while trying to establish himself as a poet.

The speaker of "The Vantage Point" [*And again scornful, but there is no one hurt*], a quasi-Shakespearean sonnet, has emerged from woods, perhaps those he stands outside of in "Into My Own" and dreams of in "A Dream Pang." But here the detachment is crisp and relaxed, quietly contemplative about the human lot. He has emerged from trees – or the thought of enjoying their special privacy – though it is only dawn, and lies down on a meadow where he can see evergreen trees, cattle, and human dwellings at a distance. The scene, opposite to obscuring woods, contains its own opposition: the dwellings of the living and the graves of the dead. The casual choice between them, "whichever are to mind," shows the speaker placidly considering the painful inevitability of death.

The poem's transition at "And if by noon" implies that he can spend many hours in such contemplation, and his turning on his arm echoes the intimate physical contact with earth from the first stanza's "reclined." Heat reflected from the earth reminds him of his own vitality, which moves toward a stronger and closer engagement with nature. As his breath shakes the bluet, he is identified with both the breeze and the flower and draws closer to earth. His body's pressure has bruised the plant beneath him, which gives forth the odors of its juices. He has turned his thoughts from mankind back to nature, where the small-scale provides a special comfort: radiance, firmness, smell, and touch without personal commitment. At last, he looks down into the simple world of the ant, a social realm ruled by instinct and tensions but without anxiety.

"Mowing" [*He takes up life simply with the small tasks*], predicting the idiom and powerfully engaged understatement of Frost's mature poems, is a hybrid sonnet: fourteen lines of very loose iambic pentameter, all except four lines relaxed and speeded up with anapestic substitutions, and the rhyme scheme irregular. Despite the speaker's aloneness, the poem exudes a stronger social sense than many early Frost poems that include people. The experience is presented in past tense, but the scene seems to live in the speaker's mind as he remembers its quiet intensity in terms of overheard conversation between his scythe and its tasks – a conversation really his own, though he must struggle to understand it. The scythe's whispering voice dominates the scene, and as he tries to understand it, he half-dreamily rehearses his physical and emotional engagements. He feels the sun's heat on his body and jokes that perhaps the scythe whispered in awe at the silence. But with "It was no dream," the tone modulates into deep seriousness as he senses that anything expressed by such labor cannot be about easy achievements or mythical fancies.

"Anything more than the truth" would be exaggeration that couldn't correspond to the satisfying feeling that joins physical and emotional exertions to their results. The sentiment parallels Frost's, the poet's, efforts to avoid overstatement and to achieve verbal power through language true to fact and feeling. The "earnest love" gathers beautiful flowers (Frost's beloved orchids) with a sympathy for their weakness and for the inoffensive small snake that darts away. Frost spares only a moment's concern for these interruptions, flower and snake providing flashes of color in the otherwise tawny harvest scene. The next-to-last line, set off as a whole sentence, is one of Frost's knotty didactic statements. Fact stands in opposition to dream in the contrast between fancied rewards and real ones already mentioned, but fact as "sweetest dream" paradoxically gives fact the rich satisfactions of dream that hover over the whole entranced scene. Thus "fact" seems to be the act of labor itself, the specific harvest, and the reality confirmed by scene, labor, and harvest. The punctuation shows that this key line is not spoken by the scythe. It has emerged from the speaker's consciousness, after which he can return to the scythe's quietness before he and it depart into the accomplished leisure which the poem has been moving toward.

"Going for Water" also expresses delight in an accomplishment, this one rare and shared rather than lonely but typical. The satisfaction here is less the result of effort than of a series of contrasts and surprises shared by a childlike couple. They do not seem disappointed that the well is dry, for their delight is in investigating the sparse or hidden brook and traversing the chill autumn fields and woods in whose ownership they delight. Once in these woods, they are briefly distracted from their goal by the entrancing moon, made vivid by the autumn bareness and making up for the diminishment of other sights. They play a game of hide-and-seek with the moon's rays, celebrating their own companionship, and then bringing each other back from this playfulness to the more serious concern of seeking water. Their listening before they looked for the brook, though slightly anxious, parallels their playing with the moon, and the repetition in "We heard, we knew we heard the brook" rises from anxiety to excitement, preparing for the last stanza's satisfactions. Here, all is delight in the spare beauty of sounds and sight, the sounds contrasting with the hush of attention. The initial sparseness of details emphasizes the brook's small-scale survival and helps make it a beautiful spot where the water's pearls and silver blade are more important than the need for water, perhaps more important than their fields and woods – a source for the future (predicting brooks as spiritual sources in several later poems). As in many of these poems, the couple are happy in their lonely ritual.

## Part II of *A Boy's Will*

"Revelation" [*He resolves to become intelligible, at least to himself, since there is no help else*], the only poem in *A Boy's Will* without a specific setting, makes a series of statements about the concealment and revelation of identity, feeling, and place, and concludes with hide-and-seek as a metaphor for relations between people and with God, though this metaphor doesn't quite fit the first two stanzas. The poem's narrative point of view also shifts slightly. Frost opens by declaring that we use teasing words to separate and protect ourselves from others but are truly distressed until others recognize our feelings and establish contact. We would prefer to be understood from behind our masks, and we say that it's regrettable that we must come out and directly show our feelings. Clearly, it is easier if we can use protective indirection and still be understood. The last stanza's "But" pushes aside the preference for partial concealment, though not completely. Those "who hide too well away" still may preserve some degree of indirection.

The scale from babes to God implies that children's games need to be put aside for maturity and that God's concealments are often too painful to endure. Hence, Frost issues a kind of cry for God and humans to come out of hiding. The speaker seems almost trapped or lost between children who don't know any better and God, who ought to know better. As Lawrance Thompson proposes (46:131), the contrast between concealing words and explicit ones may also be Frost's metaphor for poetry, suggesting a need to combine ideas and feelings with metaphors and yet be sure his readers don't miss his ideas and feelings–a method some critics feel he abuses by relying on statements and obvious metaphors. This poem communicates much urgency and pathos through such devices as the contrast between "light words" and "agitated heart" in the same person, the conjunction of "literal" and "inspire," the urgent call to God, the emphasis on "Must speak" created by its two strong syllables and the rhyme with "hide-and-seek," and the relaxed hush of the poem's last six words.

Lawrance Thompson (20:120-21) reports much about the background of "The Trial by Existence" [*and to know definitely what he thinks about the soul*] (this sentence is continued in the gloss for "In Equal Sacrifice," which is omitted from subsequent editions) This poem asserts that some of God's concealments are necessary. While still in his teens, Frost came to terms with the suffering of those he loved by puzzling out the idea that our souls, coming from heaven, could not make a valid choice unless that choice could be forgotten. Frost had put the idea into an early version of the poem, which he didn't complete for some fifteen years. Meanwhile, he had been further influenced by Plato's myth of Er (described in his *Republic* and elsewhere) that says each soul, after death, chooses a new life but drinks of Lethe's forgetful waters before being reborn, and by William James's *The Will to Believe*, which celebrates the will's struggle against adversity as a triumph usually well rewarded. All but the last of the ten stanzas are set in heaven, given a classic twist by reference to asphodel (the grass of the Greeks' heaven). The souls referred to are not newly created but those of the dead. They have all been warriors, or warriors are the ideal type.

In any case, these dead look forward to further challenges. The comparison of heaven's whole light to colors alludes to Shelley's "Life like a dome of many-colored glass / Stains the white radiance of eternity," in "Adonais," his elegy for Keats. Frost's reference partially reverses Shelley's preference for eternity, for Frost celebrates a courageous return to earth – the trial by existence – a ritual offered to all the souls and sweetly tempting to them, although most of them seem just to look on while the more courageous heed the call. The latter are told of the good they can expect (though life is a "little dream") but especially of the suffering. But now the poem switches from the "devoted souls" to an inevitable single one who accepts the challenge. As the others admire this soul, God asserts that it will find no comfort in knowing it chose its fate, for if life is to gain meaning through suffering, the choice must be forgotten.

God weds the spirit back to matter and, for one soul at least, the cycle starts again. The last stanza stands back from this scene and generalizes that all souls, or the most fortunate, choose their suffering, to "choose greatly" meaning to accept an earthly lot that encompasses much suffering. To be stripped of pride is to accept being cast down, which in turn is the price of life. The one close of pain is death. We may be crushed and mystified by suffering and death, but in the end we know that we chose our fate and that it made us what we are. Frost's elaborate and puzzlingly elitist myth turns out to be a fable of identity. His myth may be blurred, but its exhilarating conclusion suggests that we can console ourselves by trying to imitate the "bravest of the brave."

In "The Tuft of Flowers" [*about fellowship*] Frost puts aside the desperate isolation of "Revelation" and the desperate affirmation of "The Trial by Existence" to return to a gentle melancholy that quickly eases itself with assurances of human bonds. Here again the speaker is concerned with the mowing of grass and the fate of flowers, though this time neither as mower nor simple observer. He is afield to turn the already mown grass so the sun can finish making hay. Surprisingly, he doesn't seem personally acquainted with the mower, perhaps someone hired for the occasion. At first the scene impresses him by its empty silence, and his loneliness is associated with the harvest's sense of finality, which contributes to his feeling of separation. Then with the first of three transitions, he sees a butterfly, whose swift action parallels his own yearnings but whose disappointment in not finding a flower standing where it recently rested reinforces its desolation as well as his own. Questions without reply, which the speaker fancies the butterfly shares with him, must be about dear vanishing things, people, and time.

After the second transition, the butterfly is more persistent than the speaker, and the poem's passive mood leads toward enjoyment and delight as the butterfly discovers a flower, probably an orchid again, spared by the mower for his own life-loving pleasure rather than to draw attention or approval. The mover's gladness had risen to the brim of feeling, as does this poem's. No message was intended but one was delivered, the speaker says, as the third transition sweeps the poem toward various summary statements. The empty silence in the third stanza is replaced by waking birds and a whispering scythe recalled from the mowing he did not witness. The figure of the mower, recreated in the speaker's imagination, becomes a brotherly sharer of life's tasks and rewards. Frost's speaker reverses his earlier protest about separation, declaring that the shared aims and loves accompanying labor join people even when they are physically apart. Donald T. Haymes argues that here Frost's speaker has changed from his view earlier in the volume that others misunderstood him in his withdrawal to a new view that he had also misunderstood other people (92:461).

"Pan with Us" [*about art (his own)*] is a novel portrait of the woodland god of classic arcadia, part man and part goat, whose reed-pipe music represents spontaneous poetry celebrating rural beauty. Unlike the eternally youthful classic figure, Frost's Pan is old. He is pleased by the absence of people from his woodlands, whereas the classic Pan delights in the companionship of shepherds. Frost's New England landscape is growing deserted, which seems to please Pan, who is nevertheless frustrated that the sparsely settled area and the strange new nature provide little material for song. Pan tries to persuade himself that the sounds of nature don't need his augmentation. His ambiguous feelings persist as he acknowledges that his music is irrelevant to a scene satisfied by its own music. In conclusion, Frost declares that Pan celebrates old pagan virtues not appropriate here. But the natural world still charms this Pan, who lies down and looks around in frustration at subjects not quite right for his tradition or gifts. The poem combines frustration at the poet's inability to find both myths and an audience in a new world that seems self-sufficient. In this historically confusing allegorical poem the self-satire is unfocused as is Frost's puzzlement about being a poet of the new world.

The self-satire in "The Demiurge's Laugh" [*about science*] is stronger. The demiurge is a classic deity who creates the physical world according to eternal principles, and a demon can be an evil spirit, or a spirit half man and half god, or a spirit with exceptionally powerful drive or haunting force. Here Frost's Demiurge-Demon seems to be a creative force assumed to know why things are as they are (or he is the principle of being that exists without understanding its own nature). He seems concerned with power and reality, not with explanations. Frost's gloss implies that science (perhaps including philosophy) gives such mechanical answers to our thirst for knowledge that they leave us despairing. His speaker runs through "the sameness of the wood," an accurate description of unmarked forests and a metaphor for nature as massive enigma. His pursuit is joyously obsessive, but as night falls (falling light also representing failing knowledge), he receives a properly unforgettable put-down for his presumption. The Demon (like Shakespeare's Puck) is everywhere and nowhere, and it reverses things by pursuing the speaker and mocking his efforts. Its sleepiness and atavistic pleasure in wallowing show it sufficient to itself (it is a crude version of A. E. Housman's "heartless, witless nature"), and its laughter partly represents the speaker's self-mockery. At the end, the speaker realizes that his pursuit is doubly vain (self-celebrating and useless), and so he embarrassedly pretends that he was engaged in a different and casual pursuit. He realizes that the Demon is really indifferent to his pursuits and his pretenses, and at last he rests to recover his equilibrium. Frost seems to be mocking excessive rationality but not necessarily praising intuition or faith.

## Part III of *A Boy's Will*

"Now Close the Windows" [*It is time to make an end of speaking*] is another poem of seclusion and exclusion, probably addressed to the speaker's lover, who this time is asked to share his mood of strangely dreamy satisfactions that create a minimal bond. The year and bird give up their song, and the marshes sink into the near-silence of dead vegetation, their silence contrasted to the persistent wind. The speaker is so saddened by this diminution that he doesn't want to hear the restless and foreboding sounds of autumn or winter. He wants to retreat inside house and spirit and look out at motions that balance between destructiveness and a vitality hinting at eventual rebirth. His stance constitutes a strategic retreat into a calm and hypnotic wonder about the sadness of things that neither scene nor intuition can explain or change.

Not in the original editions of *A Boy's Will* and first published in a magazine in 1926, "In Hardwood Groves" first appears in its present position in the *Collected Poems* of 1930. It continues a cluster of four poems set in autumn. Its repetition, its restrained metaphors showing energy in nature, and its stoical gaiety about renewal from suffering are signs of Frost's mature style. The speaker watches autumnal transformation with familiarity, affection, and pain—all announced in the first stanza—with his disappointment at the end of shade from summer sun and his combined distress and pleasure in the matted brown leaves that neatly cover the earth. Next he looks ahead to the renewal of spring, when the tension of sunlight and shade will recur, but he remains mindful that the leaves must decay to help new birth. The "things coming up" in the spring seem reborn even before the leaves fully enter death's realm, as if the leaves must suffer the sight of the life they are losing. The thrice-spoken "must" emphasizes human resistance to death, and the personifications in the last stanza's "pierced by flowers" and "dancing flowers" intensify the projection of human suffering and delight into nature. The italicized third "must" prepares us for the self-assured desperation of the last two lines. We are told repeatedly that such a process can't be escaped, though we may fancy freedom from it in another world. The concluding "I know" suggests not only sharp observation but also personal experience, showing that the death-rebirth process here represents spiritual change within life as well as possibilities of change through death.

"A Line-Storm Song" [*It is the autumnal mood with a difference*] is a more joyous poem of renewal, blending released energy in nature with the freshening of love. Line storms are equinoctials, this one identified by Frost's gloss as autumnal, so the time must be about the first of September. The difference here is that the speaker is overwhelmed not by grief over the declining season but by the cleansing release of energy sweeping over the landscape. The initial scene shows an absence of people, the fading of hoofprints, and inundated flowers, all emphasizing the contrasting presence and vitality of the lovers. Next the speaker sings of the birds who are present but in hiding, the torn woods, the shattered rose – all contrasting to two human presences and his song. He and his lover become part of the storm as the wind propels them and creates a resistance their singing must challenge. The rain-drenched air and earth provide an occasion for their exuberant persistence, rewarded by the pressing of goldenrod against her breast, creating a decorative brooch that joins her to the season and is an emblem of her beauty and triumph. The last stanza celebrates a return to primitive and timeless being as the swelling wind and water recall prehistoric ages when the land they stand on was still sea. This sense of freshness parallels the purification that once swept doubt from their love. The last two lines help make this song part of a ritual of renewal, both placing the couple in opposition to, and making them part of, the stormy scene.

*A Boy's Will* concludes with three more autumnal poems dramatizing attempts to hold onto the past. Each is different in tone. A wish for the stasis of last moments permeates "October" [*He sees days slipping from him that were the best for what they were*], paralleling the stasis of fullness in "A Prayer in Spring." There, activity was vigorous but small-scale, emphasizing a combination of permanence and evanescence; here, the inevitable dissolution of autumn is presented as quiet, slow, and enchanting. The poem prays not to God but to the essence of the October morning. The next day's wind may waste the leaves, but the speaker prays that this will not happen yet, admitting that his is one of those hearts that wish to be fooled into seeing a delay. The wished-for slow release of leaves from the trees, reinforced by an amethyst aura of dream over the landscape, will create such an illusion. Although he wishes this delay for himself, he says it is for the grape's sake – "if they were all" meaning as if they were all, for their fullness takes on a holy quality to which he assigns his own need for tender respect. The grapes' leaves, "burnt with frost," signal the year's imminent death. He prays that winter be delayed so that the fruit can be harvested before it is ruined.

The repetition of the prayer for the grapes shows them huddled protectively against a wall, symbolizing the speaker's need for emotional protection until and while he endures the winter.

"My Butterfly" [*There are things that can never be the same*], the first of Frost's poems to have been published, again projects the speaker's autumnal feeling into nature, here represented primarily by the creature whose death he mourns. The poem is addressed to the dead butterfly as if it were still present, reinforcing the sense that the speaker's grieving self is his real subject. The poem opens by declaring that the butterfly's dear and envious flowers, as well as a predatory bird, are gone. The speaker remains alone in the scene, which he studies to see that winter has not confirmed its grip. The seasonal chill makes the butterfly's flourishing seem long past. Once it flew surrounded by beautiful companions, impulsive in its mating but frail. At that time the speaker was not painfully reluctant to see its transience; he was quietly joyful in the scene. As his memory of the creature's frailness intensifies, he projects onto it his reluctance to admit such weakness. His wishes had made him see the butterfly as almost permanent. The butterfly's destruction is softened by the speaker's view of its death as a gentle gathering by a God who could not let it achieve too much independence. For two stanzas he applies the situation to himself.

God's jealous protectiveness becomes a conspiracy against his own ambitions. His dreamy aspiration parallels the butterfly's, and he sees himself, like the butterfly, delighting in nature's magical atmosphere of grass, breeze, and flowers. When he fell silent at the thought of dangers, he was comforted by warm winds that continued their promise by flinging against his face the butterfly's beautiful but mortal-dusty wing, an emblem of hope about to be cancelled. Between the last two stanzas despair arrives; he finds the broken wing as confirmation that the butterfly and his hopes have long been dead. As it lies with the season's leaves, partly protected, the wing becomes a symbol of a resigned but not hopeless waiting.

The somewhat passive stance of "October" and "My Butterfly" persists in "Reluctance," but here the landscape is more detailed, the speaker's motion implies a more active quest, and the resistance to what seasonal decline symbolizes is more assertive. The speaker has been ranging fields, woods, and walls, Frost's typical gesture of independence. The broad perspective from "the hills of view" is across both the landscape and the world of experience. As he returns home, he accepts the end of the flowering season and perhaps some loss of independence. Then for two stanzas he describes the remnants of autumn as they lead from summer to winter. The oak tree still preserves a few leaves, whose scraping of the snow crust will perhaps disturb the sleep of others; he expects to be awake. Like some of his feelings, the leaves and flowers are no longer in motion. Part of him wants to pursue life's promises and renewals, but another part is dubious. The final stanza's generalizations gently show how the preceding scene and action represent human relations as well as feelings for nature. This stanza asks a long rhetorical question. The heart of man is a repository of faith, courage, hope, and a tenacity less dreamy than the tenacity of "October" or the resignation of "My Butterfly." The speaker is left standing with his regrets, seemingly bound to accept the season's end, just as he has had to accept love's endings, but hopeful that the season and love may be renewed.

# CHAPTER 5

## North of Boston
## (1914)

Frost's second book, *North of Boston*, was published by David Nutt in London in 1914 and by Henry Holt in New York later the same year. Several of the poems seem to have been written during Frost's first year in England, though some are probably revisions of draft material brought from America. The striking changes in style and Frost's invention of a novel blank-verse narrative form represent highly self-conscious efforts partly based on his keen attention to common human speech. The book's initial favorable reception in England and America was stronger than that given *A Boy's Will*; many reviewers recognized the novelty of Frost's blank-verse narratives, with their dialogue that combined convincing conversational idiom with traditional meters. The poet was also praised for his penetrating observations on human nature and a strong regional sense, though he later objected to being considered a local colorist. A few reviewers and some later critics, however, were so puzzled by the experimental element in his meters that they could not recognize them as blank verse, and some critics thought that Frost should turn his gifts to prose fiction. As the years passed, the reputation of the book and many of its poems continued to rise, and some critics think the volume remains his best. In 1948 W. G. O'Donnell argued that the book represented a tremendous advance over *A Boy's Will*, which he saw as uncertain in voice, excessively old-fashioned in diction, and often close to sentimentality. *North of Boston*, on the other hand, he found to be Frost's most enduring accomplishment because of its striking portrait of New England life and wonderfully honest representation of isolation and fractured human relationships (115).

Among its poems still considered masterpieces are "Mending Wall," "Home Burial," "A Servant to Servants," and "The Wood-Pile," while the frequently anthologized "The Death of the Hired Man" and "The Black Cottage" are rated only a little behind those. The volume contained only two lyric poems, "After Apple-Picking" and "Good Hours"; the first of these remains among the most praised (and analyzed) of American poems. Some critics mistakenly identified all the narrative poems as dramatic monologues, though only "A Servant to Servants" truly fits this form. Before settling on the book's present title, a phrase he recalled from advertisements for New England properties, Frost considered calling the collection *Farm People* or *New England Eclogues* (20:433). The book's dedication read: "To E. M. F. THIS BOOK OF PEOPLE," hinting at yet another possible title. The one Frost settled on suggests a cold and distant climate, as well as isolation and proud local individuality.

The much-anthologized "Mending Wall," often quoted out of context, is sometimes mistakenly said to declare that "Good fences make good neighbors," which – as Frost sometimes had to point out – is the formula of the poem's antagonist. (When Frost visited Russia some of his hosts were troubled by his reciting this poem, for they thought it might be a comment on the Berlin Wall.) Frost himself declared that he was on both sides of his poem's wall and perhaps was both of its characters, engaged in an internal debate (15:257), though the speaker resembles Robert Frost and the neighbor is unlike him. In a prefatory note to the volume, Frost says that this poem "takes up the theme where 'A Tuft of Flowers'. . . laid it down," implying a continued concern with fellowship. Before describing his wall mending, the speaker opens with reflections on forces that don't love walls: frost which makes the stones in walls spill in a pleasant tumble, and the crude disregard of hunters who run with nasty dogs. The gaps with which he is concerned are the kind caused by frost and lead to the engaging task of restoration that he shares with his neighbor.

Since the speaker is the one to initiate the shared task, his objections must be exaggerated or partly fancied. The men seem to enjoy the outdoor task and scene, but the narrator can't resist twitting his neighbor about the possible uselessness of the wall. He may be questioning himself as much as the neighbor, whom he treats like a child by ridiculing the idea of the trees on either side of the wall threatening one another and then mockingly referring to the fencing up of cows, which neither man owns. His main idea is to make his neighbor think of good reasons for what they are doing. But his questioning grows nastily sardonic when he implies that exclusions offend him personally. His "offense" (punning on a fence) becomes a sort of chant as he repeats, this time out loud, the poem's first line: "Something there is that doesn't love a wall." He follows this with the emphatic "That wants it down," reaffirming his doubts about his neighbor's formula that good fences make good neighbors. His judgments grow stronger as he compares his neighbor to a stone-age primitive with a darkened mind as simple as his stone weapons, stupidly delighting in repetitions of his father's unexplained wisdom.

This concluding crescendo suggests that at least for the time being Frost was more on one side of this wall than the other, but the poem remains as teasing as its speaker. Usually seen as a cluster of philosophical and social themes, it also depicts an appealing scene and task made more engrossing by the problematic nature of both characters. How overbearing and defensive, or merely thoughtfully inquiring, is its speaker? How dim-witted or merely taciturn is the neighbor? The large body of commentary on this poem includes discussion of it as social allegory and as an illustration of a personal struggle for balance between withdrawal and commitment, individuality and socialization, as this conflict occurs throughout Frost's poetry and life.

The readily accessible and popular "The Death of the Hired Man" also treats conflicts between individuality and social values, as manifested in the exchanges between Warren and Mary and acted out by their disloyal former hired man, Silas. As farm husband and wife debate whether to take Silas back, they examine his plight and claims, his strengths and weaknesses, and reveal their own feelings by gestures as well as words. Their talk focuses on how Silas's disloyalty is a failure to fulfill obligations, which leaves open the question of their obligations to him. The characters and values of Mary and Warren are contrasted in the foreground, while their reminiscences sketch the character and history of the decent but weak Silas. Mary's handling of Warren shows a wise, tender, and firm attitude toward both her husband and Silas. Her principles are mercy and love, whereas Warren, bordering on harshness, appeals to justice, law, and mutual responsibility. Silas's plight is greater than theirs, his attempts to preserve self-respect having divided him between loyalty to longtime employers and self-delusion about his own value and deserts.

Silas's obligation to them is halfway between the formal and the informal, and Warren feels betrayed by Silas's not respecting what Warren has done for him. A truly formal obligation is represented by Silas's rich brother, but Silas is too aware of his own weaknesses to ask for family help, though with his adopted family he can save his pride, for he knows they value his abilities and care about him. Silas's conflicts between self-rejection and inflated pride are shown in the background by his verbal fights with Harold Wilson, the former college student turned teacher. Mary understands the mutual respect between them, which was partly soured by Silas's defensive pity for Harold's bookishness and lack of practical wisdom. Mary's report on Silas's weak condition and wandering attention contrasts to Warren's self-righteous rehearsal of Silas's flaws and his own grim determination to tell Silas that his disloyalty keeps him unwelcome.

Mary's physical gestures suggest openness and control, whereas Warren's show him working out aggression. Warren does, however, show admiration and possibly forgiveness for Silas when he recalls his farm skills, especially in haying. The conflict between Mary and Warren is delicately balanced in their famous alternative definitions of home. Warren's calling it the place "Where, when you have to go there, / They have to take you in" appeals to formal, almost legal, responsibility. Rather than contradict his view, Mary's reply qualifies it subtly. For her, home is "Something you somehow haven't to deserve," meaning not an obligation fulfilled but rather a source of generosity or mercy. This thoughtful exchange leads Warren's and Mary's tones to merge, her tenderness admitting more criticism and his harshness softening but then veering back toward practicality as he goes to confront the already dead Silas, perhaps with some acceptance. Mary's last speech and the description of the cloud striking the moon provide gentle foreboding, and the couple's final handclasp, initiated by Warren, implies a bond of love including Silas.

The essentially plotless "The Mountain" says little about human relationships, but even here the farmer who is interviewed by the narrator shows independence and abrupt behavior through his failure to have climbed the local mountain and his quick conclusion to the interview. The poem may at first seem pointless, but it reveals an intense exchange of ideas. Both of its characters are in a state of wonder, but the farmer has already formulated his thoughts about the scene and clarifies them for himself in enigmatic declarations, whereas the speaker is surprised by everything he meets, and he struggles both to understand his own emotions and to handle and understand the farmer. The speaker's situation is leisurely, but the farmer interrupts daily tasks to satisfy the curiosity of a dallying stranger. After the farmer is carried away by his thoughts and reminiscences, he returns with somewhat mysterious abruptness to practical things.

Having slept in a strange village and gone out before breakfast to examine the countryside, the speaker is struck by how the mountain overshadows the town and is impressed by the waste and disarray left behind by a retreating river. After crossing a bridge and meeting the farmer in an oxcart, he wonders if all this territory belongs to the town in which he slept, but when he is told he is now in Lunenberg, he knows that the countryside is part of a different township. The farmer answers him with a clipped frankness that modulates into affectionate arrogance toward his own villageless township and its overshadowing mountain. To the speaker the mountainside looks impenetrable, and the farmer confirms the difficulty of access to it – a subject that stimulates both men's imaginations. The speaker is entranced to discover that though the farmer gives a vivid and enthusiastic description of a brook, high up on the mountain, that is cold in summer and warm in winter, he has never climbed the mountain. The narrator is also thrilled at the prospect of seeing the world from a great height and he silently imagines the grandeur of climbing the mountain and achieving such a sight.

Although the farmer is also imaginative, he is cool to this flight of fancy, but he continues to talk with delight (now more reserved) about the mountain's brook. He justifies himself by mentioning another person who partly climbed the mountain but merely offered the existence of a lake on an Irish mountain as proof of the existence of this stream, which he also never reached. Then the farmer apologizes for his not having ascended, explaining that the clothes proper for such a task belong so much to his everyday life that they wouldn't be right for climbing. The crucial line "'Twouldn't seem real to climb for climbing it'" seems intentionally ambiguous, suggesting an embarrassment at leaving the world of practical, "real" concerns to prove the existence of something less useful, and also suggesting that the vision of the brook doesn't need proof and is more real if created by the imagination. The farmer's combination of interest and detachment is reinforced by his not being sure of the mountain's name; it is probably Hor he says, but "Hor is the township, and the township's Hor" meaning that mountain and township overlap, and its dwellers live between the realms of the practical and the imaginative.

In his confirming statement about the brook's temperature in winter and summer, the farmer's intelligent insight into why the water seems to change temperature with the seasons is combined with his imaginative delight in affirming what seems: "But all the fun's in how you say a thing." He seems a counterpart to the inquiring speaker, who is a counterpart to the sharp-eyed yet dreamy poet: the everyday man, imaginative yet embarrassed by the imagination and half-conscious of the conflict in his own ways of seeing a man whose embarrassment leads to his abrupt return to everyday things. Laurence Perrine, who defends the farmer against critics who see him as an unimaginative clod, points out that the real Mt. Hor is twenty-five miles from the township of Lunenberg, which either helps explain the farmer's confusion about the mountain's name or indicates that the locale is fictional (209).

"A Hundred Collars" has more plot than "The Mountain," but its interest lies less in dramatic action than in a satirical contrast of two characters, neither of them very pleasant, but the seemingly vulgar and distasteful one proving more attractive than the refined one with his disgust for ordinary life and the body. The situation is introduced through a pithy overview of Doctor (Professor) Magoon's character as it will be illustrated in his encounter with Lafe, a collector for a rural newspaper, with whom Magoon briefly and reluctantly shares a hotel room. That Magoon, not yet named and sketchily identified, sends his wife and children to summer in his rural birthplace, where he is thoroughly uncomfortable during his brief visits, shows his alienation from the local folk.

Stuck with a late-night delay at a railroad junction and desperate for a room at the overbooked local hotel, Magoon must face the night clerk's challenge that he share an occupied room. Magoon's delicate determination receives one rebuff after another when he joins the occupancy of the countrified Lafe, who, half-naked and half-drunk, is changing into a shirt large enough for his expanding frame and drinking from a bottle that seems his regular companion. Lafe boasts that he isn't afraid and soon offers to send Magoon 100 size-14 collars that he has long outgrown – monstrously, it seems, for he has now reached size 18, suggesting a contrast between his bullish frame and Magoon's frail one. Lafe's drunken offer and his gesture to remove Magoon's shoes disgust the professor, who must endure Lafe's monologue about his country rounds as a newspaper man. Though Lafe is just a collector, his editor asks him to learn what the reading public wants. However, he seems to be half pretending and half fooling himself, and his joviality takes another turn as he describes his delight and ease among his genial rural customers. His pleasure in the country, in the people, and in his undemanding job contrasts with Magoon's alienation from country people, his grinding application to scholarship, and his stinginess.

Lafe understands Magoon's finickiness at the offer of his bottle, and perhaps he presses his soon-abandoned offer of his 100 collars as a continued assault on snobbery as well as a condescending gesture of friendliness. As Lafe leaves for an evening's entertainment (without his bottle), it is evident that Doctor Magoon will get little rest that night. His character and scholarly devotion have kept him from contact with his roots and with mankind, whereas the uncouth Lafe leads a richer life. Lafe lacks the keen sensibility of the farmer in "The Mountain," but he shows a valuable sense of humor, shrewd insights into human nature, and some understanding of his own limitations.

"Home Burial" may not be as popular as "Mending Wall" and "The Death of the Hired Man," but it is Frost's most critically acclaimed and intensively analyzed narrative. Again, Frost deals with barriers between people – in this case a husband and wife who have recently lost their first child and who handle their grief in strikingly different ways – according to their characters and expressive capacities. The locale is a New England farm with a family burial plot in the yard, illustrating familiarity with death, which partly accounts for the husband's taciturn handling of his grief. The poem opens with intense looking and severe gestures between the man and woman, as she gazes from a stairway window at the backyard grave of her recently dead child, defensively and accusatorially, both calling attention to herself and refusing her husband's concern for her grief. He seems not to have noticed the view from the window, but his tender description of the gravestones and the child's mound – not yet marked with a stone – show that he is not unfeeling but that such family deaths have become an everyday part of his life. In the initial action the wife moves away from the husband and he pursues her with hesitating dominance, but her continued withdrawal is partly a provocation, which helps account for his protest that he's not allowed to grieve in his own way. Her desire for air and her explanation that perhaps his reaction is just masculine show that her criticism may not be strictly personal.

Struggling to restrain himself, the husband sits down, speaking and reflecting on the fact that his wife goes to other people with her troubles instead of discussing them with him. He is attempting reconciliation, but she continues to taunt him with words and actions, insisting that he can't say the right thing. He musingly half-apologizes for his ways and tries to account for their communication barrier by the difference between male and female. Tentatively offering to consider certain subjects off limits for them, he cleverly notes that such a tactic is necessary for strangers living together but not good for lovers. Again she makes a taunting gesture, and again he asks her not to take her grief to someone else but rather to share it with him. Still, he shows that he is reconciled to the child's death in a way she can't be, and she regards his view that their love casts a blessing on the lost child, and expresses a promise for the future, as a sneer at the reality of their loss. His repeated protest that he's not allowed to grieve in his own way leads her to a full-scale attack on what she takes to have been his grossly unfeeling burial of the child.

Here she projects her own insistence on his unfeelingness onto images of his burial activities, not seeing that he buried the child himself to maintain his intimacy with it, to make it a part of his past, and to work out his own griefs. The spade and the stains on his shoes, which she took for signs of indifference, show his bond to the processes of life and death, just as his everyday talk after digging the grave was a way of holding back pain. But he is either incapable of an analytic answer or too stubbornly proud to offer one, so instead of protesting that she misunderstands, he can only toss out grimly oblique anger. She revels in the fact that everyone must die alone, and sets herself up as a philosopher, condemning humanity's supposed insensitivity to everyone else's grief and proposing the impossible task of changing the world.

His assumption that she has talked out her grief and his concern with the possibility of being spied by a neighbor suggest either a stronger sense of privacy than his wife's or a superficial concern about the judgments of others. The wife's obsession suggests an inflated pride in something that distinguishes her from others. Her repeated assertion that she must get away shows that she doesn't really want a break with her husband, that she can see her way to internal change. His apparently irrational insistence that she tell where she's going so he can bring her back by force suggests that he knows she wants to be subdued or at least to have her irrationality brought back to earth. Each character evinces more sympathy than the other from some readers; Amy is sometimes seen as being over the edge of madness, and her husband is sometimes seen as self-righteously callous. The poem has some relationship to Elinor and Robert Frost's loss of their first child, and although the characters do not seem much like the poet and his wife, Frost may have put into them some of her tendency toward exaggeration and his own almost willful and defensive pretense that he does not understand things that he thinks are improper. A balanced view might be that the poem shows compassion for two different human types in view of not only their loss but also their covert insistence on and exaggeration of their differences.

"The Black Cottage," written in a narrative perspective novel for Frost, celebrates a woman who had to stick to some seemingly outmoded ways in struggling to maintain her independence. The speaker visits a long-abandoned country cottage with a minister who reminisces about the old woman, his former parishioner, who lived and died in it not very long ago – a survivor of the Civil War period. The narrative has two threads: the woman's story and the minister's reaction to it. Most of the lines report his talk, but the narrator comments at the beginning and end. However, he does not judge the minister's matter or manner, though it is unlikely that he agrees with all the minister says. Implied judgment of the minister comes from clashes between the values he admires in others and in history and those he celebrates or reveals through his fantasies.

Although the two men appear to come upon the woman's deserted cottage by chance, their conversation shows that they half-consciously anticipated or sought it. They see it as a picture "fresh painted" and then "framed" by leaves, suggesting a deliberately estheticized contemplation. Through the window and inside, they examine mementos of the woman's life-style and of her husband, who fell heroically in the Civil War. The minister's voice takes over and he mournfully describes the effects of time, against which the woman struggled by preserving her husband's dim portrait and sacred memory and by valuing her unchanging surroundings to the point of being grateful to her sons for leaving her alone with her memories. The minister treasures the past to which the woman was attached, including her memories of famous abolitionists William Lloyd Garrison and John Greenleaf Whittier, her dedication to preserving the union and freeing the slaves, and especially her fondness for Thomas Jefferson's statement in the Declaration of Independence (whose disregard of slavery goes unmentioned) that all men are created free and equal. The minister reflects on the enigmatic nature of this idea, but he empathizes with the woman's belief in it and with her resistance to old and new racisms in America.

The Western states, chiefly California, would in her last days have been denouncing Asiatic immigration as "the yellow peril," and the post-Reconstruction South would have been renewing its oppression of blacks, but she rejected such views. The minister admires this stubbornness but also sees it as innocence – that is, naiveté in the face of social forces. Her stubborn traditionalism had once led him to resist a modernizing of ritual desired by liberal young attenders of his church, and he speaks eloquently about how her faith reinforced his idea that beliefs change according to fashion, not truth, and therefore should not be easily abandoned. He probably has ethical ideas mostly in mind and shows the conservative fear that change will threaten them until they are restored. But he involves himself in some self-contradiction, first by ignoring the Civil War's revaluation of deeply held beliefs and then by celebrating the idea of a land shut off from the rest of humanity by its forbidding terrain and general undesirability, for if such a land were dedicated to unchanging truths (and its infertility would make it a wretched place for nurture, he half realizes) then those truths could hardly influence many people. The passage in which the minister speaks of truths being in and out of favor may relate as much to Frost's belief in the creative interplay of ideas as to his conservatism, for such interplay, he often thinks, deepens and reestablishes basic insights. In a discussion of *A Masque of Reason*, John T. Gage suggests that this passage in "The Black Cottage" shows "the dilemma of contending truths . . . resolved ironically" (193:84).

The minister's enthusiasm for the sandstorm that might "Retard mid-waste my cowering caravan" may combine a boast with a whimper or may be a touch of self-satire. In any case, he has been swept up by his nostalgic admiration for the old woman and her isolation, perhaps forgetting that her admirable position was rather passive. The bees he summons from the wall are signs of the present life he may be ignoring, and their aggressive flight suggests a combination of a world puzzled by the old woman's stance and also continuing on with its own vitality. The blaze of sunset on the cottage windows also suggests a combination of conclusion and continuation. Perhaps the subtlest idea here is the author-speaker's intimation that old values must take some new forms if they are to live, which would validate the minister's idea of truth not changing, although in terms different from his. Margaret V. Allen argues that in this poem sympathies are divided between the old woman and the minister and that though Frost admires the strength of the Jeffersonian ideal, he is uncertain about whether it can withstand the complexities of twentieth-century life (147:228-29).

"Blueberries," the slightest and lightest-hearted poem in this collection, provides relief from the somber narratives that surround it, but it is also a tale of people who go their own way. With a minimum of plot, it is all dialogue between husband and wife. Rather than the nervous blank verse of the surrounding poems, it uses four-foot anapestic couplets (with necessary occasional iambic substitutions). The resulting jog-trot rhythm gives an exaggerated geniality to its speech and creates a few forced rhymes. A farmer-husband reports to his wife his delighted observations of the ripeness and beauty of berries in Patterson's pasture and goes on to describe the character and behavior of Loren, a ne'er-do-well farmer with a huge family who regards all berries, no matter on whose property, as his own for the taking – to eat or sell. The narrator's wife takes a more practical view, including consideration of how Patterson's berries had returned so richly to burned-over pasture land. She is concerned about the owners's feelings and thoughts, while her husband is keenly observant of Patterson's kindness toward his poor neighbor and Loren's playfully possessive intrusions. Loren's character dominates the poem. This farmer, who transports his large brood ("a democrat-load") in a light inexpensive wagon combines a genially self-mocking manner with sly humor about his supposedly surreptitious thievery. His warm relationship with his family and delight in their wild gathering, which resembles their way of life, is the poem's most vivid presentation. His joyous irresponsibility remains somehow admirable and is probably what gives the narrator's wife her impulse to remember the pleasures of berry-picking with her husband, when they had played disappearing games, and leads her to propose "for a whim" that they also pick in Patterson's pasture again this year. Her practical-playful concern fuses her mood to her husband's, and as he has the last word, several moods are mixed: a slight apprehension of conflict with the ubiquitous Lorens and a restoration of the narrator's vision of those beautiful berries with which the poem began. The poem makes thievery look like a genial game, a harmless Robin Hood activity, with the Lorens their own beneficiaries. One critic, William Goede, believing that this poem has been severely underestimated, defends it as a major work. He sees in it a forceful embodiment of several Frost themes, which themes he explains by relating them to Ernest Hemingway's portrait of his "code hero" as interpreted by Earl Rovit. Rovit finds Hemingway's fiction revolving around the relationship between "tyro," or novice, and "tutor," or teacher. According to Goede, the narrator of this poem is the tyro, and Loren is his tutor. Goede thinks that Frost here "tells us how man, unaided, is able to save himself by learning where he is weak, so to convert his weakness into strength" (148).

The protagonist of "A Servant to Servants" suffers from both too much isolation and too much companionship. The poem takes its title from Genesis I, where Noah curses his son Ham's son Canaan as destined to be a servant to servants because Ham had looked on his father's nakedness. This allusion connects the protagonist's fate to sexual shames in her uncle, her parents, and herself. The poem is the only true dramatic monologue in this collection, spoken entirely by the desperate rural wife who struggles against recurrent insanity as she is overworked by her utterly practical husband and threatened by her past. She speaks to an interlocutor identified as someone (presumably a man, though a few critics think she is addressing a small group) who is camping by permission on her land while studying local flora. Although his words are never reported, he interrupts her with brief queries and comments. He seems to be a stranger, though a sympathetic listener. The locale is Northeastern Vermont, not far from Lake Willoughby, whose presence offers the woman occasional comfort.

Before reporting that she has been out of her mind and hospitalized, the protagonist describes her dissociation of feelings from mind and body in frighteningly cold tones that reflect her resignation and desperation. She details her situation by stressing her loneliness in surroundings where she is accompanied only by her workaholic husband and the vulgar men he employs to develop the roads and countryside. Her husband has little insight into her feelings and takes a practical view of everything, denying that she needs rest and counting on medicine and continued work to help her. She grimly responds that "the best way out [may be] through," as he says, but implies that this will mean her death or relapse into insanity. She tries to give him credit for helping her, but her narrative shows that his practical decisions never improve things for her.

Thoughts of the workmen who sprawl around her kitchen arousing her sexual fear with their obscene comments make her recall her obsessions and past breakdown. Her memory of being in an asylum leads her to contrast the care it offered to home care for the insane, as cruelly illustrated in the story of her mad uncle, whom she never knew. The asylum was kind to her, but the imprisonment of her uncle in a cage upstairs in the home her mother and father occupied when first married is a frightening analogy for her present entrapment and for the states of mind that led to her mental condition. She attributes her condition partly to heredity, but probably the intense sexual shames her uncle displayed during his incarceration at home were part of the family social heritage that her parents transferred to her. She knows that her uncle was somehow silenced by her parents (perhaps by castration or even a form of murder); he was gone by the time she was born. Her sometimes having spoken of taking her turn upstairs inside his cage shows that as a child, or even as an adult she felt oppressed and in flight from her parents or husband or both. She and her husband had lived in her parents' home until her frustrations had led to her husband's agreeing that they should leave. But their move did not produce the expected change; it may have actually made things worse. Now she longs for freedom like that which she sees in her interlocutor and his companions. At the end she desperately but cautiously pleads with him not to go, for his keeping her from work is helping preserve her life or her sanity, which she surely won't be able to save much longer. Two substantial discussions of this poem, by Stuart James (254) and by Constance Rooke (255), both suggest that this woman suffers from severe deprivation of love and that she unconsciously associates a healing sexual contact with the natural scenes around her.

Frost placed the two lyric poems in this collection at the midpoint and the end. The first, "After Apple-Picking," is among Frost's most popular and esteemed poems. Here the speaker-protagonist is alone in a natural setting, but his ruminations about commitment show his concern with social life. The poem's irregular rhyme scheme and line length contribute to the sensation of swaying and dreaming which helps connect bodily movement with an intense and varying mood. His physical engagement with scene and task is reinforced by the variety of imagery and metaphor, for though visual images predominate, touch, smell, taste, hearing, and kinesthetic grasping are also striking.

The poem's time spans overlap, covering a few moments' contemplation and the scope of a day. It is evening, and having completed his fall harvest of apples, the speaker looks back at his ladder, which points toward a heaven that stands for both the sky and an ideal realm. He contemplates a few unpicked apples but is pleasantly resigned to the task's end. The aura of winter in the air reminds him of the coming night; the welcome sleepiness he has already begun to feel fuses with the lingering smell of apples, connecting the harvest's result with its end. He recalls looking that morning through an ice sheet, a sure sign of coming winter, toward fading grass, and this had made him feel that he was already entering the realm of sleep, for which his longing had increased as the day had progressed. But he was not really asleep yet, nor is he now as he recalls that even then he could tell what his dreams would be like: haunted by apples, grown larger, turning from one end to the other, and revealing their russet flecks, signs of beauty and mortality.

Returning to the present, he describes his lingering physical engagement with the completed task, the arch of his foot and the sway of his body still involved, and his ears recalling the sound of gathered apples in a way that fuses this memory into his coming dreams. The weariness with his task, hinted at earlier, becomes explicit and both reinforces and contradicts his prospective dreams. With great tenderness and exaggerated detail ("ten thousand thousand" would make one million apples) he shows how his task involved great love and a straining care. No matter how strong his efforts, he could not perform his task perfectly, nor can he bring it to a perfect conclusion. This explains his apple-haunted dreaming: he would be rehearsing a much-loved task with a combination of satisfaction with his accomplishments and regret that he could not do it over again perfectly.

The slightly sardonic "One can see what will trouble / This sleep of mine" refers back to his dream and forward to a broader significance that goes unstated. The "whatever sleep it is" intimates either an ordinary or unusually long sleep. The hibernating woodchuck might be able to tell if it would be like his months-long sleep or "just some human sleep." Considering the religious tinge to the opening symbolism and the life-weariness of the poem's end, the conclusion may point toward death and its possible rewards. But since the speaker doesn't seem to be old or worn out, and since he presents a life task as if it were typical and seems to regret that all tasks cannot be brought to perfection, his emphasis may be on the alternation of aspiration, partial failure, and renewal. The woodchuck's hibernation may be a type of death and resurrection but could also be an analogy for the human desire to sleep for weeks until one is sufficiently refreshed to have another go at ideals. The poem's title suggests humanity expelled from Eden but treats the aftermath of almost-tragic knowledge so gently that the biblical allusion is muted. Other allegorical interpretations are possible, and many have been made, but the speaker does not seem to be an old man on the verge of death or someone thinking more about the writing of poems than about life's fulfillments, as is sometimes suggested.

The rural world of "The Code" seems a far cry from that of "After Apple-Picking" and its mood of regretful tenderness; its combination of coolness and ferocity may at first seem inexplicable and unpoetic. After nine introductory lines, the poem is all dialogue between not particularly attractive men who seem incapable of direct communication except when they are distant from a crisis. The "code" of the title is simultaneously a standard of behavior and verbal restraint – a code violated under two separate and somewhat different circumstances, the first observed by the man who reports it in the foreground narrative and the second described in the background narrative, which he reports as a commentary on the first incident. In the foreground story, a town-bred farmer comments to two hired men on the need for special care in their haying now that a storm is approaching. In one of the men, this inspires a delayed taking of offense and an angry departure.

The hired man who remains tells the story and connects the error to a local code of behavior and the restraints it expects from the boss, all of which may seem fanatical to the uninitiated reader and the farmer. The man who explains the code uses the background story to clarify it. As he recalls his own story, he changes from being a quiet and decent observer of the present scene to a seemingly vicious participant in a previous one, though the farmer he had once worked for is strikingly different from his present employer. When he had worked for the self-demanding and exploitative Sanders, a farmer who abuses himself and drives his help by making nasty physical threats, he had successfully waited for an opportunity for revenge on Sanders. He had rejoiced at a chance to work alone with Sanders, and was delighted to dump a load of hay on him when Sanders had said "Let her come" rather than something neutrally descriptive. The hired man's precipitate action was like his oppressive boss's behavior, and the boss realized that he had indeed gotten just what he had asked for. Before acting, the hired man had pretended thoughtfulness, but he had proceeded with quick ferocity and had been willing to kill his employer.

He recalls this incident with frightening impersonality, as if he had responded to an intolerable insult or a wartime enemy. Although he knew no insult was intended, he took advantage of the code. He describes the farmer's reactions cold-bloodedly but gives signs that he had been afraid of the consequences had he really killed him, and he doesn't really know if he was relieved to learn that the farmer had escaped unharmed. The hand's feeling that he "went about to kill him fair enough" shows that the code has taken over for more humane feelings, an idea reinforced by the combination of drama and flatness in the farmer's acceptance of his hand's harsh judgment and murderous act. These men operate from strangely impersonal values, principles of rightness and honor that they see as judgments on themselves and others but that nearly turn them into automatons. The values and social context dramatized here reject compassionate feelings, though the plot is tolerable to the reader because catastrophe is avoided in both stories. The obsessional feelings exposed are quite different from the reactions to more universal oppressions in "Home Burial" and "A Servant to Servants," which partly explains those poems' wider appeal.

"The Generations of Men" is a genial and playful narrative in which distant cousins, a boy and a girl who are complete strangers, meet and make implicit promises for the future. The title refers to the family whose continuity the poem celebrates and to the fact of human continuity through renewed passions. The two cousins, who share speculations about the meaning of their family roots and seem ready for a self- and family-renewing love relationship, speak in voices often hard to distinguish, for dramatic tension is slight, and the characters are only superficially unlike each other. For some thirty lines the poem is spoken by a narrator whose point of view overlaps the sad tenderness of the main characters. He describes the reunion of the Stark family in Bow, New Hampshire, regretting that rain has kept all but two of the participants from a rendezvous at the ruined household of the family's beginnings. He comments on the parallel between the land's and the family's decline and later expresses doubt about the family's future as symbolized by a mountain road no one cares to ascend But he is also aware of the chances for new growth as represented by the brook that still roars below the old family homestead.

The young couple are distinguished from their scattered family by their courage in daring the rain in order to explore their roots, though their idleness gives a dreamlike quality to their daring, which must slowly develop into something more serious. As the boy and girl banter, they reveal a learned playfulness, combined with differences of temperament that promise an enriching relationship. She confesses to such interwoven roots in the Stark family that she may be mad, but her madness is mostly fancy. His saying that she riddles with her genealogy "Like a Viola" alludes to Shakespeare's Viola in *Twelfth Night*, who declares "I am all the daughters of my father's house, / And all the brothers too" (2.4.119-20) as part of her masculine disguise at a moment when she is covertly revealing her love for Duke Orsino. As the couple continue to speculate about their family, the boy expresses some doubt about their family pride, suggesting that there's little to be discovered in the family cellar hole. When she persists in seeing a significant past there, he briefly turns to deflating gestures that annoy her enough to make her look for an excuse to leave. He is sufficiently enchanted by her to counter her gesture, however, and imaginative enough to take joy in projecting his imagination into voices and visions from the scene and the brook. The two agree that what people see and hear comes from within the person.

The boy's first extended speculation is a long, flirtatious fancy in which he likens himself to Odysseus and the girl to Nausicaä in Homer's *Odyssey*. Nausicaä was the daughter of the king of the Phaecians, on whose isle Odysseus was washed up on his homeward journey. Others ran from Odysseus but Nausicaä courageously led him home to her father's palace and would have been glad to have him remain as her husband; however, his loyalty to his wife drew him home. The analogies here are limited. The passage further alludes to the *Odyssey* as the boy proposes that the voices of house and brook bid him plant a timber from the cellar and create a new dwelling place, which may attract the girl to await a possible flowering of love between them and an eventual entrance into a shared dwelling. The allusion is to Teresias's prediction that Odysseus must eventually carry an oar on his shoulder until someone declares that it is a winnowing fan, which will tell him he has arrived at a place for new settlement. The images of charred timber, raspberry vines, and a summer dwelling combine decay and fertility. The boy has correctly seen the girl as both tempting and eluding him, and she challenges him to reveal in whose voice he is speaking. He pretends to accept this challenge, but as he imitates Granny Stark's voice, Granny has pretty much the same things to say, though in down-to-earth terms. She celebrates the persistence of their people (or clan), acknowledges some room for newcomers, but backs up the boy's suggestion about planting an old timber for a new dwelling. The boy's praise of ideals leads the girl to see how much alike they are and to acknowledge a future relationship between them. She seems a little suspicious of the passion visible in his eyes and proceeds to ask for a flower as a tribute of tenderness and to dwell nostalgically on the desirability of a rainy occasion for their next meeting. Rain would be better than sunshine, for it would provide a memory of the lonely and dreamy courage that brought them together – perhaps acting as a combined shroud and promise. The overall effect suggests that sunshine will combine with rain to produce ever-new life.

"The Housekeeper" presents a painfully fractured relationship between a man and a woman, revealed almost entirely through dialogue between two other people, one of them the cold-blooded first-person narrator, who is not involved in the main action. The immediate (as opposed to historical) action occurs inside a farmhouse, where the narrator, a neighboring farmer, talks to the elderly mother of Estelle, common-law wife and housekeeper to the absent John, whom the narrator has come to visit for an explanation of rumored domestic difficulties. Estelle, who had lived with John for fifteen years, has run off and married another man, thus leaving her mother and

John in impossible situations. As the poem opens, Estelle's mother reveals first that she sews beads on shoes to help family finances and then that she is so obese she dare not leave the house and would, in a sense, have to be dismantled to be removed.

John and Estelle are characterized through a discussion of their history that reveals the frustrations that had finally led Estelle to run off and shows the combined virtues and character flaws that had led John to refuse a formal marriage and that guarantee his ruin now that Estelle is gone. Estelle left two weeks ago, and John can scarcely do anything properly for himself. When Estelle had been there, John had let the farm go half to ruin because of his eccentric perfectionism, which, combined with a nonexploitative gentleness, made him do small things the right way while neglecting serious duties toward his farm but more especially toward Estelle. She had never persuaded John to marry her, for reasons we can decipher. John thinks that the kind of devotion he shows to his hens, and his free sharing with Estelle, are more important than economic carefulness or legal guarantees. He had been thoroughly kind to her and had let her manage things as they were, but circumstances had been poor; the farm is worth so much less than its mortgage that there's little danger of repossession. He expects honor for his values and temperament, and feels threatened by official bonds and practical rules.

The obverse of his kindness is a cruelty he cannot let himself see, perhaps a deeply unconscious defensiveness about his righteousness combined with a sense that he can never be sure of the future and so must have his dependents remain as uncommitted as he is. John has let the farm run down like their lives but feels salvation in his small acts. His throwing his hoe in the air predicts the way he will release his horse and gig at the poem's end. His animals are better than his farm, but this does him little good. Estelle's mother has suffered from this situation, for she has had to watch her daughter do both the housework and the outdoor work that John neglected, and her beadwork has helped to pay for his beautiful hens. John seems unaware that he has been exploiting Estelle and her mother, and the mother sees the hell that is in store for him now that he must live without Estelle. The narrator wonders if shame has driven off Estelle, but the mother denies this, maintaining that Estelle has just turned against John, for the mother can't put into words her own frustration about John's irresponsibility.

At this point she reveals that Estelle has not only run off but also married, and her fears for John's future crescendo along with her fears for herself. John will never manage without Estelle, and the mother must realize that as her life has proven less and less, she has grown larger and larger, and she will somehow be dismantled in the process of leaving this house. Like John and Estelle she has grown into its ways of being; she could never revolt against them sufficiently, just as John could never yield his tentative ways to a firm commitment amid uncertainties. At the revelation that Estelle has married, the narrator turns joyfully cynical, implying that he thinks John has gotten his just deserts and revealing how he himself clings to conventional morality. As the mother sees John approaching the house, she wants to hide from him evidence of their financial difficulties and to avoid a confrontation. She is explosively angry but still sharp-headed enough to predict John's confidence that his harnessed horse can be let loose to take care of itself, paralleling his confidence in the ill-harnessed Estelle. John has just enough shame to want to talk privately to his neighbor before he talks to the mother, who he suspects already has news of Estelle's marriage and is perhaps gloating over it. John feels that they have conspired against him, though of course he is responsible for all of the ruin. Perhaps Estelle has found a widower who needs a wife, and she may well be fifteen or twenty years younger than the 55-year-old John. Her situation may be improved, but more likely she has thrown herself into uncharted waters. The mother, on the other hand, seems to be in the worst situation; her final cursing of John shows fury at his ruining them all, but especially herself. Frost creates a portrait of three courageous, persistent, and cantankerous people whose various stubbornnesses had sustained a not-very-constructive cooperation until the most exploited one, no longer able to stand it, had made a dash for freedom from a man whose self-imposed shackles hurt others almost as much as himself.

In contrast to the drama of "The Housekeeper" which balances between background and foreground, that of "The Fear" is mostly in the foreground; the background is harder to decipher. The stark third-person narration of "The Fear" sets the stage and then describes only simple actions. Most of the poem is dialogue between a man (Joel) and woman, whose exact relationship is never stated. Lawrance Thompson reports that the poem is based on Frost's experience one night when he went walking with his five-year-old son Carol and was accosted by an alarmed woman, as is the stranger toward the end of "The Fear" (20:344-45). Frost learned that the woman was a nurse in a Boston hospital who had run off with one of her patients and feared retribution from her husband. Many details of the poem suggest that the woman and Joel are not married and that the man she fears is the husband whom she has fled.

The poem opens with an extremely vivid scene. Shadows, darkness, blackened house windows, and a lantern just taken from a gig create an aura of intense expectancy, heightened by the man's efforts to control both the woman and the nervous horse. The dialogue starts with, and continues to center on, the woman's terror of a face that she has seen along the road as they drove home. Her agonized and knowing interruption of the man sets up the pattern of uncompleted statements that permeates the poem. Her obsessiveness makes her assume that her and his meanings are obvious without being fully spoken, and often she seems to be defending herself from fears by not speaking them. The woman's first substantial speech reveals a guilty feeling of nakedness before the eyes of the world. (Her reference to rattling a key to let something out as they arrive home parallels similar fears in "The Hill Wife" and "The Lockless Door.") She exaggerates the isolation of their home and the lateness of the hour, for "it's only dark"; that is, evening has just fallen, and families do live in the neighborhood.

She grants that she couldn't identify the face she saw by the roadside, but this very fact shows that she fears everyone and thinks her deserted husband might send someone else after them. She struggles with Joel, her lover, over the lantern and continues to insist that only she confront the intruder, again revealing guilt feelings. Joel's hardheaded skepticism about the possibility of a vindictive intruder shows a stance quite different from hers. The woman fears that if she doesn't confront the intruder he will soon be everywhere, but indeed he is already everywhere because he is haunting her conscience, not her territory, a fact of which she is at best only half aware. When Joel declares it nonsense to think the other man would "care enough," their thoughts and motivations seem unclear to the reader and possibly also to the man and woman, themselves. Does Joel mean that the husband could not care enough about the desertion to wish for revenge, or does he mean that he could not care enough about the woman to try to get her back? The woman's reply is little help, for when she says "You mean you couldn't understand his caring. / Oh, but you see he hadn't had enough–" she could be referring to revenge or affection. Her saying "I won't–I won't–I promise you" suggests that she is denying accusations, but accusations of what? That she has not been giving enough to make Joel's sacrifice worth his trouble? That her husband was more loving than Joel?

Joel tries to affirm the bond between them by taking the initiative in confronting the stranger, but her insistence on confronting him alone denies Joel's intimacy and affirms a guilty bond to the other man. The tensions lessen as an innocent stranger taking a walk with his young son comes forward into the light and explains his presence. The woman's fearfulness, however, continues, for she cannot believe that the intruder isn't somehow related to her guilt. When she is finally convinced of his innocence, she turns to her lover with a fresh burst of defensiveness but speaks with the same hush of terror that pervaded her earlier speculations. She now seems to be standing by herself. Her lover, having given up on reassuring her and maybe wondering what he has gotten himself into, presumably looks on coldly. Overcome by emotion, she drops the lantern, probably in a faint, though only the lantern's fall to the ground, and not the woman's, is described. The extinguished lantern remains an open symbol: perhaps it represents the woman's overwhelmed consciousness, her inability to deal with the fear that she has predicted will follow her everywhere, but it just as likely represents a decline in her relationship with her lover. The poem shows little sympathy for the woman and not much for the lover, whose objectivity seems shield enough for discomforts that may lie ahead. Laurence Perrine's explication of this poem argues convincingly that Joel is the woman's lover, not her husband, and cites much evidence that she has fainted at the end (173).

Despite the abundance of action in its background and foreground, "The Self-Seeker" is less dramatic than many of *North of Boston*'s narratives. Perhaps more than any of these poems, it provides the portrait of a soul – seen at a crucial moment of his life and looking forward to a problematic future. The self-seeker is never named, and the poem's epithet for him – "The Broken One" – is excessively melodramatic. The title puns on the protagonist as someone who pursued his identity as a student of beautiful flowers but who now refuses to be a self-seeker in monetary terms, although he persists in his spiritual quest. Almost the whole story is told in dialogue; only about 22 of the poem's 228 lines are objective narrative. As this man of some 30 years lies in bed with legs and feet crushed from an accident in a water-powered sawmill, still ignorant of how bad his permanent injuries will be, he talks to his good friend Willis about his coming settlement with a lawyer representing his employer. The lawyer arrives to complete an obviously unfair settlement of $500 for medical expenses and compensation, though early in the twentieth century this amount would probably have been about a year's wages for the man.

The dialogue presents a low-key three-cornered drama. The cripple's friend Willis is outraged at the smallness of the settlement and desperate to have him receive a compensation that considers his greatest loss: his inability to continue his forays into field and woodland, where he studies and gathers orchids out of profound love for them and to complete a written study. In the background the cripple's landlady, Mrs. Corbin, never appears but shares Willis's outrage. In the foreground a young girl, Anne, probably Mrs. Corbin's daughter, has a discussion about orchids with the cripple, which illustrates his tender concern for them (she must pick no more than necessary), and shows how he must henceforth depend on others to gather flowers for him. Earlier he has indicated that loss of his feet was like a loss of his soul. Anne's future work will serve as his feet and hence nurture his soul. Anne also serves as a foil for the lawyer's extreme impersonality.

To the lawyer, the cripple is even less than a person, for he doesn't even know his name. The lawyer's time seems infinitely valuable and the cripple's valueless, because his economic potential is low. The lawyer is indifferent to what time and life mean to the cripple. The cripple has no interest in struggling for a higher compensation because something irreplaceable has been stolen from him – the use of his feet as servants to his soul. He can't be paid for his flowers, of whose loss the lawyer is also ignorant; all he can do is accept his situation and try to continue his study by limited means. He is a man of considerable tenderness and has a fine but self-mocking sense of humor. He can joke about not having lost his head when his coat was caught on the sawmill's turning shaft, meaning that he freed the coat so that his legs and not his head were crushed. Before the lawyer arrives he can speak of the monetary award as if it will be settled by an auction: "Five hundred – five – five! One, two, three, four, five," showing an awareness that he's given much of himself away for very little but by his mockery affirming the immeasurable worth of what he's lost.

He is a good enough naturalist to have gotten the attention of John Burroughs (1838-1921), one of the most famous nature writers of the day. His mutually teasing dialogue with Anne shows his loving character and conservationist attitudes. His dialogue with the lawyer shows some self-denigration; perhaps he feels guilty for having injured himself. He also seems insecure about his pursuits and concerns as compared with those of the commercial world. His mocking declaration that he's "a great boy to think of number one" is the opposite of the truth. As the scene ends, the cripple is willing to allow Willis to fight with the lawyer, declaring his readiness to sign the papers in the meantime. His mind is crowded with considerations for himself and others. He asks to have Anne brought back so he can continue his study of nature, and he acts as if the lawyer's compassion were genuine. He sees both the practical and emotional pointlessness of telling the lawyer about his flowers, and in bidding the lawyer not miss his train, he acknowledges the claims of the practical world. He flings his arms around his face not in despair about losing that world but in grief over his own coming struggle with isolation.

Frost knows the agonies and enrichments of isolation and can treat all sorts of strange and intense connections between them. "The Wood-Pile" is a lyric meditation in blank verse with minimal narrative content. In Frost there are many variations on this form – most in first person, but a few, like "An Old Man's Winter Night," in a powerfully empathic third person. This poem shows the speaker concentrating on a scene in nature and progressively relating himself to the scene, a bird, and the absent and forever-to-be-unknown person who left behind the unused wood-pile. This is a lonely, bleak poem in which the speaker seeks encouragement and significance, but as he struggles with signs of it, they all prove to be distant, puzzling, and limited. The dense forest scene both radiates a mood of oppression and discovery and drives the speaker forward. His pursuit of encouragement and significance leads only to bits of it, and these prove enigmatic. The gray, barren, and frozen landscape is strikingly undifferentiated (like the "sameness of the wood" in "The Demiurge's Laugh," but more detailed). His distance from home is more spiritual than physical. The woods are a place for seeking, but they yield few discoveries.

Amid this bare loneliness, the speaker is delighted to find a bird and saddened that instead of accepting a fond comradeship from him, it sees him only as an enemy. The bird's fear carries it off the way the speaker might have gone. Its flight calls his attention to the wood-pile, and he persists in his quest of he knows not what. The wood-pile is strikingly isolated, like his own spirit, and embodies a paradox: it is passive but supported by a still-growing tree. The clematis vines woven around it are further signs of persisting vitality, but his thoughts focus on the woodcutter who has long gone and left this wood utterly unused by people. The signs that a long time has passed emphasize the persistence of the wood-pile and the distance of the man who had cut the logs. The woodcutter becomes someone whose mood he desperately needs, a person who persisted and was able to disregard potential waste. No matter what his purpose, his successes or failures, he had kept going ahead, just as the speaker does in this wood today, and had left behind only a puzzling revelation. The fresh tasks to which he presumably turned represent a willingness to accept false starts and unrewarded pursuits. The wood that now warms the frozen swamp does humanity no good, and the faint warmth it lends the swamp parallels the speaker's limited discoveries this day. But sad as the conclusion is, the limited and strangely brooding vitality of wood-pile and swamp lives on inside the speaker.

"Good Hours," was set in italics in the original edition of *North of Boston*, pairing it with the introductory "The Pasture" and helping it serve as a farewell to the volume. Its placement at the end of Frost's "Book of People" is appropriate as Frost withdraws from the lives of his characters. Possibly he is both celebrating his conflict between intimacy and detachment and pointing back to such conflict in his characters. The "good hours" of the title include those of the speaker's pleasurable walk through village and country, those that the dwellers enjoyed while he saw them only from the outside – the early hours of their retirement and the hours that his readers may spend with these poems. He is joyous in his combined isolation and intimacy, first shown as he walks alone, feeling in possession of the cottages and their windows. In the second stanza, his imaginative comradeship seizes the people and music within. But as he enjoys his aloneness and walks well past the village, he repents of his detachment enough to want to go back. On the return trip, the windows have gone from shining light to dead black, for those within have gone to bed. His increased aloneness makes him keenly aware of the sounds of his feet, and the dwellers' slumber seems to encompass their street. His presence as an onlooker is a "profanation," a slight soiling of something hushed and holy, for which he begs a pardon that honors their relaxed conventionality and yet leaves him quietly exultant in his persisting awareness. As an artist he is both abashed and proud of having penetrated the lives of his fictional (or partly fictional) characters, whose private lives he has made public in his poems.

# CHAPTER 6

## Mountain Interval
## (1916)

Frost's third volume, *Mountain Interval* (the second word of the title an alteration of the geographical term *intervale*), is named for farmland situated partway up a mountain – difficult terrain for farming. It seems symbolic of a situation between the mundane and the ideal, probably representing for Frost a pause in his accomplishments and his human relationships, as indicated by his dedication to his wife in memory of shared aspirations. The book's rather small number of reviews were generally respectful but tended to discuss his earlier works as much as these new poems, the best of which were rarely singled out. In treatment and theme the collection is a mix of the familiar and the new, and the poems date all the way from the 1890s to 1916. A few poems are reminiscent of the nostalgic meetings and yearnings of *A Boy's Will*. There are only two substantial blank-verse narratives, "In the Home Stretch" and "Snow," both now held in lower esteem than the showpieces of *North of Boston*. Frost presents an almost new type in several short blank-verse poems that combine brief narratives with intense meditation, including "An Old Man's Winter Night" and "'Out, Out – ,'" long among Frost's most esteemed poems, and the very popular "Birches," which has a mixed reputation. But a number of sonnets and lyrics with a descriptive and often understated base, some of these reminiscent of "Mowing," sound a new note for Frost and have added much to his fame; the most celebrated of these are "Hyla Brook," "The Oven Bird," and "Putting in the Seed," followed by "An Encounter" and "The Line Gang." The sharply imagined scene of warfare in "Range-Finding" reportedly precedes the start of World War I, about which Frost writes explicitly but from a distance in "The Bonfire." "The Hill Wife," much anthologized, represents Frost's only venture into a narrative told in a series of lyrics. "The Road Not Taken" remains popular but is seen as a sophisticated jest as often as it is taken for a serious statement.

In the original edition "The Road Not Taken" and the last poem, "The Sound of Trees," were set in italics, implying introduction and farewell. Frost seems to have been willing to use this initial poem with meanings not supported by its autobiographical context, for he had sent it to his close friend Edward Thomas, who was notorious for indecisiveness (but who did not see Frost's point). Some critics think the poem represents Thomas's voice, but Frost could hardly have expected his readers to recognize that, and during his frequent public readings of the poem he often warned that it was tricky and shouldn't be interpreted hastily. The poem's popularity seems to be based on the mistaken notion that it celebrates the triumph of independent choices – most likely Frost's choices as artist and man. Frost's warning showed that he hoped readers could come to see its satirical intention, which he evidently never cared to explain. But the poem's seemingly genial celebration of a fortunate choice remains seductive, even to those who perceive a satirical intention.

Yellow wood and leaves not yet trodden black place the scene in the nostalgic autumn season. The speaker's desire to take two different ways and yet remain "one traveler" is gently stated. As the first stanza ends, the future is undecipherable. In the second stanza, although the speaker chooses the less-traveled road as if he were doing it a favor, four vivid lines insist that the differences between the two roads in terms of wear as well as attractiveness are negligible. The speaker's hopes to return to the road not chosen and his reflection on such an unlikelihood seem casual. His thought that "way leads on to way" implies a symbolic choice, but his having "kept the first [road] for another day" suggests that rather than having chosen a way of life, he has made just a partial choice. As he looks far ahead and sees himself looking back to this moment and making a declaration about it, he makes a crucial change in point of view. Then – not now – he will declare that his having taken the less-traveled road made all the difference, and so the last line is part of what he will say in the future, not part of what he now declares. The core idea seems to be that he will have succeeded in fooling himself about the importance of a choice. It will have made all the difference in his imagination, not in reality. The poem may raise the question of how our casual choices affect our destinies, but if these choices are casual, they are more matters of whim and chance than matters of character and determination. Frost believes in such forces, but he also sees that the fatality of whim can be overestimated. Still, readers continue to insist on symbolic depths here. Robert McPhillips argues, perhaps with excessive sophistication, that Frost's being as concerned with the road not taken as the one taken connects to the taken road as a horizontal way and the road not taken as the vertical way, counterposing the earthly and spiritual, which must somewhere converge. Thus, Frost implies that the road of transcendence has been taken in the imagination (105:82-86, 94). John Evangelist Walsh argues that the voice in the poem is a combination of Thomas's and Frost's, and that Frost's final point is that the ability to make choices, especially when they are difficult, is a triumph over circumstances (24:212).

"Christmas Trees" is a personal blank-verse narrative with minimal plot, a few lines of dialogue, and a final brief address to the friends for whom the poem constituted a Christmas letter. Perhaps it is placed after "The Road Not Taken" because it deals with an apparent moment of indecision, during which the speaker has really made up his mind but lets himself speculate about an alternative and learns something from his hesitations. The speaker opens with a sigh of relief over the way snow seals his rural separation from city life. The city, embodied in a businessman who wants to purchase his balsams for Christmas trees, invades the speaker's privacy with the urban values of which he is glad to remain free. His trees' being a natural part of the holiness where all houses look like churches had kept him from seeing them as trees that would carry holiness somewhere else, and his heart sinks to think of how their being cut would denude his slope. But he briefly considers the stranger's monetary offer because he is used to thinking of everything (including commercial products and poetry, as shown in the later poem "New Hampshire") as deserving a "trial by market" to prove its worth. Also, he doesn't want to seem rude, and he likes hearing his possessions praised.

As the speaker silently notes the varying symmetry of his trees, the stranger coolly appraises them and then subtly offers $30 for a thousand trees, rather than stating the amount as the 3 cents apiece that this comes to a paltry sum suggesting a betrayal like Judas's. Comparing this to the dollar apiece his city friends would soon be paying for such trees, he feels nostalgic longing for the city companionship that the poem had initially rejected. He concludes by joking that he didn't know he had a thousand Christmas trees, so presumably he has a special blessing. He is also delighted to think that the trees are worth "three cents more to give away than sell"; the "simple calculation" to which he refers is the addition of 3 cents' postage to their 3-cent value, as he thinks of enclosing them with this Christmas message – a gesture that becomes part of the poem's message to his friends.

"An Old Man's Winter Night" provides a more intense scene of winter isolation. It is a brief blank-verse narrative with a minimal plot, but its blending of the speaker's and the old man's emotions contributes to a variation on the intense voice of lyric. The poem centers on an old man alone in a winterbound farmhouse, wandering between its rooms and at last falling asleep in a chair. The night outdoors, the cellar, the roaring trees, and the moon and snow are all personified as the speaker half penetrates the old man's mind, highlighting his dimmed capacity to respond to the sad company of the inanimate world. The old man can't look back to the lamp he holds, which illustrates that he is only a fading light to himself – a dim and puzzled consciousness.

His age keeps him from remembering why he lives here and why he has been moving from one room to another. The roar of outside winds against the house is as enigmatic as are his thoughts. But under all this confusion he possesses identity, determination, and concerns that no one can reach or perhaps even understand. The speaker's restrained awareness of how dim those thoughts must be combines pity with respect for privacy. The outside darkness is partly dissipated by the late-arising moon, and both are seen as ironical protectors of this dwelling; their cold preserves snow and icicle on roof and wall to create an esthetic order appropriate to the old man's fading struggle for dignity. The shifting log parallels his faint but tenacious vitality. The last three lines emphasize that in his combination of age and aloneness he can't really maintain his household but, more importantly, he can't give it the meaning of a community, as symbolized by "a house, / A farm, a countryside." The compassionate tone stresses both limitations and residual values; "or if he can, / It's thus he does it of a winter night" gathers the poem's tensions into a balance. The old man makes what preservations he can through his mysterious and diminishing communion with the natural world, his house and its appurtenances, and his half-formed thoughts. Robert McPhillips proposes that the old man has been isolated by the death of his wife and is now struggling to maintain his sanity. McPhillips further suggests that such details as the moon's assistance in maintaining icicles help keep intact the old man's diminished world, and he implies that the old man's unexpressed thoughts are about the imminence of death (105:91-93).

"The Exposed Nest" was moved to its present position after "An Old Man's Winter Night" in 1930, possibly because it shows a variant treatment of compassion for dispossession. The poem, spoken by a man to his wife, moves from a sense of delighted play to thoughtful compassion for birds whose growth to maturity is threatened. Finding his wife replacing clumps of hay, the speaker acknowledges such play as something delightful to them both and is pleased to join her – until he realizes that she is trying to protect the nest of young birds whose grass cover has just been mown. The scene combines fresh and sparkling nature imagery with an awful threat to the birds, who have been barely spared by the cutting bar of a mowing machine. The phrase "But 'twas no make-believe with you today" provides the first of several poignant transitions. The man sees how the woman has acted to protect the birds from frightening sights, and he fears that the mother bird may not know enough to return to this changed scene. His identification with the birds intensifies because he fears that human meddling might frighten off the mother bird and bring harm from an effort to do good. Here Frost expresses conservative caution against meddling with natural order and chance and defends the duty of living things to struggle for themselves.

But compassion dominates; the two people continue to build the grass screen she had begun. With a clipped phrase, the man reminds himself that this was done "to prove we cared," as if he does not trust the genuineness of his impulse and must always recognize that pity can be self-serving. This self-doubt is reinforced by the reflection that afterward they must have turned to other things (as the people do after the boy's death in "'Out, Out−'"). The two seem to have no memory of what followed – something he regretfully wishes he could deny as he asks her, "Have you?" in the hope he is mistaken. His reflection on the place they never revisited to see if the young birds had survived also shows that he is now looking back with longing and wishing that they had learned what happened. Thus the poem weaves concern, unconcern, and a recurrence of concern into a profound sense of the unity of all life and a regret that such feeling cannot be constant. The birds have been left to themselves with the limited best wishes of the human observers, like the old man in the preceding poem, but this time with tenderness about a promising future rather than the tag end of life.

The tiny scene in "A Patch of Old Snow" combines a realistic picture with a richly suggestive metaphor. The comma added at the end of the first line in Edward Lathem's emendation is a mistake, for the reflection made by the second line is essential to the speaker's description of the patch of old snow. The speaker means that he knows, after reflection, that he should immediately have noticed that the patch had a message for him. It is like a piece of blown newspaper because of its appearance and because rain wears away and speckles old snow. The grime shows that the snow has long lost its pristine whiteness, though it's hard to be sure just what that whiteness once said. That the speaker has casually forgotten it suggests that it was never important, in which case it might be just a symbol for the way the world's news grows quickly old. Or Frost might be suggesting that once the beauty of winter is gone, one forgets it, only later (as here) to realize that one hadn't appreciated it enough. The poet may be having fun in balancing his suggestions between two such ideas. In a letter of 1914 (12:111-12) Frost discussed how the poem's cadences turned the prose content into poetry, specifying how the intonation of the last two lines is essential to the meaning (which he did not explain). Probably he was referring to how the casual expression "a day I've forgotten" is followed not by an emphatic explanation or a denial but by a throw-away phrase one might speak about something of no value, playing one kind of sadness wryly against another to create a quiet sense of either self-disgust at impercipience or self-congratulation at disregard of the unimportant.

"In the Home Stretch" is another narrative with a minimal plot. It applies something of the warmth and philosophical reflectiveness of "The

Generations of Men" to an unnamed wife and her husband, Joe, who (aided by three scarcely individualized moving men) are in the home stretch of moving their household from a city dwelling to a farm. The couple are also in the home stretch of their whole lives – a desired goal, but one about whose significance they are still puzzled, the wife less so than the husband. As the couple settle into the house, the furniture continues to play symbolic roles. At first it seeks its proper place in the house, just as they do. Outside surroundings are also symbolic. Weeds and dishpan combine the sense of burden and reward in the woman's work. The mowing fields are extensions of life for the husband. The woods beyond represent the death that waits for them. The future is unpredictable, but the woman's determined love for the place and the man, as well as her faith in life, suggest continued vitality. The new moon represents a fresh start for them, and their luck in neatly fitting their old stove into place in their new home readies them for the symbolic breaking of bread and reflections on meals past and present, which contribute to the guarantee of something permanent in their relationship. The moving men's attitude toward the country, joined with their awareness of the couple's uncertainty about their move there, adds poignancy to the couple's new isolation, which must be countered by their faith in each other, in their ceremonials, and in the idea that they have achieved some kind of permanence.

Like the couple in "In Neglect," they are aware that they have been left to their "fate, like fools." As the woman's mood sinks, their loneliness resembles the descent of age in "An Old Man's Winter Night." But the husband's assurance that no one can take away the meals they've shared, leading to their breaking bread, assures permanence in their relationship. He lights the fire to give her company and they look forward to a friendly countryman showing them the ropes of living here; the fire anticipates the poem's last lines, and the expected help lends a realistic touch to their assurance that they are "Dumped down in paradise . . . and happy." At this point they have their only obvious conflict in the poem: they wonder if they have moved because of a mutual wish or just to please the other one, which leads to the poem's philosophical core. The wife declares that there are no endings and beginnings but only middles, meaning primarily that their separate wishes have joined in a necessary compromise to make them one, but also meaning that life goes on indefinitely and that their existence is part of an endless continuity.

The poem returns to a more conventional idea of permanent unity when Joe says "Perhaps you never were?" in response to his wife's saying that they are not new to each other, implying that their marriage was made in heaven and will continue there. She follows this with hardheaded declarations about things not being a beginning for them (but rather, it seems, an enriched continuity), and when he reflects on endings she gently turns this aside as gloom. The wife's concluding insistence that Joe go to bed, after which the narrative voice comments on the dancing light in their just-transported stove, contrasts their closeness to the idea that while the fire may just seem at home, they clearly are. Frost plays with ideas of transience and permanence, never guaranteeing the latter but letting his characters believe in it. Robert McPhillips sees far more conflict in this poem, proposing a major tension between the husband's trying to hold his wife inside the house as a symbol of their marriage and the wife's desire to escape, as represented by her gazing out of the kitchen window (105:89-90).

"The Telephone" continues the material, and some of the treatment, of "A Late Walk" and "Flower-Gathering" in *A Boy's Will*. The speaker has gone a long distance from his wife or lover to enjoy a thoughtful isolation but then regrets his separation, wanting to communicate with her and be asked back. In the earlier poems the speaker is more explicitly immersed in a world of sad dreams. Here his voice is deft and light and so quietly detached that he seems to hear the woman's distant voice as a whisper inside his thoughts. In the form of a dialogue, the poem allows only two lines to the woman, who seems used to extravagant metaphors such as his comparison of a flower in the field and a flower by her window to telephones. Three times he describes his actions in his contact with the flower as a kind of obeisance: he leans his head against the flower; after driving away a bee (his rival in love?) he leans and grasps the stalk; and at the very moment that he hears a reply he bows. All these gestures attribute a holiness to nature and to the woman's message. Twice he hesitates about the messages he has heard—each introduced by a dash, as if he either isn't sure what she said or can't bring himself to pronounce it because of its preciousness. His declaring that it was *"Someone"* who said "'Come'" to him shows him flirtatiously evoking the mystery of the message he is trying to draw from her after the fact. In the dialogue, he coaxes two restrained statements from her that show she also dwells in her private world. The last line implies a gentle yielding on his part and a reconciliation, though the distance and possible tension between them have been only lightly implied throughout the poem. These poems provide a quiet contrast to poems like "The Thatch," in which separation is related to conflicts that desperately need resolution.

"Meeting and Passing," a sonnet in mixed form, belongs to an apparently earlier phase of a love relationship. Here two lovers communicate face to face, the distance between them being emotional rather than physical. The scene's details become part of each one's separate and communal world as the lovers act out their tentative feelings about their present relationship and the beginning of an assured union. The hill and gate resemble the "hills of view" in "Reluctance" and the detached perspective in "The Vantage Point." Their mingled footprints imply a wordless maneuvering toward communication, a preservation of individuality, and a movement toward unity. "The figure of their being" that they draw in the summer dust is a metaphor for their bodies and spirits. It is "less than two" in that they have begun to merge and "more than one" in that they are still separate. The "decimal" is the point in 1.5. The woman's parasol reveals the early-twentieth-century female wariness of sunlight (the exposure suggesting sexual contact), and her thrusting it into the dust shows combined contemplation and hesitation. Her smiling gaze into the dust suggests her contemplation of what is to be gained and lost. In the last two lines the couple go back into their aloneness, but their sharing of landscapes continues a kind of unity and promises a fuller one. It is as if their spirits are being gently touched by a world with which they were separately unified. The repetition of "passed" instead of the use of a full rhyme creates the sense of experience brushing their bodies and faces in a holy gesture.

"Hyla Brook" and the three poems that follow it all deal with diminishments where love persists, or with the struggle to maintain love in the face of towering ideals. Despite its fifteen lines, many critics consider "Hyla Brook" an irregularly rhymed sonnet. Its next-to-last line shows that it is partly an answer to Tennyson's "The Brook," in which a brook claims that unlike transient man, it goes on forever. Here the brook is named for tree frogs that haunt its vicinity in early spring but disappear when summer's fullness lessens their water supply. Description and commentary are presented colloquially and intimately as the speaker begins by glancing sadly back to early spring fullness. The brook, personified by its groping, its secret pseudoflourishing, and its pathetic bed, either hides itself underground or disappears into mere groundwater that is sopped up by jewelweed. The tree frogs' former joy hovers over the scene in the speaker's memory, just as their earlier appearance reminded him of the winter charm that disappeared with spring.

The "ghost of sleigh bells in a ghost of snow" becomes a symbol for delicate imaginative persistence. The "weak foliage" parallels the brook's weakness, but its resistance to the water's flow resembles the speaker's clinging to what the brook was at the same time that he takes new delight in the changed scene. The "faded paper sheet" is partly the book of memory, speaking quietly and perhaps ready to record new impressions. The last four lines, slightly boastful, combine acceptance of the cycle of life and compassion for it. The love emphatically stressed by the last line is for the brook's past, its potential for the future, and the poignant reality of its decay, which resembles the decay of human life. It may also resemble that love which suffers long as it remembers the past and hopes for the real or ideal future. Robert McPhillips suggests much subtle symbolism in this poem, proposing that the dried bed of the brook represents a marriage bed that needs to go back to its sources and a sheet of paper that requires love if song is to grace it again (105:94).

"The Oven Bird," an irregularly rhymed sonnet, also dwells on the enigma of fullness in decline. The speechlike song of the wood warbler, called the oven bird because of its oven-shaped nest, is thought to resemble "teacher, teacher." As in "Hyla Brook," beauty has declined from richness and is now loved all the more for its diminishment, and the problem it raises remains an enigma. Everyone has heard the oven bird because it dominates such landscapes and because songs of diminishment are universal. The poem's striking sense of that fullness on whose decline it insists comes through in the stress on "mid-summer," "mid-wood," and "solid tree trunks," a fullness whose denial immediately begins. (Leaves outnumbering flowers one to ten looks forward to "Leaves Compared to Flowers," in which leaves stand for painful contemplation opposing fresh hope). The shrill repetition of "He says" imitates the bird's insistent screech as if the landscape reverberates with it. The bird seems to demand that the reader share its questioning, a behavior that is really instinctive but draws us into a sensitive contemplation of striking fullness followed by a rush of decline. This richness explodes before our eyes, just as sunny days a moment overcast make a tension of fullness and decline.

The "other fall we name the fall" links beautifully showering flowers to the falling leaves that augur the year's end and suggests humanity's fall into mortality. The highway dust, a signature of death, preserves an appealing shimmer. The speaker identifies himself with the bird as he declares that it would stop singing – as other birds do – except that it knows how to make its speechlike song appropriate here. The "diminished thing" emphatically announced in the last line must be more than just this scene – presumably a symbolic aura of existence. It could be the yearly decline of nature, but the placing and intensity imply something more important – probably the modern world, in which faith in ideals and absolutes is diminished. Thus the question must be how the poet should write or how we should all think and feel about such a world. Answers seem less implied than in "Hyla Brook," but Frost probably has in mind a similar stance of loving endurance. Acknowledging the poem's concern with keeping language alive in the midst of dust and decay, Mark Van Doren suggests that its core concern is with what poets are to do in a century in which singing is difficult – a concern to which Frost's answer is the beautiful subdued richness of his own work (230:75-77).

Rather than the concrete but symbolic scenes of the poems around it, "Bond and Free" embodies allegorical abstractions like those in "Pan with Us" and "The Demiurge's Laugh," but with even less sense of place. Personification of its abstractions is made plain by the capitalization of "Love" and "Thought," which are compared and contrasted in the first, second, and fourth stanzas. Love, clinging to earth, is like the feeling for natural scenes in "Hyla Brook" and "The Oven Bird," and soaring Thought is like the ideals that those poems connect with love for things mortal and puzzling. The first stanza claims to celebrate free and fearless Thought as opposed to fearful and self-protective Love, making Love feminine and Thought masculine. The second stanza gratefully acknowledges Love's physical satisfactions but seems to make greater claims for Thought's freedom. The third stanza acknowledges a special excitement in the painful forays of Thought (perhaps paralleling these to Love's painful joys), but as Thought returns to an earthly room it is constrained, as was Love in the first stanza. Thought's burning wings are like Icarus's, but its courage may be no greater than Love's holding to earth and its self-surrender. The last stanza begins to assert the true superiority of Love, but with the deliberate hesitancy of "some say," as if it's an effort to acknowledge this. By being thrall, Love must make a surrender perhaps more courageous than Thought's daring, and the all that it possesses, though it resembles what Thought finds at a distance, is richer and warmer. Intellectually the poem claims equal status for Love and Thought, but emotionally Love takes the prize.

The discursive blank-verse meditation "Birches" does not, like "The Wood-Pile" and "An Encounter," center on a continuously encountered and revealing nature scene; rather, it builds a mosaic of thoughts from fragments of memory and fantasy. Its vividness and genial, bittersweet speculation help make it one of Frost's most popular poems, and because its shifts of metaphor and tone invite varying interpretation it has also received much critical discussion, not always admiring. The poem moves back and forth between two visual perspectives: birch trees as bent by boys' playful swinging and by ice storms, the thematic interweaving being somewhat puzzling. The birches bent "across the lines of straighter darker trees" subtly introduce the theme of imagination and will opposing darker realities. Then, almost a third of the poem describes how ice storms bend these trees permanently, unlike the action of boys; this scene combines images of beauty and of distortion. Ice shells suggest radiating light and color, and the trees bowed to the level of the bracken, suggest suffering, which is immediately lightened by the strange image of girls leaning their hair toward the sun as if in happy submission.

The fallen "inner dome of heaven" alludes to Shelley's "dome of many colored glass" (also alluded to in "The Trial By Existence") to suggest the shattering of the ideal into everyday reality. Frost's speaker then self-consciously breaks from his realistic but metaphorically fantasied digression to say he would prefer to have some boy bend the birches, which action becomes a symbol for controlled experience, as contrasted with the genial fatality of ice storms. The boy's fancied playfulness substitutes for unavailable companionship, making for a thoughtful communion with nature, which rather than teach him wisdom allows him to learn it. Despite the insistence on the difference between ice storms' permanent damage to birches and a boy's temporary effects, the boy subdues and conquers the trees. His swinging is practice for maintaining life's difficult and precarious balances.

The third part of the poem begins with a more personal and philosophical tone. The speaker claims to have been such a youthful swinger of birches, an activity he can go back to only by dreaming. The birch trees, probably both ice-bent and boy-swung, stand for the order and control missing from ordinary experience. The "considerations" he is weary of are conflicting claims that leave him disoriented and stung. The desire to "get away from earth," importantly qualified by "awhile," shows a yearning for the ideal, or perhaps for the imaginative isolation of the birch swinger. His "I'd like to go by climbing a birch tree ... / Toward heaven" suggests leaving earth, but he reveals by his quick apologetic claim that he doesn't mean that. He wants to be dipped down again toward earth, but the pursuit of the ideal by going sounds like death, as his quick apology acknowledges. Frost does less in this poem than in "After Apple-Picking" to suggest a renewed pursuit of the ideal in life rather than a yielding to death. His main pursuit is continual balance between reality and ideality, but as John F. Sears (127:54) and Radcliffe Squires (45:95) point out, his vehicle for transcendence and his desire for nature to reinforce human intuition do not quite work.

"Pea Brush" has small links, perhaps satirical, to "Birches" and "Putting in the Seed." Here birches are first an annoyance: they must be cleared to make a path, and then the cut boughs interfere with the wild trillium's growth. But they also help the speaker, who uses them for a framework on which his peas, a frail early plant, can climb. These helps and hindrances parallel the images of birches as oppressed objects and then as instruments of playful contemplation in "Birches." At the end of "Pea Brush" the trilliums are pushing up in spite of obstacles, something like the sturdy seedlings at the end of "Putting in the Seed." But this playfully gentle scene contains implied ferocities. The hot sap bleeding from the birch stumps in this setting of early spring blends florescence and destruction. The frogs are happy but wary of the intruder. The birch boughs will help such garden growths as peas, but if not carted off they will burden the wild flowers. The boughs will be like cat's-cradle strings, and the peas will both give and take support from them. These trilliums will make it on their own, but this gardener, whose chief concerns lie elsewhere, helps out something that might have flourished without him. Man and nature here interact according to chance, nothing in the overall circumstances being quite sure.

"A Time to Talk" and "The Cow in Apple Time" provide lighter moments among the poems surrounding them. The first concerns a shared pause in human occupations, during which the subject of conversation remains deliberately unstated so that the human contact seems to have a momentum all its own – presumably a looking around to give significance to whatever subjects casually arise, just as the pause in farm labor gives an extra significance to its effort. The "meaning walk" to which the friend slows his horse is an unspoken call for companionship. The speaker then presents a vignette of what he isn't–someone so grim about his tasks that he resents interruptions (and presumably resents the tasks, too). The "time to talk" echoes Ecclesiastes' summary of the times of human life, and the hoe thrust in the ground is a promise of fertility and soon-to-be-continued effort. The plod to the stone wall conveys a sense of an exertion different from the farm task, and the clipped last line with its rhyme back to "is it" suggests that the pause will be brief and renewing.

In "The Cow in Apple Time," an animal, not a person, momentarily departs from routine, and the speaker contemplates the cow's reckless drunkenness with dry humor, showing empathy with her revolt but cool scorn for its seeming pointlessness. She is "the only cow of late" because the others have deserted the withering pasture (or have been driven home), which would give her reason, in addition to being drunk from fermented apples, for jumping over nasty walls. She runs from tree to tree for more nourishment and more intoxication, oblivious to the fruit's flaws. Probably, "she has to fly" under compulsion from her owner and so leaves some apples only tasted. Her bellowing indicates disgust with her plight, and her shriveled udder, dried up from lack of grass, shows the price she has paid for her drunken rampage. Though she is partly a victim of nature's caprice during apple time, the conclusion seems to make an ironical benediction over the fall of the year: summer is going, and cows, as well as people, suffer a falsely delirious leave-taking. It's done for, and that's that.

"An Encounter" returns to the mode of "The Wood-Pile" and "Birches," but with clearer interrelations of scenic detail and mood. On a typically lonely walking quest, the speaker's goals and discoveries are never wholly defined. Hard-hitting rhymes reinforce the grimly witty determination of his foray through difficult territory and disillusioning signs. A "weather breeder'" is a day promising storms, but the only storm to break here is an emotional one. He has been struggling through an overheated swamp on an undefined quest, apparently seeking an orientation or a clarification. Soon he regrets that he hadn't stayed with the familiar, and as he rests to reorient himself, his coat is grasped by a hook–probably an iron bar. As he looks to heaven for guidance, he sees that the bar is held by a tree become a denuded pole. His freedom is threatened by transformed nature. Allusion to the crucifixion seems likely: he is held by a naillike device; the once-living tree has been killed but resurrected into a barkless specter (whose offered salvation seems mechanical and superficial). The tree's fear of the speaker reflects the speaker's fear of its spectral quality. The yellow strands of wire attached to the tree, the "something" they convey, and the speaker's remark on the ubiquity of such poles all lend touches of color, vigor, and freedom to the scene, but the speaker's dismay outweighs these. Like Thoreau, he implies that wire-borne news isn't important. He defiantly insists that he isn't going anywhere of importance to the world but rather toward what might be profound for him. Insofar as he has wandered "out of beaten ways" in this narrative, he has discovered first a choking swamp and then an advancing technology that he doesn't much like. But he is still in pursuit of spiritual goals or clarifications, as symbolized by the rare Calypso orchid that grows in swamps and has been nearing extinction in New England. An additional reference to the nymph Calypso in the *Odyssey* seems unlikely, except in the sense that her name suggests the rare, exotic, and tempting. The poem's attitude toward telephone and telegraph partly resembles that in "The Line Gang."

"Range-Finding," a variant Petrarchan sonnet, is a war poem in which only three lines (and the title) make any reference to the facts of war. Surprisingly, the poem seems to have been written well before the start of World War I. But Frost's close friend Edward Thomas, a soldier who died on the Western Front in 1917, told him that it was a very good description of no-man's land (12:220). The poem centers on an intense small-scale scene in nature, surrounded by and infused with the tension of warfare, which the tiny creatures can't feel as anything but violation of an order on which they are programmed to depend. In the background looms a murderous encounter between humans, who are barely mentioned. The result is an enormously heightened perception of detail and a feeling that nature and human nature are indeed being violated, though the human destruction soon to flood this scene is only hinted at. Thus the scene is a hushed prelude to the more terrible scene the speaker won't bring himself to describe.

Range-finding, the method of initially coordinating gun sights and trajectories so bullets can find their targets, describes the rifle fire preliminary to infantry barrage and assault and also makes a pun on the range extending from tiny creatures to man. The cobweb, flower, and groundbird's nest show delicate beauty hugging the earth. The words "cut," "stained," and "stricken" fuse affliction to flower, bird, and humans; the bent and hung flower predicts how corpses will soon look here. The bird still revisiting its young shows a desperate determination not to recognize the havoc, a theme continued as a butterfly dispossessed by the same cut flower flutteringly clings to it, again showing nature's puzzled persistence, like something people feel in a childlike manner. The web like "a wheel of thread" is different from the one described earlier because it is not torn by a passing bullet (and seems larger). The bare pasture indicates a field between armies. The "straining cables wet with silver dew" combine beauty and vitality, though the web is also a spider's flytrap. The "sudden passing bullet" shows the same impersonality with which other bullets will soon slaughter men, but it merely passes through, scattering moisture from the web. The spider on that web thinks the vibrations announce an insect victim, but, finding none, withdraws with the sullenness a human might feel in its circumstances. Things so unspeakable are about to happen that the poem refuses to speak of them, leaving a contrast between human horror and the spider's sullenness as a symbol of the impersonal slaughter war tries, with some success, to teach people.

"The Hill Wife" is not Frost's only rhymed narrative, but it is his only narrative using a series of lyrics. In five numbered and separately titled parts, the poem is very much a unity, though parts I and III are written in the first person, from the hill wife's point of view, and the other three parts in a third person closely identified with it. The poem tells the story of a wife on a poor hillside farm, apparently recently married, who never seems to find deep companionship in marriage, is haunted by imaginary threats, and finally runs away from her husband. In Part I, "Loneliness," she speaks to her husband as if he shares her feelings, which seems unlikely. The scene shows her painful sensitivity to the changing seasons and to birds as companions who take the place of missing humans. The woman feels envy and regret for the birds' ability to make much out of little, which she wants to do but cannot. In Part II, "House Fear," an outside speaker describes her loneliness in terms of distances from other dwellings (their return from far away would be from shopping or visiting) and a house so empty that it is haunted by her fear. Such a need to let something out appears also in "The Fear" and "The Lockless Door." The lit lamp is a deliberately frail symbol of house as comfort and suggests entering one loneliness from another.

In Part III, "The Smile," the wife speaks again to her husband, although her hushed desperation suggests more a stream of thought than something spoken. This section focuses on her strange notion that the beggar-stranger has smiled sardonically and threateningly at them. Her compassion for him is somewhat dimmed into scorn as she thinks of him as a "wretch" (like herself). Her idea that he might have seized things from them rather than beg is foolish, for obviously they have nothing much to be seized, and there's no evidence that her husband is physically weak. Her paranoid stance is strongest in the last three lines, in which she projects her self-consciousness into the idea that the beggar would bother to pause down the road and watch them. Her idea of herself and her husband as old and dead shows her hopelessness, as if her life could have no significance before its end.

In Part IV, "The Oft-Repeated Dream," the woman's fears center on a single image combining the reality of a tree outside a window and her repeated dream of that tree. The comparison of the tree to a bird puzzled by glass shows the threatening tree mysteriously and luckily kept outside. The woman's wishing a dark saying for this experience implies that she tries to speak of it, but her husband doesn't seem to show much concern. That the dream is oft-repeated suggests a vain struggle to control it. The fact that "only one of the two" is afraid is a sardonic indication of the husband's saner mind and lack of concern for his wife's fear, suggesting their increasing separation.

In Part V, "The Impulse" (the final section), the sense of loneliness dominates with a tonal difference. The scene has an outdoor charm missing from the earlier parts, and the woman seems a bit of a wood sprite, perhaps possessing an imaginative sensitivity that the husband lacks. She seems more feeling and imaginative than he, watching the farm work, singing "only to herself," as if making her own world in the face of a lack of communication with him. She ritualistically breaks a bough of alder, perhaps as a gesture of revolt and of intimacy with the tree. Her distant straying follows naturally from her earlier contemplativeness. As she runs to hide in the fern her suddenly serious game of elusiveness expresses a hostility and disappointment she has never been able to show. That the ties broke "sudden and swift and light" suggests rejoicing on her part, and the potential lesson for the man is understated as he learns of finalities "besides the grave," where it is essential to see that "besides" means in addition to and not (as *beside* would) next to, for the woman has not died. She has managed a departure to places where her chances for independent life will be better, and presumably she enjoys paying back her husband's lack of concern or understanding.

Healthier family relationships abound in "The Bonfire," largely a monologue spoken by a father to his children, who interrupt his speech for a total of three and a half lines. Only a line and a half are not part of his or their speech. The father talks at length to his children about making a bonfire of a pile of brush gathered on a mountain and then reminisces about a similar fire he made long ago and just barely managed to bring under control. In conclusion, he analogizes about the dangers and rewards of such risks. The poem was published in November 1916, just five months before America entered The Great War, referred to at the end. The father starts by inviting the children to participate in the reckless but exciting burning of the pile of brush and to share the pleasure of rousing their neighbors, both those who would voice their outrage and those who would be more restrained. Making a volcano of the mountain and scaring themselves suggest the general but risky revitalization of letting "wild fire loose."

The father's memory of the fire of long ago is salted with biblical allusions. Fire "sweeping 'round . . . with a flaming sword" recalls the angelic flaming sword that shut the fallen Adam and Eve forever out of Eden. This suggests that reckless fire brings an end to innocence and a commitment to experience. Yet his declaring that their fire may do "much more . . . I mean it shall not do if I can bind it" shows his hesitation before a destruction that offers potentialities for good and for evil. He goes back concretely, rather than speculatively, to what happened when he once started a fire that made "a pinnacle to heaven," which resembles the Hebrews' sacrifices to their God. The fire "spread like black death," suggesting social catastrophe, but it was stopped first by a brook and then by a road and by his efforts. He had a successful struggle that left an awful devastation. His lack of weariness at the end shows combined relief at his success and exhilaration at his daring. After he tells the children that such a fright parallels what is to be anticipated from war, he warns them that their fear shows them to be ill-prepared for war, which nowadays doesn't spare children. "Now we are almost digging down to China" suggests that their hope for limiting war is as vain as an attempt to dig through the earth. War that will involve everyone seems terrible but must be faced as both a horror and a possible revitalization. The family's setting this fire will be a ritualistic preparation for what they must soon face, so he suggests that they go ahead with it. By laughing and being afraid they will recognize the ambiguity they face and be ready for it.

"A Girl's Garden" is the first of three light interludes between the threat of "The Bonfire" and the grimness of "'Out, Out–,'" both poems in which children are threatened. "A Girl's Garden" is told in third person but sticks to the point of view of the neighbor when she was a girl; her father's language resembles the poem's style. All of the narrator's comments parallel the girl's cast of mind. The girl's father had a genial but challenging attitude when he gave her a plot for her miniature garden. To succeed, she had to face limitations and difficulties. "But she don't mind now," we are told, which though slightly ambiguous about the time meant by "now," chiefly suggests that as an adult she values her former efforts. Her varied garden suggests a wide range of experience within a narrow physical sphere. Among her apparently retrospective pleasures is to have "mistrusted" that she had planted an apple tree that still bears and provides, the word meaning suspected ("mistrust" is used in the same sense in the much later "Happiness Makes Up in Height for What It Lacks in Length"). The "little bit of everything, / A great deal of none" that she produced predicts the ambiguous celebration of noncommercial self-reliance in the long poem "New Hampshire." Now the woman's chief pleasure is being able to make modest analogies between her days as a farmer and the problems, social as well as agricultural, that arise in her village.

In "Locked Out" and "The Last Words of a Bluebird" Frost seems to be composing first a parable and then an animal fairy tale for his children. "Locked Out" shows not cats and dogs but flowers being locked out of a house at night because they can take care of themselves and don't share the family's need for protection. "Cut[ting] them off from window light" shows the family keeping to itself. Locking them out is part of the house's protection from thieves and possibly suggests that the flowers too could be thieves. The speaker claims to have once dreamed that thieves tried the door but didn't molest the flowers that were out there with them, proving that flowers are safe locked out. Thus, the children need not worry about the flowers. Apparently his family did find a bitten nasturtium the next day. He may have been to blame for its fate because in playing with the flower he had made it his friend, which had caused it to get bitten trying to protect them.

The moral may be either that one can leave flowers to take care of themselves, or that it may be helpful to make friends of flowers so they will be protective, or perhaps even that one should not lock flowers out.

"The Last Word of a Bluebird" is one of Frost's few poems naming one or more of his children. He seems to be encouraging his daughter Lesley to think of birds as her friends and of the crow as reasonably friendly to the bluebird. The crow, being hardier than the bluebird, who has already been driven away by the winter, delivers the other bird's message to the girl. The bluebird had told the crow that if the girl would be good and enjoy the winter, he would reward her by returning with spring. Of course, speaker and reader know that the return of spring and bird do not depend on the girl's behavior. Frost is joking with his daughter, who was about 16 years old when "Locked Out" was first published but probably younger when it and the hard-to-date "The Last Word" were written.

"'Out, Out–'" is a concise blank-verse narrative. Told in the first person, it strikingly overlaps the points of view of the narrator, the boy whose death is its main subject, and the onlookers at this dreadful event. It also uses a blend of tones, alternating among delight, fear, tenderness, and sarcasm. The title quotes the speech in which Shakespeare's Macbeth, lamenting his wife's death, declares life to be meaningless after he has said "Out, out, brief candle!" (5.5.23). In Frost's context this becomes an angry comment on the senselessness of the boy's accidental death, though in Shakespeare's play Macbeth's fatalism is connected to his immorality. As Frost's farmyard scene begins, the animated buzz saw's viciousness contrasts with the pleasantness of the sweet-smelling wood and to the broad prospect of the world represented by the sweeping scene. As the saw continues its threat, the speaker yearningly identifies with the boy's desire to be done with work, which stresses the boy's love of life and underscores the chance nature of the dreadful accident. The animation of the saw is strangely blended with the human desire for supper, and its seeming leap implies a vicious motivation in things, while the boy's giving up his hand implies a carelessness so terrible it suggests unconscious deliberateness.

That neither saw nor hand refused the meeting makes the personifications more gentle; the tone implies that chance rather than will has guided what seems as if only will could guide it. The catastrophe is understated; the boy's "rueful laugh" suggests desperation combined with hopelessness, and the effort "to keep [his] life from spilling" associates blood with vitality. Thus fateful and fatal moment coalesce in one image. The boy "saw all spoiled" because he realized that without a hand he could not be a complete man or live a complete life. His plea for his hand is also a plea for his life, but both are almost immediately lost. The poem ends with the incredulousness of the onlookers, which the speaker can gently mock because he already knows what is to happen and has formed an attitude toward it.

"No more to build on there" externalizes the loss of the boy's life. The conclusion creates a delicate balance between sarcasm and stoicism. It is natural that others would just go on with their lives, for that is all they can do, but the abruptness of their "turn[ing] to their affairs" suggests either that their investment in the boy's life was slight or that people are not capable of truly registering the suffering of others. Frost deliberately echoes their bluntness and, as in other poems, does it with such conviction that it seems he feels their stance himself but cannot wholly approve of it.

"Brown's Descent" imitates the old popular ballads with its simple plot and conventional moral but departs from them in its mock heroic tone. The first twelve stanzas describe the adventures of farmer Brown, who lives very high up and who one frozen winter night takes a long and harrowing slide down his hill. He manages to keep his lantern upright and lit, and suffers no injury, although he has to maneuver to keep from breaking his neck or tearing his clothes. The scene is made amusing by an understated description of his neighbors' reaction to the arc of his light, as if he were making signals for a celebration, and by Brown's resigned pleasure in his childlike adventure. In six stanzas of commentary the narrator celebrates Brown as evidence that the Yankee stock is still vigorous, well-mannered, and not excessively proud. Brown makes the best of circumstances. Proud and independent, he does not mind that he seems to be going home in a roundabout way. He appears to be ready to use such indirection to gain political office, or perhaps the narrator is saying that he's inventing such a motive for Brown's indirection. In the last stanza, Brown seems unconcerned with the speaker's reasoning. He just accepts the fact that his lantern oil is almost all gone and that he has to take the long way home. Brown's comment on the oil does not reflect his need to take this way but rather shows a practical and stoical concern for the waste into which he was forced.

"The Gum-Gatherer" creates a portrait of another independent Yankee type, this one admired with a combination of genial affection and envy. Here the speaker, an active and joyous participant, shares a thoroughly pleasant downhill stride with the gum gatherer, whose independence is shown by his bag of gum being his only load and then by his pleasure in living on infertile and unpopulated land higher than the speaker's mountain farm. His shack must have been stolen because it was built where the lumber folk would be terrified of his setting their trees on fire rather than because the wood may have been stolen. Their fears of conflagration contrast with his ease in such surroundings, just as their large commercial ventures contrast with his small one. The gatherer is shown as just one outsider among others who live wildly to themselves and bring bits of produce to town to help their marginal economy. His produce is less practical than theirs, and his "scented stuff" carries an esthetic whiff of wildness. The speaker concludes with gentle envy, as he sees the gatherer communing with trees, his little knife establishing an easy and nonthreatening bond. He uses wildness without destroying it and he remains unbounded. Going to market may be business, but it is fun, and he does it just when he pleases. The puzzling line "That all your days are dim beneath" probably describes the man looking up at the shade cast by the trees in the forest, unless Richard Wilbur is right in proposing that the gatherer looks down from the heights of trees onto the shaded forest floor. Wilbur, taking the lumps of resin as symbols, sees an allegory about the making of poems, although the poem doesn't mention language and art (177).

"The Line-Gang," an irregularly rhymed sonnet, again treats the relationship between wilderness and civilization, the wilderness here invaded by men simultaneously admirable and offensive. The situation resembles that in "An Encounter," but here the speaker is visible only in terms of his attitudes. The word "line-gang," describing a group of men who cut trees and string telephone and telegraph lines, creates the sense of vigorous ruffians, and the reference to "pioneering" evokes an admirable penetration of the wilderness. However, their bringing down trees "less cut than broken" shows them as violators of the forest, as does the irony of planting dead trees. The lines they string combine the beautiful and useful in forming a "living thread" and in being "instruments"; the latter image suggests useful things making music. The words are "beaten out" (as telegraph signals) or "spoken" (through telephones). Mechanical qualities are further qualified by the "hush" through the lines before electric impulses are converted to sound. In the eighth line, the men's presence starts to dominate. Their shouts contrast to the hush in the wires, and the speaker's modulation between their violent efforts and successful completions shows his admiration for their skillful engagement. "They have it" indicates the speaker's emotional engagement with the men as he echoes their dialogue and action. Quite literally, they curse, but their scorn is for the wild as obstacle, not for the wild as something valueless. As the poem ends, the matter-of-factly useful triumphs over the recalcitrant wilderness in a way that conflicts with the speaker's initial distress. From beginning to end the poem is a tissue of mixed feelings.

"The Vanishing Red," a compact narrative with a minimal plot, uses the loosest blank verse found in any of Frost's poems. The rhythms, repetitions, and skeletal action are as cramped as the Miller's murderous anger. The pervasively sardonic tone echoes chiefly the Miller's attitude but partly the Indian's, and in some strange fashion perhaps also the speaker's grim feelings about confrontation between the two men's races. To expand on an observation by William Meredith about the title's irony (283), the red man didn't magically vanish (the sentimental veneer on the American attitude toward a destroyed people); he was murdered but, of course, he vanished from sight by means of a partly concealed and partly revealed act. It is clear that he vanished right from under our feet, if we face facts.

The first and last stanzas show the same scene; the last stanza clarifies what happened. In the first stanza, the Miller laughs with satisfaction over ridding himself of an offensive nuisance, but when a bystander expresses concern or joins in, he gives him a look "as if to say" that what the Miller has done is his own grim business and is better than talk when action is really needed. Next comes the commentary and retrospect of the second stanza. There had been such hostility between the races that the rights and wrongs weren't necessarily connected with who began the conflict between the Miller and the Red Man (John). The Red Man had been disapproving or angry about the mill's operation, and perhaps offensively curious. Angry about John's attitude, the Miller had taken him downstairs, and after showing him the opening to the wheel pit, where the water struggled in a manner predicting John's demise, had thrown John in and shut the door over him. The "ring" on the door is a handle, but the word puns on the sound it makes, ringing out a crude requiem for John. Then the Miller comes upstairs and gives the laugh with which the poem begins, within earshot of a man going about a practical task. The repeated "meal sack" shows the factual world echoing and contrasting to the murder. Not "then," but later, the man would understand what the Miller had said and what he had done. The last line locks into the Miller's thoughts, implying respect for the powers of the wheel pit as they oppose the Indian's supposed lack of respect and civilization. The Miller thinks he gave John what he deserved, and though Frost sees the action as brutal, he withholds some of his judgment in the face of a conflict one could only have understood by being there.

"Snow," Frost's longest narrative poem, is almost entirely in dialogue. Its three characters are a farm husband and wife, Fred and Helen Cole, and Meserve, presumably a part-time lay preacher for a Racker Sect. Making his way along a seven-mile stretch from store to home through an evening blizzard, Meserve stops at the Cole's more than midway to his home, at 12:30 in the morning. As the farm couple plead with him to stay, he gives elaborate, parablelike reasons for refusing, and eventually leaves—much to their relief. The poem characterizes Fred and Helen Cole through their complicated and conflicting responses to Meserve's situation and character, and makes an extensive portrait of Meserve's unexpectedly sophisticated and elusive character, which doesn't much correspond to Helen Cole's expectations. Meserve is a small man, but tough and determined. He telephones his wife to tell her he is on his way and is tenderly patronizing toward her hints that he should stay over. He is considerate to his horses and dignified and unapologetic to neighbors whom he must know look down on him.

Helen Cole claims to detest Meserve for his views, his supposed religious smugness, and his irresponsibility in having a family of ten children whose future he is risking. Fred Cole, more admiring of Meserve, respects in him what he sees as a general manliness that has an aggressive side, of which women manage to make men ashamed. But both of them have mixed feelings. Fred argues with Meserve to stay, partly out of sympathy for Helen's feelings but also out of his own concern. And Helen, who thinks that she argues mostly in consideration for Meserve's family, likes him more than she can admit and is disappointed when he doesn't display the expected religious cant.

With brief interruptions by the couple, long speeches by Meserve fill the middle third of the poem; these are rich with metaphor and analogy. He philosophizes rather like Robert Frost, mostly in justification of the daring he intends to continue. He makes a parable out of a book leaf standing upright on the table before them – one of the things in the room with them that takes its repose from the people, for repose is something that one can give even without having it. Potential motions of this leaf stand for life ahead and things behind that one would like to recover and change. Meserve wants to will change in the book leaf and in his life, as if the life represents opportunities come back that must not be missed this time, for "Our very life depends on everything's / Recurring till we answer from within." Still, the leaf's fate itself is unimportant, for to Meserve, life is more important than the analogy.

His next two figurations describe the snow outside as a monstrous and stupid creature that Meserve seems to want to challenge and then as something that when banked high against a house creates a special pleasure for those protected inside. He says that he likes the snow from inside more than from outside but that he doesn't want to be considered less than birds who can survive in such a storm and thrive on the morrow, so it is evident that he must face the worst challenge of the outside in order to enjoy the inside. Repose for him must be earned rather than just accepted. Thus, after half an hour or so, he proceeds into the storm, comparing it to a war that one would feel compelled to join. Fred and Helen argue on about him; Fred thinks that Helen wanted Meserve to disobey her.

The two of them remain anxious for him until they learn of his safe homecoming, communicated through another tense scene. Mrs. Meserve has called, angry that the Coles had let her husband proceed, but her voice stops, and a baby is heard crying. The Coles feel fear for her and her family's safety until Meserve picks up the line to explain that his wife had been helping him into the barn. Now that the Coles are relieved, they release a bit of anger against Meserve, but their feelings toward him remain empathetic and admiring, as if Meserve's quest was a kind of triumph for them. Fred's asking Helen whether she thinks Meserve will ever call again seems a suggestion that he will not and that they've had a once-in-a-lifetime learning experience – safer than Meserve's, though John Doyle suggests that the last line's purpose is to show how the Coles will continue to banter critically with each other (29:92).

"The Sound of Trees," originally set in italic type to emphasize its farewell position, also deals with the question of crucial choices and shows Frost's familiar identification of speakers with trees, as well as his view of trees as both appealing and threatening. The irregular rhymes and the interruption of rhyme patterns by periods reinforce the poem's indecisive movement of thought. Although the speaker loves the trees, he speaks of "bear[ing]" and "suffer[ing]" their wished-for noises, thus showing strongly mixed feelings about their charm and message. The trees interfere with the sense of "measure" and "fixity" because wind whips through them irregularly, creating an aura of expectancy. In the first nine lines their noise seems to come from both nature and the listeners' spirits, but when the trees are said to "talk," their personification grows emphatic, and the trees show a deeply human wisdom. Like people, they talk "of going" but remain rooted. Still, they talk on in defiance of knowledge that they will indeed stay, as if the talk were needed to ritualize impulses on which they dare not act. The speaker now feels so much at one with the trees that his feet "tug at the floor" like their straining roots and his "head sways to [his] shoulder," as if blown by the wind. At least, this happens sometimes, when he "watch[es] trees sway, / From the window or the door," symbolizing the hold of home. Without any transition, he asserts that he will "set forth for somewhere" in what will be a "reckless choice." He will do this on a day when the trees speak and toss threateningly at the clouds, as if emulating the clouds' freedom. His conclusion is sad and regretfully apologetic. Presumably, he will "have less to say" because he will have to stop arguing with himself and others, and if he is gone, he will miss and be missed by others. His sadness suggests that despite its assertive manner, the gesture—a thrust toward freedom, verging on the irresponsible—remains just a supposition (recalling the unacted flight into the lonely forest of individuality of "Into My Own"). Robert McPhillips believes that the original pairing of this poem with "The Road Not Taken," both published in italic type in *Mountain Interval* reinforces a contrast between them, with "The Sound of Trees" proposing a choice far less responsible than the balance between the real and the ideal proposed, in his view, by the first poem and by such poems as "Birches" (105:98).

# CHAPTER 7

## *New Hampshire*
## (1923)

Frost's fourth collection, issued seven years after his third, won him his first Pulitzer Prize and initially received as much praise as any of his earlier books. Some reviewers, noting the novel departure of the book's satirical title poem, acknowledged its plain and prosy style as appropriate for its intentions, though the poem has achieved little popularity with critics. The collection was divided into three parts: the first the title poem, the second a section called "Notes," and the third a section called "Grace Notes." The title poem carried a number of footnotes claiming connections to several of the "Notes" poems, but these connections are usually indirect and fanciful. The "Notes" poems – with two exceptions, blank-verse narratives – show more philosophical reflectiveness than most of the narratives in *North of Boston*. The two in lyrical form are "A Star in a Stoneboat" and "An Empty Threat." All of the "Grace Notes" poems are lyrics in familiar Frostian veins, except for "Two Look at Two," a short blank-verse narrative with much lyrical intensity. Of the volume's narratives, those most favored by anthologists are "The Witch of Coös" and "Two Look at Two," though "The Ax-Helve" and "The Pauper Witch of Grafton" continue to be held in high critical esteem. Among the lyrics are the very popular "Stopping by Woods on a Snowy Evening," "The Onset," "Fire and Ice," "Nothing Gold Can Stay," "To Earthward," and "The Need of Being Versed in Country Things," most of which are esteemed as highly by critics as by anthologists and the public.

## "New Hampshire"

Frost's longest poem except for his masques, "New Hampshire" marks a new departure. A blank-verse satire, varied in voice and loaded with allusions, its tricky attitudes have annoyed, puzzled, and charmed readers. Frost told Lawrance Thompson that the poem came partly from his desire to answer a series of articles in *The Nation* criticizing various states. Frost reportedly stayed up all of a night in July 1922 writing the poem, and during the morning hours topped it off by composing "Stopping by Woods on a Snowy Evening" (21:230-31, 236-37). John Lynen begins a lengthy explication of the poem by dividing it into four sections, which division will provide a model here (38:62-77).

In the first part, from the opening to line 60 ("We both of us turned over in our graves"), Frost argues for the spiritual superiority of New Hampshire by contrasting it to prouder, more materialistic states. He begins by making fun of people from other states for various boastful attitudes. He agrees or pretends to agree that commercial values are bad, and then he objects to excessive claims for beneficent climates and to the idea of enlisting writers in causes. Lynen thinks that Frost is arguing against commercialism and for spiritual self-sufficiency, but Frost's ideas as expressed elsewhere and his description of the New Hampshire man whose California successes soiled him with trade suggest that Frost isn't wholly serious in attacking commercial values (indeed, later he pleads for the commercial success of his own writings) but rather sees commercialism as valuable if approached rightly.

The second part, lines 61-214, surveys the world of New Hampshire and pretends to praise its noncommercial singularities. But since these are often of dubious value, Frost is probably satirizing New Hampshire boastings as he had earlier satirized other states'. President Franklin Pierce was a mediocrity, and the legendary orator Daniel Webster offended many New Englanders by his traitorous support of the Fugitive Slave Bill (an act alluded to in Emerson's "Ode to Channing," quoted in this poem). The tall tale of the preimmigrant family whom John Smith supposedly saw on the New Hampshire coast suggests local boasting and may, as Alan Gaylord proposes (214:23), satirize the New England passion for genealogy (and therefore for aristocratic standing, an idea itself undercut by the primitiveness of the people). The reformer who dislikes the smugness of artists and college boys demonstrates witty New England modesty. Frost's joking praise for the gold mined in noncommercial quantities for family use may be playing an esthetic anticommercialism and self-sufficiency off against the grosser anticommercialism of pretentious aristocrats and leveling radicals. New Hampshire's "old style" witch is the real thing, as opposed to the "new style" witch, a fraudulent combination of wealth and psychical research. But Frost may be vaguely tolerant of her, at least more than he can be of the White Corpuscles, who rush around dressed like the Ku Klux Klan as they try to censor bad-smelling writings "and give someone the Skipper Ireson's Ride" (Ireson is tarred and feathered in Whittier's poem of the same name). Frost's smack at censorship excludes him from the "prude[s]" mentioned later.

Frost seems genuinely regretful about the poor quality of New England land (some readers are tricked by the ironic claim that "quality makes up for quantity"), though it helps protect the region and once aided his purchase of a neighbor's envied property (but without the coercion he claims here). Frost's delight in the purity of New Hampshire's unsprayed apples is balanced by knowledge that they end up going partly to waste. The problem of commercialism comes home to him in relation to his struggles to market his poems. New Hampshire's difficulties may promote the creation of literature, but commercial values make it hard to market. Frost makes Vermont share New Hampshire's qualities in order to praise their New England solidarity and to prepare us for the poem's conclusion. He may delight in the smallness and good humor of New Hampshire communities, but he recognizes a certain provinciality.

In the third part, lines 215-357, Frost concentrates on his role as a poet and his relationship to other writers. He quotes from Emerson's "Ode to Channing" a line that condemned the supporters of the Fugitive Slave Act. Then he cites Amy Lowell's claim that Frost's own poems (she meant those in *North of Boston*) show the degeneracy of New England's people. Here and later, he acknowledges that New England's difficulties are representative of the human condition and are thus the source of his deepest inspiration, though he seems unsure about the contribution of suffering to great literature. Frost's calling himself a "sensibilitist" means that he is overly sensitive to his surroundings. An environmentalist is one who takes what he can from his surroundings without trying to change them. As a sensibilitist, Frost quotes Christopher Marlowe's *Doctor Faustus*, in which Mephistopheles declares "Why, this is hell nor am I out of it," which supports Frost's claim that ordinary life provides plenty of suffering to make him an artist. He finds New Hampshire life sufficiently symbolic of humanity to make his work representative, though he also congratulates himself that he has wonderful friends throughout New Hampshire (better than the people he has fled from) and declares that life in America is not terrible enough to provide material for Russian-style novels. Here Frost partly contradicts his Marlowe-quoting mood as he praises the beneficence of New England life and goes on to make fun of Communist (as opposed to Czarist) Russia for legislating cheerfulness in literature rather than (presumably) being as fortunate as we Americans, who have no cause for intense gloom. The farmer who cites "John L. Darwin" (a conflation of the names of John L. Sullivan, world heavyweight champion, and Charles T. Darwin, great biologist) as the cause of Victorian gloom is either jocular or ignorant. Darwin knocked faith out of the Victorian world and created the kind of gloom that would contribute to the writing of Russian-style novels. But perhaps this New England farmer is deliberately talking sage nonsense. The man who burned his house for the insurance money and bought a telescope with it tried too desperately to satisfy his curiosity and looks like a figure in crisis who should have sought calm differently.

This is a very mixed bag of New Hampshire people, but Frost says that they are good enough for him, that he would rather elevate the land than the people – though as John Lynen argues (38:72), he elevates the land to make it a symbol for his perspective as a poet. He is someone who would bring the ideal down and join it to the real, an idea given a second illustration by the lumberjack gang-boss who dances wildly across a logjam and finds it an ideal because its difficulty leads him to a triumph of skill. Lynen sees this activity paralleling the poet's "maneuvering in the world of ideas" (38:74). Alan Gaylord speculates that Frost may have initially ended the poem at line 357 and added the last part early in 1923 after a bitter conversation with the literary journalist Burton Rascoe, who attacked Frost for lack of sympathy with Eliot and Joyce (214:35).

In the poem's fourth part, lines 358-413, Frost confronts a "New York alec" who sees sexual frankness as the hallmark of genuine literature and gives Frost the choice of being "prude or puke" – that is, someone afraid to be realistic or someone so devoted to the brutal truth that his work will make people vomit. "'Mewling and puking in the public arms'" parodies Shakespeare's "Mewling and puking in the nurses's arms" (*As You Like It*, 2.7.144). The praise of realism seems to uphold the necessity of brutality, which turns out to be what Frost cannot accept. But he refuses to accept the dichotomy. He flees to the woods, where he doesn't have to choose, but he emphatically rejects people who fear nature and see it only as a source of brutality. On the other hand, he won't engage in nature worship like the idolatry of Ahaz in the Bible, thereby implying that the puke is a kind of nature worshiper, or at least an idolater of sex. John Lynen argues that Frost is opting for a healthy relationship with nature as a "penetrating exploration of reality" (38:77).

## "Notes"

In "A Star in a Stoneboat" Frost follows through from an ambition mentioned in "New Hampshire": "To tap the upper sky ... / Down from the stars to freeze the dew as starry," as a fallen meteorite symbolizes poetry's attempt to build its own world and understand the cosmos. Combining realistic description with extravagant yet ironically controlled metaphor, the speaker issues a challenge against those who would doubt his imagined vision of a plodding farmer who has picked up a meteorite but missed all its microcosmic splendor, yet the mocking tone expresses both sympathy for humanity's limited vision and a comic self-deflation of the speaker's imaginative vision. The farm laborer's ignorance of the fact that he might move the fallen star from the spot is puzzling – until one sees that his immediate reaction has led to a harmful florescence of the soil, whose substitution of flowers for grain grieves him until he loads the meteorite into a stoneboat (a handcart for moving stones) and carries it off to use in building a wall. But he does the wrong thing, for the fallen star, representing imagination, should not be dragged to the earth but should be kept flying.

The speaker now fully enters the realm of imagination and blames himself for not taking up the laborer's proper burden. However, he is divided between different proprieties. He doesn't know a more proper place for the star than in a wall – a notion that suggests a merging of the real and the ideal. Or perhaps the star should have been left where it fell to find its own purpose. As the speaker gazes from stone walls, representing both reality and limitations, toward stars, representing the ideal, he realizes that he cannot quite understand either. He looks for final meanings in such stone walls – combinations of the real and the ideal – rather than in creeds and churches, knowing that with the right effort he can bring the rare stone of imagination to life, for the fallen meteorite has now become a version of any stone as microcosm. When his imagination works, it asserts its vigorous thrusts, which can't easily be controlled. The last stanza reverts to the initial irony about the laborer, though the poem is permeated with irony. Frost undercuts the laborer's powers to find a world in the imagination or to really understand whatever he finds. But the preceding lines have already suggested both the limits of his symbol (it was not "a star of death and sin") and his inability to control it. Frost's conclusion helps connect him to the ordinary people whom he seems to satirize at the poem's beginning. Richard Poirier thinks the poem comments on Frost's own poetry and poetry in general (42:313).

"The Census Taker" returns to the waste world of "The Wood-Pile" and "An Encounter," but with a big difference. In those poems the speaker's lostness and pursuit of significance were central. Here the landscape displays a human-created ruin of dwelling places, and the speaker is desperately hopeful that such ruination is not inevitable. He seems literally to be a "census-taker," having been delegated to see if anyone still lives in a large tract of land from which the lumber has been ruthlessly cut down, where he finds an abandoned house. The scene is profoundly sorrowful. Women have never lived there, with their promise of the race's continuance. All the people remaining, though they are just fantasies, are hiding from the outward eye, as if they had deliberately fled from the speaker's hopes and left him to locate them with the inward eye. It is autumn, but all trees that might have been flourishing have been cut down to rotting stumps. As if he needs company, the speaker personifies the wind and sees it swing the door of the abandoned house in place of the rude men who have vanished. These men come to life in his imagination, and he counts nine of them before he himself becomes the tenth one and enters the house, only to obsessively see numerous signs of their absence. They are "people to [his] ear," perhaps because he hears them in the wind.

The comparison of the one-year decay of this house to the ruin of ancient civilizations makes the present scene seem very old – another example of the worst that can happen to civilizations. In order to confirm the absence of humans, the speaker performs a sort of inverse marriage ceremony, asking that any person still living there come out of hiding or that anyone objecting to his pronouncing a divorce between the area and the haunts of humans should speak up. Frost combines a final outburst of aggrieved resentment with a hope that he may be wrong, and the juxtaposition of this last hope with the pained resignation of the next three lines prepares us for the desperation of the concluding statement: "It must be I want life to go on living." This line seems to resound over the emptiness, like a prayer directed toward the speaker's own breast, but also quietly outward toward humanity and God, without making a direct plea that such things not be allowed to happen.

The simple story of "The Star-Splitter" presents subtly varied ideas. Brad McLaughlin, having failed at farming, and caring more for stargazing than working his fields, burns down his house for the fire insurance, purchases a pretty good telescope, and having secured a job on the railroad, enjoys gazing at stars, often in the company of the speaker. As the poem opens, Brad's loving talk about stargazing contrasts with his "smoky lantern chimney," and though the stars see his clumsy farming, he still has rights they should respect – presumably both his way of farming and the dishonest act he is about to perform. Brad's description of his plowing suggests that he had not been a completely lazy farmer and shows what poor land he was working. The story of the house-burning and telescope purchase is told a second time, the repetition showing Brad's obsessiveness and throwing his questionable morality at the reader's face. Immediately thereafter, Brad is allowed his core philosophical statement: "'The best thing that we're put here for's to see'" – a hard generalization to argue against, except that it doesn't adequately include human relationships.

Twenty-five lines are given to amused but uneasy justification for Brad's act: he needed an opportunity to somehow undo the crime; his childhood deprivations somehow justified it; the house wasn't really hurt; perhaps some good would come of it. Through all these rationalizations, Frost mildly satirizes modern social views that he does not like but by which he seems tempted. Satire continues in the description of Brad's railroad job, which includes the posting of railroad signal lights, whose resemblance to stars suggests by contrast that he is still stuck with the mundane. As Brad and the speaker gaze together at stars, delighted with the firmness of their feet and the telescope's, looking at stars split in two or three (the effect that a medium-power telescope gives at the first sighting of a star), Brad is still not getting a whole view of things, suggesting that one cannot get a whole view. The star-splitting is further satirized when the speaker suggests that splitting stars is good if it is to be "compared with splitting wood"—that is, if it's useful, which it quite clearly is not. Possibly the speaker's point of view is being satirized here, though the comparison of star-splitting to wood-splitting calls to mind the end of "Two Tramps in Mud Time" and contrasts with the limited praise of grasping the stars' meaning in "A Star in a Stoneboat."

Still, the two men "Said some of the best things we ever said"—a triumph of experience for both of them. But this triumph, which is not detailed, seems strongly contradicted by the speaker's "We've looked and looked, but after all where are we?" (implying that we do not get very far with our insights) and suggests more skepticism than does the conclusion of "A Star in a Stoneboat." Furthermore, the man with the smoky lantern takes us back to the earlier Brad and implies that things do not stand differently for him now; that is, he doesn't have much more understanding or ambition than he first had. Such an interpretation is questioned by William S. Waddell, Jr., who thinks the poem is built around two aphorisms: Brad's statement "'The best thing that we're put here for's to see'" and the speaker's "For to be social is to be forgiving." Waddell suggests that the questions at the poem's end, rather than expressing severe doubt, are intended to go unanswered, and that the gain in relations between men is more important than the relationship between men and stars (262). This view denies an obvious melancholy in the last five lines but does help account for Frost's affectionate view of Brad and the nostalgic survey of the speaker's experience. John C. Kemp defends the poem's unity somewhat differently, maintaining that the narrator is not intended to be wholly reliable and underestimates the lasting value of the two men's conversations. Frost, Kemp thinks, dramatizes the "speaker's vacillation from regional to nonregional and back to regional attitudes," and implies that the regional view's criticism of Brad need not be wholly trusted (36:215). James L. Potter offers a compromise view: that Frost is trying to balance the importance of trying to "find one's metaphysical position against the necessity of man's limiting himself to his own worldly realm" (43:133).

"Maple" is another narrative poem about incomplete vision, this time the result of the protagonist's hesitation. Maple's problem is to learn why her mother, moments before she died after giving birth to the girl, gave her this novel name that is so widely and troublesomely taken to be Mabel. Her mother may have had a deliberate intention, and her father's feeling that pursuit of the name's meaning might be dangerous implies that it concerns something worth keeping hidden. Perhaps his explanation that her mother meant her to "Be a good girl—be like a maple tree" is a cover for an embarrassing concealment. Maple's pursuing of her name's meaning, but not in the spirit of "the parent seed," suggests that she looks for things to satisfy her own values, not those her parents (or mother) might have held. Frost jokes about the contrast between her name and ordinary names by citing the names of his own four children. The narrative takes on the aura of a mystery story when Maple finds a maple leaf in the family Bible but finds no significance in the marked passage and then loses the page forever, though later she tells her husband a possibly significant phrase she recalls from it.

Her name does in fact influence her fate, for her self-seeking curiosity induces her to become a secretary in New York City. Her boss's observation that she reminds him of a maple tree (though he also thinks her name is Mabel) leads to their marriage, after which they continue to search for her name's meaning. Hoping to find a revelatory tree near her father's country home, they find no trees, let alone a grove of sugar maples, but this venture leads Maple to tell her husband what she recalled of the Bible passage. The phrase "wave offering" appears about 18 times in Genesis, Leviticus, and Numbers, where it is associated with "heave offerings," a description of sacrifices of ram's flesh and bread that the Lord bids Moses and Aaron conduct ritually. In one Bible passage these sacrifices are shown to be recompenses for trespasses, but Maple can find no relevance to herself in this. Her husband makes some progress with the problem by recognizing that the name may have been part of something exclusively between her father and mother, or at least something that her father may understand but not want to explain. Evidently he senses the likelihood of a sexual meaning, for he compares her father's reticence about the past to his indirect reference to Maple's present pregnancy ("About the way he saw it was with you") now that Maple is the same age (twenty-five) as her mother had been when she died. In a last attempt to decipher the name, they examine a grove of sugar maples. It is autumn, long after the springtime sugar harvest, about which they decline to think. Their most significant discovery is a maple tree that has recently shed all its foliage and now stands naked with arms uplifted and appears to be just a little younger than Maple. That "They hovered for a moment near discovery," indicates that this is a crucial symbol, but they lack faith "in anything to mean / The same at different times to different people." They cannot trust a true communication from the past. This and a possibly "filial diffidence . . . kept them / From thinking it could be a thing so bridal." That is, they perceived the bridal quality of the denuded maple but could not apply it to Maple's past.

This was their big mistake, for surely the name had been given in connection with feelings for the sexual and bridal, a likelihood reinforced by the message coming too late to be significant for Maple and by her covering her eyes in what looks like unconscious shame as she decides that they must abandon the quest as useless. She and her husband had shared this sexual hesitancy in not thinking about the sugar-yielding maples. But the name has had its effects. Probably the mother was telling Maple, through her name, to possess the giving sweetness and symmetry of a maple tree. The Bible passage may have been in her mind in connection with the offering she was making in bringing Maple into the world out of risk to herself and devotion to her husband. This connects indirectly to her desire that Maple be open and loving. Maple had not understood, but the name had given her the forthright sweetness and independence that won her husband. The last three lines must be satirical, for Maple's name has left much "to nature and happy chance" yet increased her chances of blossoming rightly. Still, had she had the courage to see through her father's and her own sexual diffidence, she might have taken an even deeper joy in her powers and understood the bond that her mother was trying to make between them. John Morris offers a radically different interpretation of this poem, citing a long passage from Numbers 5:11-29 (which he misidentifies as coming from Leviticus 5:25). This Bible text associates wave offerings with a test to determine if a woman is guilty of adultery, which test results in the woman's death if she has indeed committed the crime. Morris suggests that Maple's mother is directing her daughter toward awareness of such a crime on the mother's part and also warning the girl against committing such a sin. This reading seems unconvincing in light of Maple's innocent sweetness and the likelihood that her mother's message was more a blessing than a warning (110:127-28).

"The Ax-Helve," based on an incident between Frost and a French-Canadian neighbor named Guay, combines realistic narrative and allegory. The allegory displays at least two cutting edges: one the message his neighbor is both acting out toward him and speaking, and the other the analogies between the neighbor's values and Frost's artistic creed. The speaker admires the strength and prowess of his neighbor Baptiste but is troubled when Baptiste, coming from behind, arrests the speaker's chopping arm and seizes his ax, as if there might be an argument coming. But Baptiste wishes only to point out the deficiencies of the speaker's ax-helve and make him a new one – a neighborly gesture. The ax-helve is machine-made, and the speaker recognizes it as a commercial product, the grain of the wood crosswise to and not parallel with the length, "like the two strokes across a dollar sign." The speaker remains defensively hostile but accepts Baptiste's invitation to go to his house for a really good ax-helve. Still defensive as he arrives that night, he senses that Baptiste is trying to demonstrate his need for and right to recognition. Baptiste's wife is uneasy and ingratiating to the point of endangering herself at her fire, and Baptiste is uneasy about keeping his guest's attention. But when Baptiste displays his ax-helves, he comes fully into his own, for he judges the wood masterfully, seeing the natural flow of lines wedded to the shapes cut from it. Baptiste handles an ax-helve lovingly, as if it were a woman.

Perhaps Baptiste's slow proceedings are further motivated by his desire to talk to the speaker about his children's education. He needs justification for keeping them from school and he implies that school work is artificial and inferior to life experience, a view he demonstrates with his ax-helves, and one the speaker at least partly shares. The speaker begins to realize that Baptiste is anxious to have him support his notions about education, especially his feeling that he has as much right as the more educated to judge what should be done with his children. The concluding stanza reveals an overall good feeling between the two men, for the question of the children's education is put aside, perhaps as tentative, while they admire Baptiste's handiwork in shaping and inserting an ax handle. The ax stands on "its horse's hoof," which compares the ax-helve to a hoof held to a horseshoe by nails (as an ax-helve is held to the blade). It is proudly erect but "not without its waves"—that is, it has flowing lines that stand for both its grace and the wavelike difficulties that Baptiste's views may create. It resembles the snake in the garden of Eden, standing erect before it seduced Adam and Eve and was forced to go on its belly; this suggests a possibly dangerous pride in both Baptiste and the speaker, though Frost is probably satirizing the idea of such a danger. The ax is now "top-heavy" in a way Baptiste's "hand [makes] light of," a pun on the strength of his hand and a satirical challenge to its sharp dangers. The ax-helve now resembles a head rather than a foot, holding its "steel-blue chin" with a French cockiness. This image implies a combination of skepticism and assertion in Baptiste, a view evidently admired by Frost and his speaker. The adjustment of natural materials to artistic craft has been widely commented on as an analogy for Frost's poetic method: the balancing of reality against order-creating imagination and craft.

"The Grindstone," one of Frost's most subtle and difficult poems, strikingly resembles yet differs from "The Ax-Helve." Also focusing on a conflict between two men over a farm tool, this poem presents a less realistic and more emphatically mythical scene. The speaker begins by looking at the grindstone in the present. It is winter, and he is a grown man. The grindstone is anthropomorphized and viewed angrily for its inability to get anywhere as it stands "under a ruinous live apple tree," suggesting a fallen Eden. The speaker then recalls a scene from his boyhood, probably during a warmer season, when he had ground a blade on this stone with a "Father-Time-like man," with whom he had had a terrible battle of energy and will. He had turned the stone while the older man pressed down the blade, and he had grown angry over the man's control. The situation had been dangerous, but he had almost wished that a disaster would end it and had also hoped that the man wouldn't take the risk of grinding the blade away but would settle for something less than perfection. Frost commented in a letter that the grindstone was "an image of the naughty world" (38:91), which suggests that it might get out of control under the exertions of boy and man. Detail after detail shows artificial heightening that implies allegorical meanings, but the symbolic representations are open to speculation.

John Lynen proposes an opposition between the speaker, representing energy and the flesh, and the older man, representing intellect and the devil. The speaker's effort stands for the suffering necessary to creation, and the older man's for other elements of creation that are essential but dangerous. According to Lynen, the blade is not identified and hence suggests an instrument of both good and evil. But the blade may be the scythe carried by the "Father-Time-like" figure, which would associate it with the wearing away of time (38:90-98). Another problem is the line "I was for leaving something to the whetter," for the whetter would presumably be the person who controls the blade—that is, the older man. Thus interpreted, the line contradicts the speaker's desire that the older man desist from his perfectionism. If the whetter is presumed to be the speaker, showing his willingness to accept limitations, that would contradict his representing energy rather than intelligence. If the whetter is indeed the older man, why should the speaker want something left for him, unless "something" means only something and not the whole judgment? At the end the speaker wants a compromise so the task can be finished, suggesting a grim acceptance of reality.

The poem's curious combination of passion and jocularity is distinctive, even for Frost, and contributes to the possibilities of different allegorical intentions. The poem may have come from great psychic depths, without the author having quite known his intentions; this would reinforce the likelihood that the poem is both a comment on the conflict between perfection and the need to complete poems, and a comment on the dangers of perfectionism in life's conflicts between energy and intelligence. Now mature, the speaker seems to accept the existence of this spheroid grindstone (an image of combined pain and accomplishment) as, or in, a fallen world. When younger, he found the situation more desperate, though he experienced both pleasure and revolt as he worked his way toward a grim acceptance.

In "Paul's Wife" Frost adds a delicate chapter to tales of the boisterous American lumberjack colossus Paul Bunyan, a figure on which Frost builds cleverly. The popular Paul Bunyan is celebrated for unprecedented feats of strength and skill, usually defying the laws of nature, and Frost briefly incorporates two tall tales of such acts. But Frost's Bunyan has a different sensibility: he is a man obsessed with his wife and embarrassed to the point of running away whenever she is mentioned. The narrative declares that Paul's fellow lumberjacks bear him no ill will, but the way they taunt him about his wife shows competition, sexual jealousy, and a sexual embarrassment that often abounds among men who work apart from women. The narrative initially surveys five reasons why Paul might have run away whenever he was asked about his wife, and then illustrates the fifth reason at length. While machine-slicing pine logs with fellow workers, Paul finds a hollow log whose top opening at first seems to be a "streak of grease," suggesting the sinful nature of the sexuality he will soon realize. Working alone on the log, Paul discovers a strange piece of pith in it, which when immersed in the loggers' stream turned into a beautiful woman. The girl catches her breath with a laugh and then proves adept at walking on floating logs. She resembles Pygmalion's Galatea and, having been born from the soul of a tree, is a proper mate for the world's most famous lumberman. After Paul goes off with her for their abbreviated courtship, marriage, and honeymoon, they are pursued by rough lumberjacks who delight in making fun of them. The girl is like a star and Paul like a shadow, suggesting his subservience to her and a degree of shame. The "brute tribute of respect to beauty," as the lumbermen's vulgarity is called (with only partial irony, for these men can accept sex only by vulgarizing it), made her light "go out like a firefly, and that was all." Some commentators think that the woman has disappeared, but the next line and the concluding stanza suggest that she lives on. "Everyone had been wrong in judging Paul" refers only to their having thought he had a bride to be ashamed of, for they had not been wrong in sensing his embarrassment. Murphy's idea that "Paul / Wouldn't be spoken to about a wife / In any way the world knew how to speak" implies that Paul is excessively self-conscious about love and sex and also that he has an exalted sense of his wife's value. Frost's Paul Bunyan is a combination of artist and ruffian, subdued and embarrassed by his finest instincts but secretly triumphant in his loving accomplishments – a description that partially fits the poet.

"Wild Grapes" is also a poem about the tenderness of love in unexpected places, here revealed in a woman's heart, but it leaves to our imagination the human situations that illustrate it. The poem is narrated by a woman whom Radcliffe Squires calls "charmingly erudite" because of her ability to cite the Orpheus myth and a variation on the saga of Leif the Lucky (45:57). She also alludes covertly to *A Midsummer Night's Dream,* in which Peter Quince tells the ass-headed Bottom, "Bless thee. . . . Thou art translated" (3.1.107). She makes her own personal allegory out of an incident involving her brother and herself when she was a little girl. They had been picking grapes from vines entwined in birch trees, and he had persuaded her to hold onto a birch bough he had bent down, but when it swung up, she had held on and would not let go, and hence had been "translated" into a different and frightening but thought-provoking realm – until he had finally drawn the limb down, enabling her to escape. Her memory is of his unkind attitude, her frustration, and her final relief, but chiefly of what she learned. As Squires points out, her ascent into the birch tree resembles that of the speaker in "Birches" (45:57). It represents the ideal, which in this case turns out to be painful and hard to sustain. The mind returns her to earth, but her heart clings to the ideal in the form of love. The first step in knowledge, "to let go with the hands," refers to giving up physical possessions, but holding on with the heart means persisting with love where circumstances seem to make it impossible. Struggling with the difference, she says "The mind – is not the heart," sensing that mental and emotional possessions blur together and that though she can try to forget the pains of her most precious concerns, she has no reason to give up the love that may go with them. Such choice resembles the difficult one at the end of "Reluctance," in which the speaker resists the end "of love or a season." The classicist Helen Bacon, working partly from unpublished sources, has demonstrated that this poem takes its origin from an autobiographical anecdote reported to Frost by Susan Hayes Ward, poetry editor of the New York *Independent,* who published several of Frost's earliest poems. Bacon also points out that the images of the grapes and the tree-suspended and maenadlike girl owe much to Euripides' *Bacchae,* and she identifies "Leif the Lucky's German" as Leif Eriksson's companion Tyrker, who helped him explore the New World and who resembles Dionysius, which allusion enriches the poem's reference to Vinland. The poem, Bacon maintains, was partly designed to honor Susan Ward's independence as a person and as an intellectual (289).

Love is treated more coolly in "Place for a Third," whose dilemma centers on where Laban is to bury his dying third wife, who pleads not to be laid to rest with her predecessors. The title also refers to whether as a third husband he is to rest with any of his wives. That for Eliza and Laban "The score was even for them" in number of marriages puns on "score" as counting and suggests a settling of resentments – a sourness balanced by the endurance and loyalty that, more than deep affection, mark this aging couple. Laban has difficulty sympathizing with his wife's wish, but he recognizes "the lingering person in Eliza" – her individuality – as something he once treasured in himself. Eliza and Laban are worn out, and he lives perhaps more by formulas than by deep feelings, for his first thoughts stress decent gestures: a plot especially for her with an expensive stone that would express the grief his prudence honors. Then he has a much better thought: to bury her next to her first husband, who had died young, and who had shared youth's joy with her, rather than the weight of cares – a sobering and nonpassionate reflection. But Laban must get permission from the sister of Eliza's first husband, John, if she is to be buried next to him, and this requires tact; he can't tell the sister that Eliza doesn't want to lie near his other wives or that the idea of her burial near John is his, not Eliza's. Eliza resents sharing Laban with other women, and Laban shows both envy and self-sacrifice in his thoughts about sharing her with John. The description of the relationship between John's sister and Eliza after the death of Eliza's second husband throws additional light on Eliza and Laban's marriage. At that time, the sister had offered Eliza a temporary home, but instead Eliza "went the poor man's widow's way" and kept house for a man out of wedlock. Thus, her marriage to Laban would have been a rescue for her, perhaps mutually initiated more by prudence than by love, though Laban was "a decent product of life's ironing out." The sister's determined rejection of Laban's proposal is an echo of Eliza's, who did not want to be scanted in death by being the third to Laban's other wives. The sister does not want to demean John by placing his thrice-married wife by his side, and Eliza's other men include more than her husbands. So Laban has to get the special new plot for Eliza, leaving him a "choice of lots" for himself ("lot" meaning both gravesite and fate) when he "comes to . . . settle down," a reference to burial and to the end of his moving from one woman to another. Frost focuses on proprieties but also, more importantly, on the problem of emotional investments in diminished loves as they face eternity – a theme treated vigorously in the next two poems.

"The Witch of Coös" and "The Pauper Witch of Grafton," brought together in *New Hampshire* as parts I and II of "Two Witches," were first published in 1922 and 1921. Their order of composition has not been established. I have elsewhere published a detailed analysis of the two poems as companion pieces that form a two-paneled picture, "Coös" studying sexual failure for one kind of witch and "Grafton" showing sexual triumph for a different kind (281). "Coös" has been mistakenly seen as a tale of the supernatural, but most recent commentators recognize that the witch's story of a skeleton that came from a corpse buried in her cellar is her guilt-ridden fantasy of a lover murdered by her husband. All but the first and last four lines are dramatic dialogue by the woman, long widowed, and her not-very-bright (or badly disturbed) 40-year-old son.

Mother and son believe in spirit rapping, and she is a medium whose Sioux Indian control suits her French-Canadian background. She claims to still hear in the attic the skeleton whose flight up the stairs forty years ago is mentioned by her son before she describes it. She alone hears it, just as she alone had seen it in the dark kitchen on the night of its ascent, when her husband was upstairs in bed, thinking about how she was always asleep before she entered their ice-cold bed, two symbols for her sexual reluctance with him. The skeleton, she thinks, began ascending the stairs out of the snowed-in cellar, another symbol for emotional enclosure. Its puzzlement, shaky walk, and flashes of fire and smoke represent her disorientation and sense of sin. She "knew them and good reason" because of her former desperate intimacy. The bones waiting "for things to happen in their favor" are trying to dominate her again but fail as she tries to knock them apart. She warns her husband, whose annoyed expectation of company contrasts with her terror. She admits that in the light she cannot see the bones, which shows that they are imaginary. She vividly pictures the bones as her lover singing a song about a daring vagabond who resembled him.

She and her husband fancy they have trapped the skeleton in the attic, which they nail shut. In the attic the skeleton, as haunting guilt, is closer to the woman's consciousness than it was when buried in the cellar, and it goes on tormenting her. She admits that the bones are those of the lover her husband killed for revenge and to protect her from her wild impulses. Though she must have told parts of this story before, this is the first time she has confessed to the murder. But she has grown numb about the meaning of what happened, just as she supposes her husband would have done – probably because she is tired (as he would be) of pretending that the lover stole passion that the husband might have claimed, because the lover had really spurred passion that the husband could not release. The husband would be, and probably was, drained of concern about her – the opposite of the husband of the Grafton witch, with his passionate concern in life and, imaginarily, afterwards. The husband's name, Toffile Lajway, is a pun on "to file away," which the couple had tried to do with the dead lover, could not do because of the wife's guilt, but finally managed to do with their tender concerns. The woman's jocular recounting of some details represents defense against her guilt, and her husband's buffoonery creates an ironic heightening of their suffering and waste.

"The Pauper Witch of Grafton" narrates its speaker's life history and her present desperation as she struggles to be declared a legal resident of Wentworth rather than Warren (where she once lived) so that Wentworth will be forced to support her. The Grafton witch, unlike she of Coös, is a social outcast and had once been feared by the community. But she had been vital, good-humored, and passionate, and had had a deeply rewarding marriage, before her husband's death had reduced her to loneliness and poverty. Still, she has precious memories and a jocularly wicked wit that seems to be good protection against the hypocrisy and parsimony of her society. She begins her story and her opposition to Wentworth's disclaimer by demonstrating that her husband could not have been a citizen of Warren, for the Arthur Amy who had run there for Hog Reeve (an officer who impounds stray hogs) must have been her father-in-law, not her husband. Furthermore, her husband, who had not voted often, had voted in Wentworth against its maintaining a tote road to his neighborhood – doubtless because he had wanted to keep away lustful men who were distracted by his fetching wife. The story of Mallice Huse (whose name answers the question, Whose malice?) pops up in association with Heman Lapish, whose name suggests lechery, to demonstrate the reckless, self-deluded passion of local men for the young Grafton witch and their blaming their infatuation on her supposed witchhood. However, she had not minded being taken for a witch, because it showed her power and was a put-down for pretentious men, and she had been somewhat angered when her future husband (Arthur Amy) had tried to prove that she was not a witch. He had done this with the not very logical argument that since Mallice Huse was a crib-gnawer, Huse's claim that the witch had ridden him around the county and hitched him to posts must be false because there were no marks proving that he had gnawed the posts. Thus Arthur Amy had begun courting her, and after marriage he had delighted in celebrating her as a witch, for he shared her jocular attitude toward society—but more importantly, he was intoxicated by her sexual powers. He was a quiet man but passionately in love with this responding woman, who now recalls their outdoor lovemaking that reeked of the earth, of riskiness, and of nature's mysteries. Now that she has come to nothing, she hopes that if he can see her he will be spared awareness of her suffering. She wonders how she could once have been rebellious in the face of such prospects. But she does not really seem to have come to nothing. Unlike the Coös witch, she stands outside of mainstream society and its values, but she had once been deeply satisfied and lives with brave and magnificent memories. Still, both women's lives have come to a kind of arrest that suggests the possibility of fate's indiscriminate unkindness.

The title phrase of "An Empty Threat" is directed against people with whom the speaker is living, whose demands make it hard for him not to run off to a grimmer—but at least independent and, frankly, doomed—fate. This fantasy, in the form of a retaliatory daydream, is an unusual departure for Frost, but it echoes the domestic discords of several preceding poems. The abrupt lines, irregular rhymes, and fiercely colloquial condensations reinforce the speaker's attitudes. He begins with close-mouthed resentment at having to stay in a painful situation in which successes remain in doubt and require endless talk for compromise and clarification. He would almost prefer going off to the frozen wastes of Hudson's Bay, where only a French Indian trapper and a few seals would share the bleakness. John-Joe, the trapper, seems dimly aware of the fate of Henry Hudson (1575?-1611), who was set adrift on the bay by mutineers and perished knowing he was being abused. But the trapper's unwillingness to tell what he does or does not know is a frank intransigence, easier to endure than warmer relationships gone wrong. The speaker may dimly yearn for other companionship but is relieved that he sees seals and not men at a distance and that John-Joe is not around much. He despairs over the desolation of snow and mist, yet he thinks it may be a proper reflection of reality. He feels that such a vista, not understood by Joe, may represent Hudson's fate as it would apply to his own quandary, for Hudson's failure "to find or force a strait" (he had been looking for a Northwest passage to Asia) represents human dilemmas, and Hudson's abandonment is an appropriate expression of the speaker's wish to be vindicated by destruction. At the end, addressing Hudson, he sees both of them, like the extinct Great Auk (a flightless bird that could not run), almost better off defeated than forced to make compromises. George Nitchie sees additional depth in this poem and its title phrase; he proposes that its empty threat shows that "excessive concern for the single life is a violation of nature" (41:24).

In "A Fountain, a Bottle, a Donkey's Ears, and Some Books" the elements of experience also tend to fly apart. Such dispersion applies to the motivation of Davis, the guide who leads the speaker wildly across the map – in pursuit, it seems, of everything except what the speaker wants to see. The jocular title refers to three landscape features and the pile of identical copies of a volume of poems they inspect in a deserted house. Davis wanted to show the speaker his mica mountain, which may turn out to have great commercial value (mica is a transparent, heat-resistant mineral much used before the era of plastics). But the speaker is more interested in seeing a fountain, the outdoor Mormon baptismal font on Kinsman mountain. Possibly offended, Davis reluctantly agrees to go there, though he's sure the font will be a ruin. He leads the speaker up and down mountains where they see vegetation that marks out the shape of a Bottle and then avalanche formations that resemble a donkey's ears. In response to the speaker's complaint that the Bottle is empty, Davis declares "So's everything," anticipating the poem's conclusion. Davis also angrily rejects the speaker's accusation that Davis is leading him astray – as punishment, one suspects, for the speaker's having declined Davis's first suggestion. This possibility is reinforced by Davis's insistence that the speaker much prefers books to such natural things as the Bottle and donkey's ears, whose names seem to mock nature and intelligence. Davis leads him to the house with its pile of copies of a volume of poems, self-published by a long-dead "poetess" who had written from the perspective of a shut-in who looked out of her window at birds and flowers. The appearance and fate of the books are satirized at length, but the speaker does his best to take an interest in them (or, rather, it) – and for all his general scorn, Davis isn't unsympathetic. However, interest in the woman's work cannot overcome the notion that "In time she would be rid of all her books," implying that they will come to almost nothing. Perhaps Davis is right; everything is empty. The speaker had refused to see Davis's mica mountain, and so he had been led around to see the near-vanity of bottles, a donkey's ears, and some books. The demonstration, like the poem, seems to be an elaborate joke.

The concern for nothingness in "I Will Sing You One-O" is serious and personal. This intense lyric, with its stabbing two-foot lines and hard-hitting rhymes, shows the momentum of the speaker's sleepless speculations, stirred up by a stormy night. The title is like a child's chant, but it also suggests that the number one has become zero, as it does toward the poem's end. The winter storm makes the speaker visualize the piling of personified snow and the clashing of winds along otherwise empty streets – a vision that focuses his thoughts on the vast expanse of time and the universe. As he waits for day, he wants to hear the clock tower tell him how far he has to go toward dawn. He worries that perhaps the cold of the wind and snow has frozen together the hands of the clock, whose sound he awaits – a parallel for the universe's becoming frozen. At last he hears the stroke of one from a tower clock and then again from a steeple farther off; they converse mostly between themselves, for few people are not protected by sleep. Their sounds fuse with those of the storm as it assaults his house, and his thoughts plunge into cosmic distances as the sound of One recalls first the solar system, then individual stars, then constellations. The sound seems to go out to the limits of speculation, in which the universe, as a clockwork, interacts with its individual components. At last the sound stirs the farthest star, whose distance at first makes it appear still. But what seem to be its active "whirling frenzies" are soon revealed to be its death throes, for it had once expanded into a nova (an exploding or shooting star), and so the light now pouring down really comes from a long-dead star. The light has been seen by humans throughout their existence, during which they have been engaged in actions as destructive as the star's burning. The fascinating energy of the universe leads only to destruction and is connected to the impulses by which humans destroy one another and their societies. The oneness for which the speaker has been listening is the unity of the universe as a process of both creation and destruction. The speaker's thoughts have come to a kind of rest, but neither in sleep nor in calming revelations.

Cosmic concerns appear differently in "Fragmentary Blue." Rather than presenting a scene for speculation, this poem asks wistfully ironic questions. It assumes in its listeners a cheerfulness about the fragmentary occurrences of blue in the natural world ("wearing stone" probably refers to slate being worn by the steps of time), as if these were merely symbols of the ideal, making them minimally satisfying or, perhaps, downgrading the evidence of the truly ideal blue of the heavens. But the second stanza partly undercuts this idea. As if to continue his argument, the speaker cautions us that earth isn't heaven – as social radicals expect it to be and as scientists crudely make it out to be when they note that the earth's atmosphere (whose refractions create the sky's blue) is part of the earth. For the blue of heaven is really far above us, sharpening our desire for the true ideal. Are we to wait until we go to heaven to realize the ideal? Or are we to be cautious in hoping to synthesize it from fragments around us? The speaker makes fun of the second idea, probably as much in himself as in others, and issues a warning about his impulse to turn up the ideal in simple things.

Metaphorical concern with ultimates continues in the more harshly ironic "Fire and Ice." The metaphors of this poem are less concrete than those in "Fragmentary Blue" insofar as the end of the world is not really visualized, but they are given hardness through the idea that human existence is dominated by desire and hatred. Tone is crucial in this poem. The repeated "Some say" looks like a casual comment on an awful inevitability, showing both stoic confrontation and vindictive acceptance. The reference to tasting desire suggests both juicy satisfaction and distasteful shock, and the casual "I hold with those who favor fire" pretends to a choice the speaker would prefer to avoid, making "favor" an ironic combination of intellectual approval and haste for the end. The speaker's voice grows coldly objective with his speculation about "perish[ing] twice," as if this were all a matter for scientific examination or control (that there is no control is a further irony). The poem closes with his arch and understated observation that an end from ice "would suffice." It would surely do the trick and would also reassure him that hatred is massively destructive and gets what it deserves.  )

"In a Disused Graveyard" follows three poems that glance with various degrees of wistfulness at disappointed ideals that end in uncertainty or death. Here the speaker gently mocks people's unwillingness to die and gives stones the ability to see and say that death has ceased. The scene, however, is concrete: a New England graveyard no longer used because its community has faded. But visitors still come to read the tombstones, not out of affectionate attachment but out of curiosity. The attraction of these living by the dead emphasizes the contrast between vitality and arrest. The tombstones' inscriptions speak of how those reading them must eventually join the dead. The tombstones' personification gently contrasts with their real incapacity; the speaker satirically focuses fear in the word "shrinking." At last he shifts voice and denies the kind of cleverness in which he has been engaging. He speculates that he could lie to the tombstones by expressing the human hope not to die as if that hope had become true, and he makes his strongest personification of the stones as dead people by sadly reflecting on the likelihood of fooling them. The last line radiates meanings: the stones "would believe the lie" because they know what fear is like (except that they know nothing), they would believe it because no one seems to join them anymore, and they would believe it because the speaker has projected his life-haunted feelings into them.

Perhaps Frost placed "Dust of Snow" after several gloomy lyrics to demonstrate the mystery of suddenly lifted spirits, though here the cause of sadness goes deliberately unmentioned so that scene and change can dominate. This tiny poem consists of four lines of sharp imagery and four lines of pithy commentary, all made firm by their compactness and crisp rhymes. As Laurence Perrine's thorough explication shows, the poem is a highly suggestive study in contrasts (171). The crow's black color implicitly shines out against the snow, and both contrast to the dark green of a hemlock tree, which in turn suggests the redolence such trees lend to winter scenes. The crow's gesture seems spiritedly independent, a challenge to the speaker's presence and self-centeredness and, thus, to his mood. "The dust of snow" suggests a contrasting lightening of scene and emotion, and the second stanza makes the inner change emphatic, suggesting a lifting of the eyes as well as the heart and then a looking back across the day's preceding gloom with a deft judgment of it. The slightly archaic flavor of "rued," plus its mournful sound, intensifies the gentle criticism of the self-indulgent sadness that is being put aside for the remainder of this brightening day.

"To E. T." is the first of Frost's four poems about his dear friend Edward Thomas, who had become a poet largely through Frost's encouragement and who, as an artillery officer in France, was killed at Vimy Ridge on 9 April 1917 (some while after Frost had returned to America). Here the gloom is specific, especially with the biographical material in mind. It is a gloom whose lack of resolution is essential to the poem. Frost had fallen asleep while reading Thomas's poems, and the book's dove-winged shape becomes a metaphor for his hope that his reading would lead him into a dream. His friend had died before Frost could fully praise him for his poetry and his soldierhood, which now raise him to a hero of his race. Addressing Thomas as "brother," Frost indicates that not all had been said between them, and he seems to be struggling to express what went unsaid. The capitalization of "Victory" indicates that the Great War's end is meant; Frost wants to have shared that Victory with Thomas as a triumph for the soldier and his people and, paradoxically, as the triumph whereby Frost lost Thomas. The soldier's having met "the shell's embrace of fire" implies an apotheosis of Thomas that has deprived Frost of him. Thomas's death had made the war seem over more for Frost than for himself because the thing Frost most cared about in it had been killed, whereas Thomas's tragic end seemed to be all that was left of him. Now, however, things seem reversed – except that they really cannot be reversed, for though the war is over for the living, Frost cannot get it out of his mind, because he is unable to celebrate his friend's personal victory and go back from the world of war to that of poetry, in which his work had pleased Thomas. The yearning dream state with which the poem begins persists at the end, for the sense of loss has been ritualized but cannot be dispelled. There is no healing here except for the possibility that the comradeship between the two as men and as poets persists in the imagination.

"Nothing Gold Can Stay" combines condensed metaphor and vivid description. "Nature's first green is gold" because the pale green leaves of early spring are goldlike in their light-reflecting tints, as well as in their preciousness and promise. It is the "hardest hue to hold" because its appearance soon changes and its ideal beauty flees the mind. The green-gold leaves darken quickly, a change that symbolizes the brevity of all ideal heights. As John R. Doyle points out (29:175), the word "subsides" provides the poem's point of balance. It is a gentle replacement for an expected term of expansion or growth, and suggests a sigh of disappointment as leaf turns out to be not flower but more leaf – that is, as immature leaves are replaced by advancing ones. The fall of humanity in Eden came by such a process. Starting from a height, it plunged the race into knowledge of natural decay. Frost's view resembles Emerson's idea that being born into this world is the fall, implying that the suffering and decay brought by natural processes are what we know of evil. Dawn's going "down to day" is another touch of the unexpected, for day should be life at its height, but Frost implies that at the moment when sunrise ushers in day, diminishments begin. The "Nothing" of the last line, repeated from the title, receives special emphasis; the gold that cannot stay comes to represent all perfections. Like W. B. Yeats, Frost thinks that "Man is in love and loves what vanishes."

"The Runaway" creates a vividly active farmyard scene, combining a little Morgan horse's point of view with that of the human spectators (especially the speaker), who watch the scene with affection and compassion. The horse, amazed by his first snowfall, races about like a puzzled child, to which he is compared through references to his absent mother, who probably would not be able to explain the snowfall to him because he would not believe a commonplace explanation of something so rare. The speaker, who has been talking to other people watching the scene, is surprised that the horse has been left out alone. Watching the horse act increasingly alarmed, he expresses a gentle resentment about its mistreatment and speaks aloud a muted plea toward those who ought to lead it indoors from the scary scene. Again, Frost treats a thought-provoking change of season, but the young horse's point of view is more limited than people's, and so the scene is gently pathetic rather than philosophically mordant as in "Nothing Gold Can Stay."

Wholly metaphorical, "The Aim Was Song" comments on poetry as a combined expression of nature and man (since Frost uses *man* as a generic term, it cannot be avoided here). Without the help of man, nature – in the form of wind – created "untaught" sounds, loudest at places of friction. Then man came along and instructed the wind to avoid the rough places and to blow more gently so it could make song. The third stanza details the continuation of the lesson: Man held just a little wind in his mouth so that the fierceness of the north became the gentleness of the south, and then blew it out carefully "by measure" – that is, by artistic planning. The song seems to have come out right: "word," or meaning, is combined with "note," or sound. Man thus achieves what the wind had tried to do by itself but could not. The last two lines repeat the lesson: not too much at a time and with the aim of song (not just noise). The phrase "the wind could see" implies that the wind has learned its lesson. This playful conclusion shows nature achieving a capacity that the poem really assigns only to humans. Frost amuses himself by projecting the creative impulse partly back into nature, which he usually sees as supplying only the energy for art. The stress on restraint and care shows Frost's artistic aims, and the slight anthropomorphization of the wind reveals a nostalgic desire for purpose in nature. The concern for gentle expression throws light on the tenderness of "Nothing Gold Can Stay" and "The Runaway," in which resentments are expressed with nostalgia or restraint rather than with brute anger.

"Stopping by Woods on a Snowy Evening" is Frost's most popular poem, and the poet himself was very fond of it. Despite its apparent simplicity, it has inspired numerous detailed analyses. Its vivid scene combines contrasts between white snow and dark woods, and adds other sensuous appeals in the sound of harness bells, the sweeping wind, and the snow's softness. The time is the winter solstice, "the darkest evening of the year" (usually December 21). The speaker is alone but sets up relationships with his horse, the absent owner of the woods he has stopped to contemplate, and the people to whom he has "promises to keep." He has been riding home on a horse-driven sleigh, and he delights in his feeling of contemplative possession of a snow-filled field that is really owned by a man in the village, as he also enjoys his momentary isolation. The horse's fancied questioning of their stopping reinforces the sense of his nonpractical delight in the pause and in what he sees. The absence of farmhouses increases the pleasure of his isolation, and the time of year adds a gentle note of ease about the darkness and the coming winter. The horse's questioning emphasizes that there has been no mistake, and perhaps its shaken bells make more vivid the quietly appealing sounds of wind and snowflake. The appealing softness of the snow gracefully increases the speaker's feeling of deep and comforting beauty in the snow-filled woods, which seem so inviting. Many critics have debated whether the speaker is tempted to yield to death, and his attraction to the snowy woods has often been referred to as a death wish, in correspondence to Freudian ideas of a death instinct. Frost was angry at such suggestions, perhaps because he didn't understand them. Surely, the transition from the picture of the appealing woods to the speaker's thoughts of the promises he must keep and the miles he must travel before sleep represents a desire not to give up, or at least not to yield to passivity in the face of duty. As Theodore Morrison argues, however, it is important not to let this interpretation dim the fact that the poem is primarily oriented towards the pleasures of the scene and the responsibility of life, and that sleep is a restorative as well as a metaphor for that end which, in this poem, looks a long way off (111:186-187). Interpretations of possible symbolisms in the traveler, the owner, the horse, the woods, and the goal will doubtless continue to proliferate.

"For Once, Then, Something" is a personal philosophical poem, in which Frost addresses those who accuse him of never being able to take a firm stand about his ideas of truth. The situation is dramatized through a comprehensive metaphor in which he gazes down through the water of a well toward something at its bottom that represents those firm truths to which he can never quite commit himself. He starts with irritated reference to people who say that when he looks down into such wells, his angle is always wrong—and so instead of seeing into the depths, he sees just a reflection of himself on the surface, appearing self-satisfied and rather cherubic, which suggests self-celebration and whimsy. With an italicized *"Once,"* the poem shifts back to a time when he had taken such a stance with the hope of more success. Then he had seen a picture (perhaps again himself reflected) but had also been able to see, through the depths, something "white, uncertain." He had lost that vision, however, because water had dripped from above him, causing a ripple that had "blurred it, blotted it out." So when he had made his very best effort, he had not really succeeded. Had he seen truth, or just "a pebble of quartz"? The title phrase, repeated as the poem's last sentence, expresses both his frustration at his inability to get a final vision and his irritated questioning of those who doubt the seriousness of his efforts. The something he saw may have been a hard piece of reality or just the quick, blurred impression that is the most anyone is allowed of truth. The complexity and mystery of nature seem to be as responsible for our limited vision as are our efforts. The poem is a whimsical partial admission of self-preoccupation, as well as a whimsical defense of Frost's own tentative vision of ultimate meanings.

"Blue-Butterfly Day" looks back to the color symbolism of "Fragmentary Blue" and the aura of beautiful transience in "Nothing Gold Can Stay." On a spring day, the air is full of blue butterflies that "flurry" down like snowflakes. The pure blue of their wings is more prevalent than the blue of flowers that have not yet fully bloomed. In the second stanza, the butterflies are described as if they were partly flowers. They fly because of their nature, and they "all but sing" because they announce the joys of spring. But they have "ridden out desire"—that is, they have exhausted themselves from mating, showing how quickly spring's new life moves toward its end. Now, with wings folded, they cling to the ruts made by passing wheels. The first harbingers of spring, these creatures also predict the quick death of everything that rushes toward fullness. Nevertheless, the poem ends with a pleasing picture of the butterflies' attempted persistence amid the fertile freshness of the scene.

"The Onset," among Frost's most celebrated poems, presents two vivid scenes in which the cycle of the seasons dramatizes the speaker's faith in the struggle of life. The first stanza surveys his desperate resistance to the bitter onset of winter, represented by the first snowfall, and the second stanza shows the preservation of hope in thoughts of the slow but sure arrival of spring's new life. The first snowfall is always the same in its force and in the speaker's resistance to it. As the gathered snow lets go, tension is released and the inevitable is grimly accepted. From start to finish, the whiteness of snow symbolizes both evil (freezing death) and the conventional ideal of purity and goodness, perhaps implying a complicated relationship between them. The white snow is at first vaguely heartening in contrast to the oppressively dark woods. Falling, it sings, but it also makes a hissing sound, like the snake that appears as a metaphor for the second stanza's disappearing stream. So overwhelmed that he almost stumbles, the speaker compares himself to someone who admits his powerlessness and gives up the effort to stay alive, feeling as much a failure as if earth never had life. The second stanza looks ahead to a spring not yet arrived but firmly and calmly believed in. It is described with gentle restraint; all the details suggest early spring. The precedent for hope lies in nature's recurrences.

Winter has never overcome the earth. No matter how deep the snow (its being measured against trees shows their persistence), nature has again come to life. Winter cannot keep the tree frog from croaking joyously as the threatening snow melts into a slim brook whose charming flow promises growth. But the brook also represents the "disappearing snake" of evil, even as it moves through the persisting sadness of "last year's withered brake." The description of spring is still transitional and subdued; realism is preserved, shouts of joy are withheld. Full growth is far off. The image of whiteness reappears, with the emphatic "Nothing" showing joy in the displacement of the death-dealing snow. The snow remains a two-sided symbol, reminding us that whiteness recently stood for destruction, while the birch tree lifts its slim white beauty, and the white houses and church reveal the persistence of the human community and its shared values. A few critics, including John Lynen (38:43), maintain that at the very end, whiteness remains ambiguous in order to show that the defeat of winter is only temporary and that the whole threat and struggle must be endured again. The whiteness of snow as both comforting and threatening appears in other poems, sometimes with other nuances.

"To Earthward" is an intensely personal lyric. Its details hover between sensuous presentation and metaphorical resonances. The speaker, an older man, looks back at the experiences of his youth, chiefly those of love. Then, "love at the lips," or kissing, had seemed too intense to be borne (an exaggerated way of showing his reluctance to accept the complications of pain), and he preferred the sensual pleasures of smelling flowers. He had wanted "strong sweets," but his experiences of them had seemed stingingly sharp. Through exaggeration, he recalls how little it took to satisfy him then and how threateningly intense his experiences had been. With "Now no joy but lacks salt," the poem changes direction. The comma introduced at the end of this line by Frost's editor, Edward Connery Lathem, is surely a mistaken emendation; Frost always published the line with no end punctuation. "That is not dashed with pain" cannot be intended as an appositive for the preceding line; rather, it must be a restrictive modifier, indicating that joys lack salt if they are not dashed with pain. Now that he is older, the speaker's need for intense experience has increased. His fear of its stinging quality has diminished, and he has come to realize that pain is of joy's essence. Images of human love, such as "the stain / Of tears" and the physical marks that love can leave, combine with smells of burning clove and the pressure marks from leaning on one's hand on the ground as examples and symbols of the necessary blending of pain and joy. That the hurt from these things is not enough is a call for a total engagement with experience, though the speaker's desire to have his body fully pressed against the earth suggests experience so intense that it may be a promise of complete fulfillment in death, a view reinforced by the speaker's sense of longing.

"Good-By and Keep Cold" is a meditation about a winterbound apple orchard, in which the speaker talks to himself playfully in preparation for a formal farewell to his orchard, though he actually seems to be addressing the orchard throughout the poem. The four-foot anapestic lines contribute to the light tone and run curiously against the poem's seriousness, as if to help bridge the gap between human and trees, which are addressed as if they were naughty children. Apple trees form hard buds in the fall and are endangered by early thaws, which make the buds expand and the sap flow, thereby making them vulnerable to killing frosts. Before saying the words of his formal good-by, the speaker reflects on winter's dangers. The trees' bark can be eaten by small creatures, the twigs nibbled off by deer, and the buds eaten by grouse. He fancies summoning these creatures and warning them with a stick instead of a gun, for he is almost as tender toward them as he is to his trees. But his biggest fear is of warmth, so he warns the trees to stay cold, though of course they have no say in the matter. His advice mimics the usual warning to children to stay warm, but the trees are not people. He goes away, unwillingly, in order to trim or cut down other kinds of trees–a task he speaks of as wearisome and less dear than caring for his apple orchard. He wishes he could lie in bed and think of comforting these trees with a light as their hearts sink under the earth–rather like those of dying people, as Richard Poirier suggests (42:193)–but he must leave their comforting and protection to God. Curiously, the plight of the trees requires that they accept the cold that would make people's hearts sink, so perhaps Frost is playfully suggesting that these hearty beings won't suffer the way people do. Having done his best, the speaker feels that the trees' final chances are in God's hands–unless the conclusion is satirical, as Poirier thinks (42:195); he argues that the speaker has done his very best not to leave anything to God and so must be poking fun at that idea. Lawrance Thompson, on the other hand, holds that the poem shows an assertion of Frost's religious faith in the face of his wife's skepticism (46:139-40).

"Two Look at Two," a compact blank-verse narrative with a simple plot, presents an experience shared by two lovers rather than a story of conflicts. These lovers, lost in their feelings for each other, have been climbing a mountainside and are ready to turn back. The return path's desolation makes the trip seem like a disillusioning phase of life. Their "onward impulse," expended in a longing look upward, is a symbol for the quest of continuing love and life. The "tumbled wall" that halts them stands for barriers between the real and ideal and between humans and nature. Thus, when they see beyond this wall a fearless doe, the vision immediately begins to break down barriers. The doe's seeming to think that as two "they were safe" implies that the bond of love extends out from the couple toward this creature and nature.

The doe's lack of fear contributes to their vision of more than they had hoped for when they had stopped climbing. But more is to come: a buck appears, and they must check their responses to see that it is not the same deer they had just seen, just as the two deer in the poem constantly test the accuracy of what they see with their vision. The buck seems to question the nature of the humans' existence and vitality, showing that they still feel a barrier. They almost reach across the wall, but instead remain deeply satisfied with their vision as the fearless buck, "pass[ing] unscared," offers a second guarantee of their own loving harmlessness. As they say "This *must* be all," they experience a deep conviction of communion with nature, "as if" the experience had come from the earth itself. The use of the metaphor of a wave to describe the experience connects to the forward impulse of the poem's opening, suggesting that a partial disappointment has been changed into a convincing union with nature's loving spirit – albeit a tentative one. The deer's emotions have been only supposed, not guaranteed, and the wave at the end is more a wave of feeling than a certified spiritual message. The poem is the obverse of the later "The Most of It," in which an isolated man receives a message (or feeling) of alienation from a suddenly appearing buck.

"Not to Keep" is a short blank-verse narrative with little characterization. Its simple plot is based on mostly silent communication between a wounded soldier, sent home for a brief rest, and his wife, who hopes that he has returned permanently, about what is in store for them. The poem is based on experiences of Frost's close friend Edward Thomas, who was similarly wounded and then returned to the Western Front. Deliberately shadowy references intensify the sense of doubt, confusion, and hope, and show how the couple make a world to themselves. The "they [who] sent him back" are the impersonal authorities. She reads their letter to her with anxious speed, grasping only that her husband is coming home. When he arrives she studies him, sarcastically amazed that he has been allowed to keep his life, anxious about how he has been hurt, and desperately glad that he is hers again – the *"they"* of "And still she had all – *they* had – they the lucky!" referring this time to her and him, not to the others. Relaxing into the joy of her possession, she is still compelled to ask what the situation is, and his reply is grimly understated. His wound will quickly heal with her help. They have sent him back not to restore him permanently to her love but to enlist her aid in making him well and fit for war, so the couple are quickly back at the beginning of their fears. Communication between them is agonizing; she can only ask with her eyes how he feels about once more facing the trial of war. As "his eyes [ask] her not to ask," we see his parallel desperation. In the last line, "not to keep" turns the preceding "They had given him back to her" into heart-wrenching pain rather than healing.

In "A Brook in the City" the country-loving speaker questions himself and his listeners about the fate of a brook encompassed by an expanding city, and wonders what ruination may come from its being driven underground. A farmhouse adjusts to the newly surrounding city, but he wonders about the fate of the brook in whose waters he once delighted. Such country things as grass and trees can be covered by concrete or cut down and burned, but the only way to control the brook is to plunge it into a sewer, which becomes its "dungeon," emphasizing the speaker's view of the brook as a living person. The innocent brook continues to run underground, but the speaker concludes by solemnly wondering if its suppression will haunt the city's dwellers and disturb their work and sleep. The difficult line "Is water wood to serve a brook the same?" probably asks if the water of the brook is like the wood of the apple trees and can be similarly seized and used to get rid of another intruder. The poem radiates a tangy affection for the brook and a vivid sense of its transformation and its current activity under the city. But the symbolic force of the brook does not relate to the city people's concerns, and so the personification seems at the end to justify a moral that the city dwellers will not care about.

"The Kitchen Chimney," the first of three poems about illusions, moves from lightheartedness to pathetic disillusion. The speaker pretends to tell a housebuilder how to install a real chimney for him, rather than a false chimney propped up by a shelf over the fireplace. Phrasing and repetitions make the voice slightly childish, thus reinforcing its plea and creating an innocent empathy, a tone that shows the speaker trying to create a spell for the builder and himself. The smallness of the house suggests a sorely needed intimacy. False chimneys may not promote house fires, but the stains from the tarred backing and the rain they allow on the fire are troublesome in themselves. Mostly, they predict that the falseness of the chimney will detract from the real and symbolic solidity of the house, especially as a symbol for life. A shelf bearing clocks and decorations would seem cheerful, but if it were used to hold up a chimney, it would remind the speaker "of castles I used to build in air" – that is, it would show that the real must be the basis of life and that the false or fanciful endangers one's efforts and hopes.

In "Looking for a Sunset Bird in Winter" the longing for something illusive is gently pathetic rather than misleading. Here the speaker is snowshoeing home across a winter landscape and has a brief vision of a cheering bird overhead in a tree. He recalls the sweet birdsong he heard from this tree in the summer, but when he looks closely, the tree is empty except for a single leaf – the remains of summer and a forecast of another. He walks around the tree twice in his determination to see if he was wrong about the bird's presence. His delay has sharpened his awareness of the freezing weather. Its "adding frost to snow / As gilt to gold that wouldn't show" suggests that he derives rapture from the deathlike quality of the scene, though he can find nothing more beautiful than he did at first. His upward look at the sky, revealing a brushstroke of "cloud or smoke," shows an imaginative perspective resembling that reflected in his earlier vision of a bird. The "piercing little star" shining through is the only epiphany he can summon, but it seems enough. Hope glows down toward him from the distance, showing that his imagination is not wasted and that the scene promises the return of cheering things.

"A Boundless Moment" presents another winter scene, surveyed by the speaker and a companion who talks to him as they walk through the woods on a windy March day. His companion stops at the sight of a scary but hopeful apparition among the trees. The speaker catches his mood, thinking that they are seeing the bright flowers of the Paradise-in-Bloom, for the day's weather is "fair enough" to let him believe a May flower had arrived. The two stand in a world seemingly transformed, the speaker enjoying the success of his self-pretense. But at this moment he perceives the truth – or admits it to himself – that what they saw was really "A young beech clinging to its last year's leaves," an image of blighted youth hanging on to remnants of beauty and displaying utter desolation. Thus the poem warns against projecting false hopes into nature and, though not denying the coming spring, asks us not to run from the truth of nature's decline. Nina Baym suggests that the title mocks transcendentalism, and that the poem proposes that hope and faith "cannot be based on the assumption that nature tends towards renewal and regeneration" (64:716-17), though one might argue that since Frost rarely disregards the seasonal cycle, the poem merely criticizes any leap of excessive hope.

Fanciful visions are playfully proposed and accepted in "Evening in a Sugar Orchard," in which the speaker watches and encourages the late winter gathering and distilling of maple sap. At a time when the maple sugar harvesters must keep their fires going steadily, the speaker sees a lull in the activity, which allows him to ask the fireman attending the boiling pans to stoke the upward-arching fire. His aim is esthetic and not practical; the sparks' ascent is his chief delight. Charmed by the moon's glow, slight as it is, he hopes that the sparks will add to its illumination of this lovely scene: a sugar-gathering bucket on every tree, and on the ground a smooth "bear-skin rug of snow." The sparks, however, decline to become part of the moon. Instead they are "content" with what would seem a much harder task – forming constellations of stars. The speaker's playful imagination goes from modest to extreme daring, and the poem ends with a cozy assurance and satisfaction. The fireman has been a magician, but less successfully than the imaginative speaker. The sparks, as stars, are perhaps as risky as castles in the air. They are not at last seen for the dying things they are, like the dormant beech in "A Boundless Moment," but this is because the speaker is satisfied with a playful vision that transforms a moment.

In "Gathering Leaves" Frost makes a lighthearted return to a season of decline, which the speaker tries to bring to an end by struggling – endlessly, it seems – to fill bags of autumn leaves. Concise, homey similes show the difficulty of the task: spades are spoonlike in their slight ability to gather the overflow of leaves; the airiness of the leaves makes full bags resemble balloons; the noise of rustling leaves, "like rabbit and deer / Running away," seems out of proportion to his progress. Gathered leaves make mountains, yet these are small. Once-colorful leaves, separated from their trees, have turned dull. But the task is joyous as well as frustrating in its playful physical engagements, and the elusive leaves become an amusing burden. The task seems endless and the gathered leaves slight and valueless. Still, the speaker celebrates what feels like a triumph with no end in sight – a matter of pure exuberance. This endless and elusive gathering may symbolize the persistent pursuit of unseen ends or the difficulty of artistic triumphs, but more likely Frost playfully treats the combined frustration and joy of a necessary cleansing whose chief goal is preparation for seasonal renewals, though his baffled exertions create a pure ritual of activity enjoyed for its own sake.

Changes of daytime rather than season create the focus of "The Valley's Singing Day." This poem is reminiscent of such different works as "A Dream Pang" and "Never Again Would Birds' Song Be the Same," for the speaker warmly addresses a loved woman in celebration of a dawn ushered in by birds whose song she had wakened while he was still sleeping. Most of the verse consists of his reflection, in retrospect, about what he intuited had happened while he slept – though perhaps he had heard in his sleep the woman's closing of the door as it all began. Her feet had been silent in the grass because it was wet from rain. Personified dawn had pried open night's lids and released the birds' lovely song, which had announced the conversion of the rain's "pearls" into day's radiance. But the focus of his delight is the woman's having started the song while he slept under dripping roof and inside wet sills. After awakening, he had been able to confirm what she had done, knowing by faith and love both her powers and her truthfulness. Thus, he has had a kind of dream vision he can believe in and remember as a confluence of nature and human being.

"Misgiving" describes an autumn scene, with leaves flying through the air, but the details are pervasively allegorical as they filter through the feelings of the speaker, who hears the leaves speaking to the Wind as if both were alive. The leaves are at first willing to go with the Wind to another realm; they have realized from the time of their birth that this would be their fate. But then they show various reluctances that parallel humans' reluctance to die or to take the risks of a realm beyond life. Their asking the Wind to stay with them implies that the life force or the spiritual realm could share their reluctance. Their hesitance is further dramatized through their vague and limited movements, which create a realistic picture of how leaves can be swept afar by winds or, at other times, merely rustled. In the last stanza, the speaker switches to the first person and applies the scene to his apprehensions, calling death freedom and hoping that when he comes to die he will have the courage to want his spirit to pursue boundlessness rather than to settle into a restful nothingness.

"A Hillside Thaw" treats a special seasonal transition with amazed delight. Frost pours on one metaphor after another, yet holds them in a neat pattern around the central image of melting snow as lizards released by the sun's warmth during the day and refrozen at night by the moon's cold. The speaker claims an amazed lack of understanding of what is happening and frustration at his prospective failure if he were to try to hold onto these fleeing lizards amid celebratory birdsong. This pretended naiveté makes the metaphors represent a surprising mystery. The poem divides neatly in half, with the speaker expressing amazement in the second part, as the moon succeeds where he would have failed. For the moon's chill seizes the lizards and transforms them from melted water into hard-formed shapes that lie both parallel and crosswise. The speaker pretends disbelief at the quiet of the scene and the pervasiveness of the moon's spell, which at the end creates another magic tableau: one lizard held by each moon ray. He looks back abashedly at his foolish thoughts of attempting such a hold on frozen water, so miraculously achieved through nature's magic. The poem as a whole, however, celebrates the speaker's imaginative powers in seeing – or creating – these transformations. Absorbed with the fun of his performance, Frost seems unconcerned with philosophical meanings, except for his delight in the powers of imagination to expand on the beauty of the scene. He may be expressing some reservation about the swift arrival of spring, though, paralleling the reserve of the second stanza of "The Onset."

"Plowmen" is a sardonic epigram about winter's unfertile desolation. The speaker reflects on the strange name of the snowplow, for rather than preparing for planting and growth, it reveals the barrenness of earth below the snow. "At having cultivated rock" ambiguously refers to the attempt to grow things out of rock, and to rock as the product of removing the snow. The poem imitates the disheartened feeling of plowmen, as if they seek some relief in mockery of their task's relationship to productive ploughing.

"On a Tree Fallen Across the Road" is a philosophical sonnet whose realistic portrait of a tree blocking passage down a road leads into the bold personification of the tempest as nature's power, then into the image of a road as a metaphor for human progress, and then, more daringly, into the fantastic metaphor of people challenging astronomical forces to guide the earth itself toward their spiritual destination. The subtitle, "To hear us talk," undercuts the boastfulness, but the poem's tone remains joyously bold as it plays off the vicious yet creative power of nature against people's grim delight in resistance, creating the aura of an exulting game on both sides. The barring tree knows it cannot hold humans back but takes pleasure in making them reconsider their arrogance and sharpen their abilities. Thus, the delay is a fruitful challenge. Our capacity to achieve is given fantastic dimensions as people are seen defying all the laws of nature to guide the earth's body itself into the farthest challenges possible.

"Our Singing Strength" is another celebration of imagination's persistence and triumph, this time embodied in a flock of snow-beset birds who come to stand for those poetic powers that stem from nature and drive it on. The three stanzas form neat divisions: the first showing the birds' initial frustration, the second their puzzled efforts to adapt, and the third their coming triumph. The speaker begins with a strikingly detailed picture of how during early spring, snow slowly manages to accumulate on grass and earth, even though at first it vanishes or makes only small formations. At last it takes hold, both crushing the grass and adding beauty by resembling fruit in the new buds. The road's remaining muddy rather than snowy invites the flocking birds that dominate the second stanza. They arrive in spring in amazing abundance, various in breed and destination, but all frustrated by the surrounding snow that keeps them off fields and trees and so makes them concentrate along the road. Here they ignore their differences to make a great unified crowd. The speaker almost drives over them with his car, for the birds are too tired to fly far; they just shake snow from trees and return to the road. They move forward in front of the car, for this single storm did not give them time to learn that they might settle behind the car. Thus the speaker becomes a "Drover" (the capitalization suggesting a parable), contributing, although not very willingly, to their continuing concentration. Despite the birds' distress, he has been delighting in the vigor and music of the scene and concludes with restrained praise for the storm for having brought together "the country's singing strength." The weather will not hold it back. Soon they will join the growing forces of nature, which have been confined like them.

Lawrance Thompson reports that "The Lockless Door" is based on an incident in 1895, when Frost, sleeping in a cabin, was awakened by knocks on his lockless door, called out "Come in," exited through the window, and fled to town. Thompson thinks the poem centers on an image "of escape from something feared," an urge persisting throughout Frost's life (20:206-8). But surely Frost makes this material into a complex parable. The speaker's long wait for his lockless door to announce something significant suggests a strongly evasive stance toward life. His blowing out the light and tiptoeing show his need for secrecy, and his prayer to the door tries to stem a threat. His subsequent exit through the window again suggests a self-protective quest for isolation. He bids the unknown force come in so he can run from it – perhaps as if he hopes to trap it, despite the lack of locks. The last stanza enriches the connotations, for in seeing his dwelling as a cage, the speaker acknowledges that he has fled a dangerous self-confinement, which makes the knock a claim by the world for special action or change. Even in the broad world his need for evasion persists, so instead of hiding in his indoor cage, he "[hides] in the world." Still, new experience must alter him, and so presumably he becomes more accepting of human engagements.

"The Need of Being Versed in Country Things" presents an outdoor scene devoid of humans, except for the observing speaker and the memory of dwellers in a burned-over house. The title is heavy with pathos and puns: "versed" refers to knowledge and poetry, "country" refers to the rural and to the sexual cycle, and "need" refers to a reluctant acceptance of decay and natural renewal, such as the birds seem to feel, but which humans put off. Looking back at the quick fire that had destroyed a farmhouse, the speaker sees the "pistil"-like chimney, which makes the vanished house resemble nature in decay. Only the barn is left, as the winds had not swept the fire across to it, and now it alone carries the place's name. The speaker laments the desertion of the barn, where once horse teams scurried and brought in hayloads; Richard Poirier compares these actions to the sexual activity of abundant life, also suggested by the images of chimney, pistil, and birds' nest (42:x). After three stanzas, the birds – the chief actors in the drama – appear, flying in and out of the house with sounds that seem like "sigh[s]" over loss, but which are really no such thing. What the birds experience is the renewal of nature in the lilac and elm, and the persistence of a fine dwelling place, as marked by pump arm and fence wire, where they can happily perch. Abandonment and decay have left them what they need. The speaker tries to see nature lamenting over the disappearance of people and their dwelling, but the birds refuse to cooperate. Appearances to the contrary, the birds are not sad and rejoice in their nests. They, indeed, are "versed in country things" – in the naturalness of the cycles that sustain them – but humans need to make a special effort to be versed in country things in order not to misperceive the birds as lamenting. The poem radiates a sweet tension between celebration of country things as the persistence of life in the face of decline and defeat, and a deep grief about the disappearance of humans and their dwelling. It asks us to be versed in country things, but it more than half hopes that we will refuse at least one way of country seeing and will indeed "believe the phoebes wept."

# CHAPTER 8

---

*West-Running Brook*
(1928)

---

Frost's fifth volume, *West-Running Brook*, originally contained thirty-nine poems, to which three were added for the 1939 and subsequent collected editions. Even so, the collection fills only a third as many pages as *New Hampshire*. The title poem, in which exchange of ideas is more important than plot or character, is the volume's only blank-verse narrative. With few exceptions, this collection was received more coolly than were Frost's preceding three, though most of the disappointed critics acknowledged that Frost's was still a remarkable talent and that some of the poems were wonderful accomplishments. Several reviewers felt that Frost had included too many trivial poems. Others lamented the dearth of narratives. Anticipating later disagreements about its value, some critics singled out the title poem as either a masterpiece or a talky failure. Of the poems that eventually gained high critical esteem, the most frequently praised were "Spring Pools" and "Once by the Pacific." What have probably become the most celebrated of the other poems in the volume—"Acceptance," "Acquainted with the Night," "Tree at My Window," and "A Soldier," received occasional high praise. The volume's original division into six numbered and titled groups of poems, three of them carrying epigraphs, established loose groupings that are moderately useful in understanding the collection. The comments in this chapter are organized according to these groupings.

## "Spring Pools"

The first poem provides the title for a group of eleven poems, many of which depart from the poem's wary treatment of how nature's powers resemble threats to human hopes. "Spring Pools" is a stark contemplation, during early spring, of a forest scene. The speaker sees spring pools reflecting the sky and senses the coming growth of flowers and trees as a combination of growth and destructiveness. Everything trembles with transition. The forest shrouds the pools, but they still reflect almost the whole sky. It is spring, but pools and flowers shudder with cold, a foreboding of the death of both, as the trees will drink up the water through their roots and then shed deadly shade over the flowers. In the second stanza, in an ominous yet enthralled voice, the speaker reiterates these observations and warns the trees that through their summer fullness and dark foliage, they can eliminate the mutually animating and beautifying pool and flowers. The concluding line looks back sadly at the transition from winter's cold to a fertility that carries its own destruction. As the speaker reflects on the awesome experience, both admiring and fearing it, his warning to the trees suggests that little is possible except an awareness of life pulsating with its own decline.

"The Freedom of the Moon" attributes powers to nature that are really the speaker's. He claims to move the moon across the landscape in various designs, but he is actually changing his perspective by moving his position. The poem suggests everyday amazement at how altered perspectives can look like external changes. The speaker pretends amusement at taking credit for something he does not really accomplish. In the second stanza he moves to both plainer and more elaborate challenges, unloading the moon from a packing "crate" of trees and dropping it into water, where the reflection's elaborate mergings make a small saturnalia of creativity. At the end he covertly admits that the flowing pictures occur spontaneously, but his continuing wonder implies admiration for powers that he seems to share with nature.

"The Rose Family" also toys with a natural image, but ends with a serious personal application. Frost plays with the idea of roseness by alluding to Gertrude Stein's famous "a rose is a rose is a rose," which suggests how words become reified as the essence of what they represent. Now the word will not work so well, however, because botanists have assigned roses to the family Rosaceae, which includes various plants. The blurring reference of this precious word troubles the speaker, but he reassures himself by telling his lover that she is and always has been a rose, as if this guarantees that her essence preceded its naming but is still described by the name.

"Fireflies in the Garden" shows another small-scale natural scene close to home. The speaker takes pleasure in imagination's powers and then gently doubts them. His alternating perceptions of the fireflies as starlike and life-size resemble an alternation between feelings of aspiration and skepticism. He gives fireflies a sort of small final blessing, acknowledging that he can sustain only his powers of comparison and recognition.

Stressing endurance rather than fleetingness, "Atmosphere" shows its speaker delighting in a garden. The poem memorializes a wall's transformation of a garden and its atmosphere. It contrasts bleakness with fullness – the first associated with transience, the second suggesting a lingering experience. In open places, the wind destroys the grass, but the wall, absorbing the sun's heat like an old protector, weakens the winds so that they can't sweep away growing things. Thus the plants within retain their moisture, color, and smell, all of which blend into a unity that transforms the sense of time. Daylight may not last, but the gathering atmosphere's solidity fills the time with significance.

Devoted only to human relationships, "Devotion" connects to the poems preceding it through its yearning for permanence amid transience. Its first brief metaphor of the heart thinking about devotion shows intellectual activity becoming emotional and then, metaphorically, physical. The core metaphor shows the lover as a shore against which the ocean of the beloved continues to beat. The shore's unchanging position is its eternal faithfulness and its endurance of trial after trial; the endless repetition shows that love cannot grow stale.

A note in *West-Running Brook* dates "On Going Unnoticed" at 1901, though it is sparer in style than most of Frost's poems from that period. Here Frost returns to his early sense of isolation and neglect and sustains a note of unpitying self-protection. Contemplating leaves high in a tree as they compare with the flowers of the coralroot (a low-lying orchid), the speaker personifies the leaves but addresses only himself, something perhaps obscured by Lathem's addition of a comma in the middle of the third line. From the shadow of trees, the speaker sends his emotions high into their leaves. He envies their free movement in the light and breeze, which symbolizes power and recognition and contrasts with the low-lying small-flowered bushes he resembles. The leaves shaken from the tree escape his grasp; they do not bear his name, for he has not acheived anything to capture the world's attention. The woods remain as abundant as ever, even without the small flower he takes with him as a memento of his efforts. Although he has gone unnoticed, he still seems joyful in the abundance of his lonely experience.

Like two of the poems that precede it, "The Cocoon" is about obscurity, this time belonging to the unidentified inhabitants of a smoke-shrouded house. Out alone at night, the speaker sees smoke pouring from the chimney. The house is so tightly closed against intrusion that its dwellers won't light a lamp until later and have not "set a foot outdoors," not even to do chores. He sees the inhabitants as "inmates," as if the house were a prison, and thinks they may be "lonely," fearful women. He wants to talk to them and explain how their prudence encloses them in a cocoon "anchor[ed] . . . to [the] earth and moon." They seek permanence but risk isolation. Winter gales may be threatening, but the loosening they bring seems more useful than these dweller's stasis, for the cocoon they are spinning is more like a shroud than a protection promising new life.

"A Passing Glimpse" is subtly connected to themes of isolation. In this poem Frost finds his everyday perception so limited that he fears he is not living in the real world. The poem is dedicated to the fine minor poet Ridgely Torrence (1875-1950), whose volume of poems *Hesperides* alludes to the realm of the golden apples – symbols of an ideal like the spiritual insights that the poem both celebrates and suggests Torrence possessed. The passing glimpse is into a world of spiritual beauty that can be seen only dimly in earthly things, a radiance beyond reality but sometimes intuited in it. The flowers briefly seen along a railroad track are the central symbol. Their identity can never quite be grasped, but still they hold something of the elusive ideal. Had the speaker known just what he had seen, the vision might have been complete, though the flowers he names suggest this vision through their special qualities. Fireweed springs from destruction, bluebells grow where a tunnel plunges into obscurity, and the lupine flourishes where nourishment and water are scarce, all showing the miraculousness of spiritual creation. "Was something brushed across my mind / That no one on earth will ever find?" uses a trickily passive construction to ask if an unspecified force had brushed across the speaker's mind and given him an insight all his own. He concludes wistfully that the best insights come only by accident and must be taken on faith.

Elusive ideals are also pursued in "A Peck of Gold," a reminiscence of Frost's youth in San Francisco, where one of the world's best harbors is haunted by winds. The poem plays with the kind of story that might be told to chide or comfort children. During the days of the gold rush, small quantities of gold did enter the atmosphere, and the image of it might have served as a palliative and incentive to youth. Sunlight can make dust look like gold, but the speaker is annoyed that he had been told some of it really was gold. Well aware that whatever had dusted his food and drink could not have been gold, he continues his chant – as if back in the time of his childhood – but with the added witty allusion to everyone's eating his peck of dirt, as if the splendors of San Francisco life had converted this truth into something more attractive. If the poem expresses annoyed speculation about the discomforts of pursuing the ideal, no passing glimpse of the rare seems suggested.

Concluding the section called "Spring Pools," "Acceptance" is both a hymn to night and a prayer of resignation. A perfect Shakespearean sonnet in outline, its sense runs across the quatrain divisions to emphasize uncertainty. Watching a magnificent sunset, the speaker projects his feelings into the birds, who alone seem involved in the scene, for in some sense he has already withdrawn. The broad silence and the horizon's gulf, which receives the sun, portend the frightening emptiness of night. Though the birds are silent, the speaker feels that they "at least" (for they are small and seem the only sentient beings present) must know what the change to darkness means. Two birds are individualized – first a maternal one, whose sounds are low and self-soothing, and who closes her eye for protection and accepts the day's decline. She contrasts with a young bird, "some waif," hastening home and possibly thinking or exclaiming "Safe!" Except in the last three lines, the speaker lets this bird's expression expand into his own thoughts as he draws himself into an inner protection, declaring that he willingly accepts the darkness as a different protection – a barrier against seeing into the future, with all its possible evils. The final "Let what will be, be" is a prayer or benediction over all possibilities. Such a prayer is easy to make from the resigned stances he and the birds have achieved, and continues the softening of tensions that began with the bird's flight from night into nests and with the speaker's sympathetic identification with them. The poem dissolves into night, rest, and peace – perhaps with as much hope as fear for the future.

## "Fiat Nox"

"Let there be night," declares this section's original heading, providing a link between the conclusions of "Acceptance" and "Once by the Pacific," and giving the latter's title an additional irony: whereas the peace of "Acceptance" seems desirable, the peace of "Once by the Pacific" means the end of the world as we know it. A note in *West-Running Brook* dates the poem "as of about 1880," and Frost said to at least one audience, "And this, mind you, was before the first World War," implying that even as a boy he could see in the stormy Pacific a massive symbol of dangers to civilization. The poem is pervasively sardonic, metaphoric, and understated. The speaker, watching as if from a great distance, laconically issues a warning to humanity about terrible threats that seem more their concern than his. The image of clouds "like locks blown forward in the gleam of eyes" reflects the aggression in the waves' stares. The sardonic understatement of the "something" the waves thought of doing implies unspeakably awful acts. Yet the speaker draws back as he says "You could not tell," pretending uncertainty about his apprehension but possibly vindictive in his thoughts about punishments deserved by humanity. As he descends to the colloquial "lucky" and "being backed," he pretends casual concern about desperately needed reassurance. Such mock casualness continues with another "it looked as if," this one broadening the threat from "a night" to "an age" and thus changing the merely geographical to the historical – that is, to the coming of another dark age. Then two crowning understatements strike – the "Someone" (meaning everyone) who should "be prepared for rage," and the "more" (meaning everything) that would be broken. The conclusion's reversal of the biblical "Let there be light" is also an exact quotation from Shakespeare's *Othello*, in which the hero says "Put out the light, and then put out the light" (5.2.8) before killing his innocent wife, which act soon proves painfully tragic. Does God put out the light in anger or in regretful tenderness? Readers have reacted differently, but the allusion to *Othello* and the quietness of the words surrounding the pronouncement argue for a regretful God.

Nature serves explicitly as a symbol for human suffering in the epigrammatic "Lodged." The speaker sees rain and wind as personified conspirators against the garden flowers. "Smote" suggests murderousness (as in biblical language), and "that the flowers actually knelt" suggests the speaker's and their surprise at an assault from usually kind forces. They "knelt / And lay lodged" to protect themselves from what seemed to be injustice, like innocents nursing their wounds. The final line understates the speaker's similar experiences; he is close-mouthed regarding his resistance to suffering and injustice.

A mood of personal gloom continues in "A Minor Bird." The speaker lets himself be disgruntled by nature's refusal to share his mood but then realizes that his attitude is wrong. He is out of sorts with the world, but instead of saying why, he shows how his mood had made him threaten a persistently singing bird. Still, he admits he had not been right, for the bird could not help singing in a manner that mocked him. At last he recovers a small cheerfulness, realizing that any song is good and should not be silenced. The bird is "minor" because its song is not particularly pleasing, and the speaker is annoyed at it for reminding him of his own failures as a singer.

The speaker of "Bereft" feels a sinister world directly assaulting him and leaving him open to danger and mockery. He stands alone before a house whose porch has a "sagging floor." The wind becomes more fiercely threatening, summer is over, and night is upon him. He sees the personified wind as destructive and consciously inquisitive about his feelings. The door he holds open is "restive" because he seeks escape, and the "frothy shore" represents the stormy world he has internalized and wants to flee. The porch cannot hold him up, and the leaves strike as if he deserves their assault. But his "secret" is that he is completely alone, suggesting that the assault is an internal punishment for a situation he chose. However, that word has gotten out that he has only God left makes his lament a partial plea for the strength to resist hopelessness. Richard Poirier argues that "no one left but God" can be read as a small-town platitude and that Frost may be snickering at this view (42:196); others see it as an affirmation of faith.

A dark mood persists in "Tree at My Window," but its whimsical gentleness adds a brooding warmth. The speaker addresses his "window tree" as if the window both classifies the tree and posesses it. At night he lowers his sash but wishes no curtain to intervene between himself and the tree; he recognizes the difference between their worlds but craves the tree's companionship. Its dreamy and "diffuse" head resembles his in sleep and, perhaps, even during his waking thoughts. But its leaves – "tongues" that can say nothing profound – mark the big difference between them, though the poem as a whole suggests that the speaker is not as adept at expressing his feelings as he wishes to be. Their strongest connection lies in the fact that both tree and man have been "taken and tossed." He projects onto the tree an awareness of his restive desperation, which awareness the tree might have if it could watch him as he slept and dreamed. At the end, he draws back into quiet, imagining Fate to have "put [their] heads together" for a gently mocking purpose; Fate, however, was really his own reflective power. The last lines breathe an understated relief: the contrast between the tree's concern for outer weather and his for inner weather implies that the tree has less to bear than he and that his attempted comradeship with it can only go so far. The reference to inner weather shows the speaker's restraint about his discomforts and his determination to endure thoughtfully.

"The Peaceful Shepherd" seems spoken by a master artist reflecting on his desires to redraw the universe. As shepherd, he may be a god, or just a pastor planning to contain his flock, but the fact that he is going to draw the lines between stars that form the imaginary shapes of constellations suggests the process of connect-the-dot drawing, and gives him a touch of the childlike. It isn't clear how lines marking out and naming constellations and star clusters relate to the confining "pasture bars" of heaven. In any case, he wryly declares that he would be tempted to leave out such old formations as the Crown of Rule (the Seven Sisters, or Pleiades), standing for government; the Scales of Trade (Libra), standing for commerce; and the Cross of Faith (the Southern Cross), standing for Christianity or religion. As he remarks casually, the rule of these formations has been characterized by so much war that they might as well have been replaced by the Sword, the formation made by the stars below the belt of Orion, the hunter, representing warfare. This suggests that religion, trade, and government are responsible for war. The speaker's peacefully leaning on pasture bars, combined with the resigned "may all / As well have been," expresses a weary detachment unlike the submerged vindictiveness of "Once by the Pacific"; it lends this poem the aura of a moment's thought rather than a preface to destruction. Things, it seems, will go on as they have.

"The Thatch," probably an autobiographical poem about a struggle between man and wife, is set in the darkness of emotion and night. David Clark thinks it is based on Frost's wish to stay in wartime England when his wife wanted to return to America (161:119). Its four-foot couplets move in a rush, but the poem is divided into three parts. The momentum shows how one emotion runs up against and alters another. The speaker waits persistently in the darkness outside his home, engaged in a battle of wills with his wife, who is indoors, behind a lighted window. Clark suggests that the struggle is about whether she will go to bed before he comes in or will insist on restoring his comforting presence. Pulsating, vindictive, and stubborn feelings are matched by the deathlike atmosphere created by the cold rain and earthy-smelling wind. Suddenly he accidentally flushes several birds from the straw, and their frightening plight as they struggle – wet-winged, mired down, and unable to regain their nests – moves him so deeply that his grief seems less than theirs. Tenderness surges up from this sight of a helplessness he cannot relieve. They remind him that he can help his own situation, and thus his own "grief [starts] to melt," probably leading toward a reconciliation. In the curiously abrupt final section, he looks back from the vantage point of the present to the now-ruined house. This look continues the comparison between protective nests and human dwellings, but rather than speak of healing, he suggests that all griefs are eventually swept away – implying that it is best to do what one can about them before natural ruin takes over.

The comparatively cheerful "A Winter Eden" may have been placed with poems about the night because it describes an all-too-brief interruption in winter's oppressiveness, though the touch of gloom at the end is qualified by "might seem too short." A sun-drenched garden spot briefly makes the winter earth become a delicate spring-like paradise, but the atmosphere doesn't end winter's deathly hold. It is not warm enough to melt the snow or awaken the trees, and last year's berries, though shining, can not be very vital. The browsing deer is gaunt from winter but luxuriates in his feast. The difficult line "So near to paradise all pairing ends" may be an allusion to Andrew Marvell's "Two paradises 'twere in one / To live in paradise alone" (from "The Garden," which playfully congratulates a person alone in a paradisal garden for avoiding the risks of sharing it), for Frost's speaker declares that the birds flock as "friends," not as lovers, and are content to inspect the buds, whose indeterminate state shows the world riskily approaching spring. This is a realm of cautious joy, whose end is announced by "a feather-hammer" – a bird pecking at a tree trunk. In the last two lines the speaker comments sadly that this single springlike hour might be too short to make it worthwhile to awaken into joy – perhaps more a qualified hesitation than a reassertion of oppression.

"The Flood" is a gloomy but ambivalent metaphoric comment about war. If not a holdover from the first World War, the poem may express feelings about the rise of international tensions in the 1920s. Its fatalistic view of bloody human conflicts carries overtones of Frost's aggressive nationalism and admiration for manly pride. The flood is human passion, symbolized by blood, exploding into conflicts, usually war. Throughout history, the blood of international passions has been contained by plans, treaties, and hopes, but has eventually broken out into armed conflicts. Humanity attributes this to such external promptings as the devil, but "if power of blood itself releases blood," then aggressions call forth answering ones. These are culminating passions that the speaker partly admires. Blood's "unnatural . . . level" shows its desperate need for forbidden expression through war weapons when struggles for dominance through persuasion and trickery are not successful – but these are merely "points at which it finds release" and cannot stem its source. The "tidal wave" of blood about to sweep across humanity and leave its mark everywhere confirms the speaker's initial judgment that passion must find one outlet or another. The attitude toward war is less grieving than that in "Once by the Pacific" and closer to that in "The Bonfire," which combines tragic awe with relief about the inevitable.

"Acquainted with the Night," drenched in internal and external darkness, appropriately concluded the original subsection "Fiat Nox." The poem was probably written in Ann Arbor, Michigan, more of a city setting than a New England town would have been. If Frost did indeed write it in Ann Arbor, that is an additional reason for seeing its "luminary clock" as a real tower clock rather than as the moon, a likelihood argued by Laurence Perrine (139). The poem fuses calm feelings with inner turbulence, and its title – the core phrase of the identical first and last lines – is strikingly understated, hammering home how profoundly knowledgeable the speaker is of outer and inner night. The understatement intensifies the accepting mood and, at the end, delivers a crowning sense of this acquaintance. Persisting rain increases the sense of gloom, and the speaker's circular movements of body and mind range across the city in pursuit of something elusive. That human dwellings are sad to him and that he is unable to face the watchman suggest the guilt of painfully private feelings. The feet whose sound he stops are his own, showing how deserted are the streets. The "interrupted cry" suggests both conflict and broken communication between people; it is not even directed toward him, suggesting that he has suspended his own relationships. The tower clock is an extreme sign of his loneliness, detachment, and faithlessness, for its sound cannot orient him but only indicates a time at which commitments of mind and heart are not possible. Such a rehearsal of loneliness justifies the depths of his acquaintance with a night that he now seems able to bear until wisdom or kindness bring relief. Several critics feel that the alienation and lack of commitment depicted in the poem reflect the despairs of modern life rather than something distinctly personal – a view that sees "the time was neither wrong nor right" primarily as a social comment.

"The Lovely Shall Be Choosers," added to *West-Running Brook* in collected editions, would have made a strong conclusion to "Fiat Nox," its muted anguish and subdued celebration echoing other poems in that section. Lawrance Thompson discusses the poem as a portrait of Frost's mother, details of whose life may be essential to a full understanding (20:291-93). As close to unmetered verse as Frost ever came, the poem maintains a compulsive rhythm, partly iambic with striking variations. Except for eleven words of stage direction, all is dialogue between a Voice and a set of choric Voices, pronouncing the fate of a woman in a manner showing that it is exactly what will happen (or has happened) to her. The single Voice is Fate and the plural Voices its instruments. The woman is to be hurled down seven levels of the world during twenty years, and Fate declares that what happens will be by the woman's choice. The "task beyond her choosing" refers to the results of which she is not wholly aware, though the poem suggests that she has gladly embraced her suffering and disappointments, making a parallel to the doctrine of "The Trial by Existence."

Ironically, she is to be hurled down by one joy after another, for all that happens to her is both enriching and disappointing. The first joy is her choice of a husband taken in preference to someone more safe and honorable. "Something they know, he and she" may represent Frost's incorrect assumption that his mother was pregnant with him at the time of her marriage (20:554-55). Her second joy, hidden from her friends, may be her husband's unfaithfulness. Her third joy is that when friends do learn of this trouble, they are too distant and self-concerned to think about it much. Her fourth joy is her two children, who learn of her former happiness and see how its aura still clings to her, unlike friends, who would never believe this. Her fifth joy is that she never needed ("deigned" meaning stooped) to tell them about her happiness, for she was so humble that she did not care about their judgment. This attitude fuses into her sixth joy: that not being understood or cared for by her friends, she knew she had descended too late to the world of their values to learn their kind of pride. This joy is added to by the admiration of one person who was amazed by her combination of lowness and endurance but was perhaps too proudly curt to wait for an explanation. Her last joy (the seventh) is her heart's going out to this person and almost declaring all her feelings to him. This admiring person is probably her son, Robert Frost, who would have intuited the depths of his mother's character and fate but might have been too hurried and self-concerned to show it. At the end, the Voice and Voices are joyfully mocking, for this woman never had more than she could bear. She triumphed over adversity and treasured loves she could not fully act out.

## "West-Running Brook"

The book's title poem was originally given a section to itself to show its importance and perhaps to mark the transition from poems of struggle and gloom to more affirmative ones. The only blank verse in the volume, it is more a philosophical dialogue than a narrative, presenting a conflict between young husband and wife on the level of ideas and leading to a warm reconciliation more playful than dramatic. Evidently recently married, Fred and his unnamed wife are surveying their neighborhood together for the first time, though he knows the terrain well. Seeking orientation, the wife learns that their brook runs west, against the direction of the other brooks, which must mean against the slant of the land toward the Atlantic. She is delighted with this contrariness, for it reflects the couple's ability to remain close despite their differences, and she thinks of the brook as enriching their marriage by joining them to nature. The bridge they will need to build over the brook is described by the wife as "our arm thrown over it asleep beside it," paralleling their own embrace. She delights in calling it West-Running Brook and fancies that the rush of white water backward from a rock against the current is a wave toward them. But her husband, who has long noted this phenomenon, explains that it is not.

His speech recalling them to reality is interrupted by an eight-line parenthetical passage without quotation marks, spoken not by Fred but by the author, who, in explaining how a sunken rock creates this white wave, compares it to the feathers of a struggling bird that seems almost defeated. This passage prepares us for an element of Fred's final speech. The wife, however, persists in her fanciful thoughts, which Fred disclaims with gentle annoyance – but she knows he has his own speculations. He proceeds into the poem's central philosophical discourse, showing a highly educated sophistication, and leaning heavily – as critics have pointed out – on Henri-Louis Bergson's idea, in his *Creative Evolution*, about a creative élan vital that takes precedence over universal forces of dissolution. Fred sees in the white wave such a novel contrary force: the source of all life, an initiation of humans more important than evolution from lower forms of life. Some people, he says, see life as an eternal dance, like the Pirouot and Pirouette of French mime, who rehearse the same actions and never get anywhere. But he is ready to admit that existence pours itself into emptiness and fills it beyond its own dissolution. "The universal cataract of death" carries away all matter and their love as well, except for a resistance within it, which he finally defines as that which most makes them human. But he also sees "a backward motion toward the source" in physical things, and though it may be mostly "the tribute of the current to the source," he seems to imply that it may promise some form of permanence. Thus what "is most us" may be a part of the universe's design. The poem ends with a brief reconciliation, in which the naming of the brook and Fred's affirmation of faith join to form a firm memory for the couple.

## "Sand Dunes"

A lyric meditation on conflict between nature and mind, "Sand Dunes" picks up themes from "West-Running Brook," though here the speaker and the people he represents are bravely content in their loneliness. For two stanzas, nature assaults humanity as the sea washes the land and, where it cannot go, sends storm-washed drifts of sand—forming dunes to bury those men it cannot drown—unless, like Frank Lentricchia, one thinks the sea is portrayed as a "ubiquitous god" (37:93). At the poem's midpoint, the sea is personified as a woman who understands border areas but not people, who will not yield independence of thought to nature's destructive shapes. The last stanza adopts a gentle fatalism in the face of losses already suffered. "Men left her a ship to sink" (one of many? one from which the crew was removed?), and thus can also leave her a simple dwelling close to the shore. In so doing they can cut their losses, for the ship and hut now stand for excessively formal thought or materialism. By accepting their losses, people can gain in intellectual freedom and move toward wisdom beyond anything the sea has to offer. Lentricchia, while granting that confidence and control are evident in this poem's voice, thinks it shares much with the fearful voices of "Spring Pools," "Once by the Pacific," and "Storm Fear" (37:92-93)—a view which may slight the delight in independence that increases as the poem progresses.

Triumph continues in "Canis Major," named for the constellation of the great Overdog, who stands forever upright in the sky, with Sirius—long beloved by Frost—shining from his visible eye. In this poem, however, the triumph is more joking than philosophical. As night emerges, the great Overdog leaps in the east and then stays upright all night, seeming never to need rest. The speaker is an "underdog"—that is, he is a mere earthling, far from the heavens, or he is not properly recognized, or he is identifying himself with the self-pitying view of liberals, who want everyone to be an overdog. In any case, for this night he takes his inspiration from the Overdog in the sky and barks along with it, even though he cannot achieve its height or uprightness. Thus he seemingly combines disgruntlement and triumph.

The sonnet "A Soldier" makes a metaphoric statement about a representative soldier who has been killed in battle and who has achieved a triumph the speaker believes in passionately, however difficult it is for humans to understand. Frost is probably looking back again at his dear friend Edward Thomas, whose death in battle, he had written to Thomas' widow, was a final ennoblement (12:216). The poem compares the fallen soldier to a lance lying where it has fallen, subject to the assaults of dew and rust (probably representing attitudes of neglect) but still determinedly maintaining its direction. If we living persons look to where it traveled, we can see no important objective for it because we do not see the curve of its trajectory around the world. Unlike the soldier's, our own efforts do not go far; rather than accept the challenge, they are blocked by the curve of the earth. They fall short of their goals and break their arcs and points with clashing sounds. The implication is that we are skeptical of war's aims because our vision is limited. But all is different for the soldier. The arc of his fallen lance has struck a different kind of obstacle, one that destroys the body but sends the spirit far forward, toward objectives that we have never really been able to see but that the speaker believes in profoundly and asks us to accept.

In "To E. T.," Frost had seen Edward Thomas as a hero of his race. The epigrammatic "Immigrants" makes national heroes of the voyagers of the *Mayflower,* the ship on which the Pilgrims came to America in 1620. The poem sees the gathering of subsequent immigrants to America's shores as a kind of homecoming and the forming of a nation. The *Mayflower,* its Pilgrims still manning it as if in protection of the dream they began, brings new pilgrims past fresh perils. Thus their dream persists. Frost, typical of his generation, forgets the slave ships with their unwilling cargo headed for generations of death or involuntary servitude.

"Hannibal," another epigrammatic celebration of a national hero, praises the persistence of a man who ultimately failed. Could Frost have known that Hannibal (247-183 B.C.) – the Carthaginian general who led a massive force across the Alps into Italy, coming close to defeating the Roman Empire but retreating home in defeat after 14 years – was partly black and would become a hero to black people? The poem asks a long rhetorical question, implying that however lost was Hannibal's cause and however impossible was the hope he held on to, he nevertheless set a model worth elegiac celebration.

Also celebrating triumph as the original grouping of "Sand Dunes" concludes, "The Flower Boat" centers on a retired fisherman and his dory, which now stands full of flowers on the earth of the "harbor" formed by his house and barn. His retirement is dramatized by his swapping stories at the barbershop, and by the contrast between his present (represented by the dory's overflowing flowers) and his seagoing days. But his need for adventures has not passed. Memories of the catch and of the vigorous sea winds lead to fresh desire for adventure, which blends with the image of the flowers as "Elysian freight" (Elysium, the Greek heaven, generally stands for paradise) to suggest that boat and fisherman want the rougher weather that stands for death as a venture toward "the Happy Isles," a heaven for seagoing men.

## "Over Back"

This title for Frost's original grouping of four poems suggests a retreat into rural simplicities, but the simple circumstances of the poems provide for varying attitudes. "The Times Table" tells a little parable of a farmer whose horse – understanding the human need for a pause – always draws his wagon into the wet sand near a spring where people drink; the "broken drinking glass" suggests that the terrain is nearly abandoned. Seemingly exhausted by the steep climb, the horse sighs heavily, which leads the farmer to quote his oft-repeated epigram about the pointlessness of life – for, as he tells his wife (who must have to put up with a lot of gloom from him), all our breaths, standing for efforts, compel so many sighs, and as sighs mount up, they count out our passage to death. This is the "multiplication table of life" – the effects of effort, multiplied by time, equals death. In a slightly childlike voice, the speaker acknowledges that this may be true but warns that it should not be spoken, for the effect of that would be to make people abandon the preservation of civilization and the continuation of the race. Though he does not say so, the speaker must feel that humanity's persistence is significant in the face of death. Unlike other poems, "The Times Table" treats the replacement of nature by people as a disaster – not even a partial mitigation of something spoiled.

The farm couple in "The Investment," a sonnet whose form plays amusingly against its down-to-earth material, live in a place so desolate that the residents see existence there as just "staying" rather than living. The poem describes one family's investment in new paint and a piano for their house as an attempt to renew their lives. The speaker is a curious and sympathetic observer whose view blends briefly with the farmer's. From a distance he sees the "old house renewed with paint" and hears the piano playing inside. Next he sees the farmer outside digging in the cold, half-listening to the piano as he calculates the number of dinners to come from the potatoes – a scene that dramatizes the conflict between practical concerns and more personal ones. In the third stanza, the speaker's voice lifts into controlled joy as he wonders what led to this change. Did the couple inherit some money, or did "young love" lead them to extravagance, or was it that "old love" was suddenly determined not to worry about the expense? As the concluding couplet asks, was it done to avoid the crushing routine of just being man and wife, to reinvigorate life with color – as in paint, emotion, and music – as in the delight a piano brings to she who plays and he who listens?

"The Last Mowing" returns to Frost's engagement with pastoral scenes of mowing, as in "Ghost House" and "Rose Pogonias," in which the fields' returning to an unmowed state is occasion for both sadness and joy. In this poem, for reasons never really given, a meadow is to be abandoned, as people at the farmhouse suggest; perhaps it is impractical to continue mowing it. This news fills the speaker with delight for the flowers that hate farmers and want to flourish undisturbed. These flowers must make their move fast, however, because the absence of mowers will help the spread of trees, whose shade will keep the flowers from blooming (as in "Spring Pools," with its more ominous tone). His voice falling into one of ritual celebration and exorcism, the speaker says that he fears only the trees, not "tame" men; the field is now free of men and is subject to wilder forces. For the moment, he declares, the place "is ours / For you, O tumultuous flowers," meaning that the people who care have handed their possession over to the flowers for a passionate flourishing that contrasts with human doings. He "needn't call [the flowers] by name," because they are familiar – or perhaps he means that they know their needs and role well enough not to need summoning.

In "The Birthplace" nature again recovers what it yielded to people, but the speaker's attitude is joyfully relaxed. His family delighted in their life on the mountain slope before they went on to different rewards and let the mountain have its way without them. Spoken by someone from a farm family of twelve children, the poem uses one of Frost's few distinctly borrowed personas. The speaker narrates his return to childhood scenes for a happy reminiscence. Before he was born (it seems) his father had founded a farm higher on the mountain than seemed prudent. But he had succeeded, and the farm life, as described, had been perfectly pastoral: the growing family had been pleased and thriving in their isolation and confident of the future. Seen as a personified friend, the mountain had fussed over them and smiled beneficiently. But now that they have grown up and moved away, it would not recognize them. Like a mother, it pushed the maturing children "off her knees" to make place for a new brood – this time trees, which seem more proper and satisfying to her. The scene moves from wildness to settlement and then back to a relaxed wildness, as if to suggest that having had what the mountain could offer, the speaker is glad to give it back to its original nature.

## "My Native Simile"

The last nine poems of *West-Running Brook* were first grouped under this grab-bag heading that suggests a variety of playful comparisons. A few of these poems do feature such comparisons, though only three seem to stress self-satirical skepticism. "The Door in the Dark" is a grimly amused account of being struck in the head by a door, which the speaker fails to avoid as he moves around in the dark. The blow that jars his "native simile" seems to have knocked the common sense out of him; he no longer sees things clearly or categorizes them as he used to. Some playful symbolism seems intended. His attempt to "save my face" could refer to his intellectual capacities, and his "native simile" might refer to having a head for things, which would reinforce the idea that being off one's guard reduces one's imaginative and intellectual capacities.

Such an occurrence is viewed as somewhat desirable in the next poem, "Dust in the Eyes," which centers on a metaphor rather than an experience. The speaker faces up to accusations that he claims too much knowledge and needs some dust in his eyes to limit his pretensions. He claims to be willing to face the worst, which would be a "blizzard [of] snow" serving as dust. If this were to "blind [him] to a standstill," it might make him reconsider and solidify his position, a challenge he seems grimly willing to accept.

"Sitting by a Bush in Broad Sunlight" also treats problems of knowledge, but with no sarcasm. As John Lynen points out (38:46-47), unlike most of Frost's poems, it follows a single image with a series of reflections. Compromising between evolution and conventional belief, the poem makes one of Frost's strongest religious affirmations. As Radcliffe Squires notes (45:52-53), science here receives support from religious myth, as the Bible's burning bush becomes an analogue for "sun-smitten slime," which takes on life to begin the evolutionary process. Thus, although the speaker is frustrated by the elusiveness of the sunlight between his fingers, he takes assurance in reflecting that it once animated dust—such as himself—from which all life has been perpetuated. That we do not see the miracle repeated before us is no reason for skepticism about its once having happened, the speaker says. He offers the analogy of the disappearance of God after he had appeared as a burning bush and his declaration that he would no longer manifest himself directly. God's withdrawal is symbolic of his continued presence in the fires of life. The creative flame from God persists in our lives, and the word of God persists in our faith through the evidence of life itself.

Knowledge is also a theme of "The Armful," which combines seriousness and dry humor to make an allegory from an everyday occurrence. The speaker has something more in mind than the problem of getting home with all his packages intact, though the poem seems to originate from that event. For three lines he states his frustrations in keeping balanced a pile of differently shaped burdens, but then, in calling them "extremes too hard to comprehend at once" but still not to be abandoned, he uses a formula for the difficulty of balancing ideas, not packages. Next he shows that his burdens require heart and mind as well as hand. Their being balanced at his breast, though realistic, chiefly connotes inner feelings. His describing himself crouched and sitting in the road continues the realism and shows near-defeat. The conclusion's matter-of-fact assertion lends quaint determination to the underlying idea of ordering one's complex ideas well enough to go on with them.

For "What Fifty Said," not originally in *West-Running Brook,* there are two possible interpretations, one general and one specific. If the theme is general, Frost is contrasting the classical mode of education he experienced as a boy, when both the treasures of the past and conventional modes of thinking were stressed, with what he now finds around him: a world of youth that celebrates open ways of learning and thinking. However, these innovations create a painful strain, about which he is jocular. The more specific theme may be Frost's resistance to new poetic modes, a theme appropriate to a section called "My Native Simile." From this viewpoint, the title shows the poet in full career. He is sarcastic about keeping up with poetic techniques as they change. When he was young he tried to subdue personal passions to the requirements of poetic form, with the great English poets as his models. Now things are reversed. He is old, and the scene is invaded by modernistic poets whose prosodic experimentalism issues a challenge – especially their use of harshly varied meters, as in what Gerard Manley Hopkins called sprung rhythm, a new adaptation of old accentual verse, in which the lines or feet are ruled by stress count rather than by a regular alternation of stresses and unstresses, and in which a variety of semiviolent sound effects abound. Perhaps Frost is remarking sarcastically that such lessons provide a painful strain, both in the new poetic mode and in his supposed difficulty in imitating it. Although he seems to give grim assent to what is happening, his mocking tone shows that he is dubious about such violent disregard for the past.

In "Riders," Frost returns to his native similes – or, rather, metaphors – in his determined use of an everyday figure for a favorite theme: human persistence in the face of dangerous challenges (as in "On a Tree Fallen Across the Road" and "Sand Dunes"). The speaker seizes his material with gusto, experiencing himself as one of the riders on the wildly plunging earth. People have been "guiders" of all challenging things, which now include aircraft. The "what" of "what we ride" is the object of guiders and represents all of humanity's vehicles and principles. In the second stanza, the speaker sees us as having originated as infants "mounted bareback" on the plunging horse of the earth, which we must hold by the hair, suggesting that humanity is still in its infancy but fiercely determined to go on with life. Last, he sees the earth as "a headless horse" – a compendium of power and drive, tending to dangerously random movements and unresponsive to our calming efforts. But he has not given up: if we go on with all our possible ideas, we are likely to tame this horse, or at least to ride successfully toward our goals.

"On Looking Up By Chance at the Constellations" does not contradict the challenging affirmation of "Riders"; rather, it takes a self-assured look at the universe's apparent unchangingness, as if to suggest that humanity not take itself too seriously. More literally, however, the speaker just says that we cannot look to the stars for such "shocks" as we can count on in our lives to prod us toward sanity, so we had best enjoy the temporary peacefulness. Generalizing as he gazes at the untroubled sky – thrilled by non-threatening astronomical phenomena, most of which are visual illusions – the speaker can see no disasters imminent there. (The speaker of "I Will Sing You One-O" saw disaster behind a shooting star and anticipated the universe's running down.) Declaring that "We may as well go patiently on with our lives," he pretends disappointment in the lack of heavenly violence, as if it might reinvigorate our spirits. But his knowledge of the "shocks and changes we need to keep us sane" is a guarantee that life on earth will provide them, and also a challenge to utopians, who think we can eliminate them. He pretends to patience about the end of peace in China and the end of "drouth[s]" anywhere. These images make a curious pair, for the end of such peace would at best seem to imply a fatalistic acceptance of evil, whereas the end of drouth would be an anxiously awaited good. The pairing suggests that alternations of the desirable and the not-so-desirable are healthy for humanity. The speaker's switch to "Still it wouldn't reward the watcher to stay awake" pretends bemused boredom with the need to see similarly startling changes in the heavens. Here the poem's mood (and this is very much a poem of mood) focuses sharply. The speaker is enjoying a deep personal security, reinforced by confidence in an unchanging universe that makes his concerns (at least for the time being) comfortably small. He is happy in his own unthreatened stability, for – intellectualize as he will – this night's peacefulness seems to guarantee his own calm as well as that of the heavens. A kinder paraphrase of the thematic mood might be that we should not look for any more trouble than we have to, though the poem's genial stoicism is not necessarily unkind.

"The Bear" originally concluded *West-Running Brook*. It and "The Egg and the Machine" (now the final poem in this collection) continue a sardonic view of humanity, without the relaxed speculation of "On Looking Up by Chance at the Constellations." "The Bear" contrasts the natural freedom of a bear – ranging wildly across the countryside, enjoying ripe fruit and not much bothered by the damage it inflicts and receives – with man seen as a caged bear. The speaker moves from bear to humanity by declaring "The world has room to make a bear feel free; / The universe seems cramped to you and me," though the bear's freedom brings limited rewards and man's cramp turns out to come from too much thinking, for which the poem offers no remedy. Man as caged bear rages between sets of ideas and learns nothing valuable through such scientific tools as the telescope, for grasping the cosmos, and the microscope, for searching the nature of life – both of which spread a "nearly equal hope," which turns out to look profitless. Turning to philosophy, man swings from looking straight ahead to looking far aside, his philosophical stance making him look dumb as he sits on his "butt" (a pun on the qualifications of *buts*) with his eyes really shut and his religious faith mostly a pretense. As he sways, he resembles the ancient Greek philosophers in Aristotle's academy (called the peripatetic school), who strolled in a garden while exchanging ideas. His quick changes of intellectual stance "may be thought, but only so to speak," for his chatter doesn't represent real thought. All in all, he is a sloppy and sad sight, whether sitting or walking around. Yvor Winters argued that the poem criticizes rational man and implies that he would be "a wiser and a nobler creature" if he shared the bear's impulsiveness (137:572). This view, however, neglects the bear's mindless roughness and disapproves of Frost's moody frustration with the human situation.

Annoyance at human entrapment by civilization remains strong in "The Egg and the Machine," in which the protagonist (seen from a grim third-person distance) resembles a Thoreau gone wild. Without apparent explanation, he explodes with anger at the railroad's invasion of his wilderness. His string of aggressive actions begins as he hears a railroad engine approaching and regrets that he is not able to pry its tracks open and wreck it. Coming like "a horse in skirts," thrusting out its cowcatcher, the engine frightens onlookers with its "squirts" of steam and swelling noises. The train-hater screams out against "the gods in the machine"–the crew. The satirical allusion to the deus ex machina (god from the machine) of Euripidean tragedy, who descends at the drama's conclusion to make things right, suggests that these men-as-gods are false saviors. The speaker follows the trail of a turtle–unlike the train, a slow-moving and unaggressive creature–and arms himself with a load of its eggs, which he promises to throw at the headlight of the next passing locomotive, a futile assault on its vision and movement. Expressing as much misanthropy as hatred of machines, he wants peace but does not seem likely to get it this way. With "The Bear" and "The Egg and the Machine," Frost concludes *West-Running Brook* with two gestures of puzzled disgust and flight from humanity rather than with poems depicting his more typical struggle to resist destruction and absorb whatever creative possibilities nature offers.

# CHAPTER 9

## A Further Range
## (1936)

Frost divided his sixth collection, *A Further Range,* into six sections. The collection contains no real narratives and very little blank verse. Its many satirical poems, often directed against liberal social thought, frequently reveal Frost's reaction to the New Deal and perhaps show him secure enough with his poetic reputation to risk making such criticism of a popular movement. Only some half a dozen of the volume's poems are now rated among Frost's best, including "Desert Places," "Neither Out Far nor in Deep," "Design," "There Are Roughly Zones," and "Provide, Provide," though many critics would also rate "The Master Speed" and "Unharvested" very high. "Two Tramps in Mud Time" remains very popular, though critics now downgrade it, and the manner of assaulting social amelioration in such poems as "A Roadside Stand," "Build Soil," and "To a Thinker" has not worn well, even with some conservatives. Now that Frost's strong resistance to social change is accepted as a personal crotchet, the collection continues to yield rewards from poems other than its best, and Frost's new departures – often verging on light verse – have fresh pleasures to yield.

### "Taken Doubly"

Frost originally grouped the first fourteen poems under this rubric, and his table of contents assigned each an alternate title, supplied here in brackets, suggesting how each poem might be taken as a parable or fable. He was partly joking, for he wanted most of his poems to yield the universal in the specific, yet more than half the alternate titles focus on social ideas, and the poems tend to be discursive. Several are in the first person but offer little of the concentrated emotion we expect in lyrics, though later parts of the collection contain many poems that fulfill such expectations.

"A Lone Striker" ["Without Prejudice to Industry"] is based on an incident from Frost's work in a spinning mill in Lawrence, Massachusetts. In the third person, the poem tells of a man shut out from a mill for an obligatory half hour's loss of time and pay because he had failed to arrive before the gate-closing signal. The first stanza satirizes the presumptuousness of the industrialists for equating their laws with God's, for reducing the man's already miserable pay, and for making him feel like an outcast. Looking at the mill, now shaking from the machinery's operation, he cannot see inside to its impersonal operations, but he imagines what is going on there: a tense activity, with workers rushing to join broken strands. Despite the aura of tension, he admires the cleverness of the machinery and the workers, but finds it "easy to resist."

Then, with lifted spirits, he thinks of beautiful woodland ways, apparently close by, that seem to need his attention – places where he can develop his thoughts and revive his ability to love (presumably to love people, as much or more than to love nature). Approaching a world far more attractive than the one that has shut him out, his spirits are close to soaring. His thought that "the factory was very fine" is satirical, and his "wish[ing] it all the modern speed" is more an aggressive farewell than praise for a rejected alternative. His worry that industry might die because of his neglect, or might sometime have a special need for him, shows increased satire, and the bid that industry come looking for him is more a challenge than an invitation, for he will be deep in the woods and glad to be rid of it. He is taking on a newly won independence, a determination to make do on his own, and the last line reflects a hard assertion cast back over his shoulder. The alternate title, "Without Prejudice to Industry," seems sarcastic, except for its secondary reference to the speaker's choice of his own kind of industry.

The speaker-protagonist of "Two Tramps in Mud Time" ["A Full-Time Interest"] looks like the hero of "A Lone Striker," now in midlife, asserting his independence against a different kind of social claim and lucky enough to live mostly outdoors. His full-time interest is investing his energies in things he loves and finds rewarding, but now the interference comes from conscience, not personal economic pressures. The scene starts with striking immediacy. Chopping wood in his yard, the speaker sees two men (the tramps) approach and address him with mindless sardonicism. One of them pauses to see if they can get his work for themselves. His attention shifts back to his joy in his efficient chopping, which uses an energy deflected from aggression into useful activity but which is still unimportant enough to allow for exhilarating emotional release. Next, three of the poem's nine stanzas describe the outdoor scene and its delights. It is an April day, but the weather is so delicately balanced that small changes send it back into March or forward into May. Cloud and wind are personified as almost conscious parts of a difficult balance that the bluebird can also warily feel. He is blue in color rather than in mood, but still he is not taking chances with his song or assuring nature that it is safe to blossom. The water underfoot tells a similar tale, filling the speaker with joy at the promise of full spring but making him wary of its potential for quick freezes.

The ambiguous feelings in this long interruption increase his pleasure in his task, as does the challenge of the men's claim. He boasts of his outdoorsmanship, connecting it to his joyous activity. When his thoughts return to the tramps he shows some disgust with their "hulking" forms and simplemindedness, though he is proud enough of the axmanship on which they base their judgments. The men say nothing, for the regional code requires the speaker to recognize their combination of skill and need and give over his amateur pleasures for their professional right to earn a living. Ideas begin to focus as he acknowledges that when love and need coexist, need has the moral victory. He never reveals what he chooses to do; he simply shifts to a justification of his desire to unite vocation and avocation. His ideal is to find situations in which love and need are one, for then the accomplishments will make "the work . . . play for mortal stakes." The pun on "play" as gambling implies that to do one's best is to play for life itself in the hope of winning something permanent, such as "Heaven."

Laurence Perrine argues that the speaker has decided to give the lumberjacks his work. He bases much of his argument on "They knew they had but to stay their stay / And all their logic would fill my head" and on the evidence for Christian charitableness in Frost's general beliefs (279), though these lines seem to reflect irritation at the lumberjack's self-assurance, and Frost strongly opposed conventional ideas of charity. John C. Kemp, who shares Perrine's conclusion, thinks that the speaker's object in living has no bearing on how he acts toward the tramps and that the poem focuses on his woodchopping as an act of love that strengthens his love of life (36:197). Other critics complain of the poem's uncharitableness but many have a less important point than Richard Poirier's: that the poem does not really demonstrate a connection between love and "the creative promises of seasonal change and poetic inspiration" (42:274). But one can argue that the poem does not show speaker or poet thinking about poetry.

"The White-Tailed Hornet" ["Doubts about an Instinct"] is a blank-verse satire on a less social and more philosophical issue: Does instinctual behavior guarantee efficiency in the animal world? And if it does not, are we making a mistake in insisting on our evolutionary continuity with lower forms of life? The speaker elaborates on his two-fold experience with the white-tailed hornet, for whom he shows a patronizing affection. In the first stanza he admiringly observes the hornet's aggressive accuracy in having kept him away from its balloonlike nest on a woodshed's ceiling, though he is rather offended that the creature would not recognize his essential gentleness and lack of interest in making its nest into a decorative trophy. He even takes a kindly attitude toward the hornet's having relentlessly stung him out of anxiety for its family's safety.

All this had occurred when the speaker went to visit the wasp. When the wasp comes to his house, where its behavior is more polite, its pursuit of flies shows a lack of perception and efficiency. Again, the speaker takes a kindly view of the creature; sympathetic with its need for prey to feed its young, he gives it instructions about its errors. The hornet cannot tell nailheads and huckleberries from flies and so wastes a lot of effort hunting them. The speaker notes that one "huckleberry" is really a fly, but the hornet fails to hit it. Alluding to *Hamlet,* in which Polonius stupidly agrees with Hamlet about the possible shape of clouds ("Very like a whale" [3.2.367]), he playfully notes that the hornet, unlike poets, is not concerned with comparisons.

The last stanza abandons description for a little essay. The speaker complains that we have been mistaken to think instinct infallible and humans less than fallible, for this view makes us admire brute behavior as getting good results and discarding morality in favor of efficiency. Thus Frost attacks ideas such as social Darwinism and perhaps also naturalistic determinism, which see people dehumanized by the grip of instinct. At one time, people saw themselves as just a little lower than the angels (the perspective, of course, was religious), and so comparisons were upward, and we strove in that direction. Now we supposedly compare ourselves to what is below us and discard our decencies in order to survive. If "nothing but fallibility was left us," we could be consoled by the uncertainty that distinguishes us from animals, but the speaker's observations of the hornet show it to be as fallible as man, offering no model for useful behavior. Frost seems to be attacking a crude version of survival of the fittest as social philosophy. Evolutionary comparisons by serious thinkers have usually been as much upward as downward, frequently acknowledging the equivalent of gods and angels as goals of human development, though historically many people have had difficulty adjusting evolution to their religious faith, especially faith in revelation.

"A Blue Ribbon at Amesbury" ["Small Plans Gratefully Heard Of"] is a balladlike celebration of a prize hen. The "small plans" of the alternate title are those of her breeder, but the words also stand for an ideal that people might well aim for. Perhaps placed after "The White-Tailed Hornet" to show a more genial view of animal life, the poem describes a calm and small-scale perfection in a pullet, revealing the breeder's dedication, and treats the hen's unruffled determination as if it were a matter of choice, not instinct. The speaker tells the story of a neighbor's success with his pullet, which has just won first prize at an exhibition. He describes her perfect form, which might have been painted by Robert Van Vorst Sewell (1859-1924). The owner's viewpoint blends with the bird's, as the hen is shown delighted to be back home, where her owner gives her every deserved attention as he works inside his many-doored henhouse. He is so pleased with this bird that he thinks she might start the best race on earth (evidently displacing people) and that her egg-laying abilities may get her yet another prize. The pullet takes her time about feeding, not letting people – a "human specter" – hurry her, and rising to her roost with full dignity. Once roosted, she seems fully comfortable, protected from the winter storm outside and providing a model to people by her reserve, confidence, and pride. Frost has found a downward comparison that pleases him, though the tone is more jovial than serious.

"A Drumlin Woodchuck" ["Be Sure to Locate"] is another balladlike comparison of the animal and human, this time with a grimmer tone and a terminal admission that the speaker has been pretending to be a woodchuck but is really a human being seeking an analogy for his ideal of self-protection. A drumlin is a small oval hill of glacial drift, which suggests extra fortification for the woodchuck. He surveys other animals' nests and then boasts of the special security of his own rockbound retreat with two doors for emergency entrance and escape. Thus prepared, the woodchuck can risk being outside and pretending friendship in a dangerous world. Like most groundhogs, he is equipped with a warning whistle, and when emergencies send him underground, he stays safely inside while the hunt goes past him. He compares the "double-barreled blast" of guns to warfare and social stupidity.

This grim view of a hostile world from which reliable protection is essential modulates into tenderness in the next-to-last stanza. The woodchuck addresses wife or lover, as if his retreat were planned to bolster confidence and survival for her sake. But he ends with a low-key boast that though he does not amount to much, he will enjoy a limited triumph because he has "been so instinctively thorough" in choosing and digging his place of dwelling and retreat. The last two stanzas smile with apology for the slight paranoia of his position. The alternate title's advice that we "be sure to locate" implies that wise choice of position and determination are essential for survival. Robert Frost seems to be describing his own formula for protection and escape: intellectual elusiveness, prudential avoidance of the commonplace, and preparation for the worst.

"The Gold Hesperidee" ["How to Take a Loss"] is a parable about one Square Matthew Hale, who seems to be an early American farmer. The title "Square" may be a dialectical variant of *squire*, perhaps inspired by the character's physical bulk. The title is an invented name for a kind of apple and, as Robert Fleissner points out, alludes to the golden apples of the Hesperides, which represent an ideal pursuit. In this case, Fleissner believes, the ideal is the golden mean (85:213-14). Matthew Hale had tended a grafted apple tree for five years before it had begun to bloom. Finally, it had borne three stems that produced apples, referred to as "downy wax." Upon first examining these atmosphere-blessed apples, Hale had perceived only two of them, but had thought them a good beginning. He had shown the apples to his five-year old son, warning him not to touch them and identifying them by name. Later, Hale – having seen all three apples – had cultivated them devotedly, sure that when they were ready to be eaten, their name would be appropriate.

But one Sunday, the approach of frost making him think he might pick and eat the apples, he discovers that they are gone. He is on his way to church, but he puts his hat on the ground and jumps on it angrily. Then he realizes that he had engaged in evil – something resembling the worship of hewn images, or the sin for which the biblical Ahaz was punished in Chronicles 2.29 (the destruction of his own children). He had worshiped the apples before they were ripe and overestimated the value or meaning of their gold, thus violating prudence and counting on God for gifts before they had been ready. But God understands and forgives, and keeps the crowd of Philistines (represented by the city of Gath) from seeing Hale's proud behavior. This mercy leads Hale to renounce his anger and presumably to walk more humbly. He had learned, and now shows the world, "how to take a loss" – that is, not to let it bring out one's presumptions and vanity, for certainly Hale had been too proud and had thought that his ideal was certain of achievement. Frost may have placed this lesson after the self-congratulatory "A Blue Ribbon at Amesbury" and the excessively defensive "A Drumlin Woodchuck" to suggest a contrasting humility.

"In Time of Cloudburst" ["The Long View"] starts with a realistic scene, and rapidly turns to genially sardonic fantasy. The speaker is a farmer who watches as the garden of his mountain farm is inundated by rain that will bear away some of the topsoil. Realistically, he reflects that the fertility brought by the rain makes up for the loss of soil, but then his philosophizing turns slowly Emersonian as he cautiously reflects that perhaps the harm is not real, since it may ultimately produce a magnificent renewal. Glancing far ahead to the garden's being washed entirely away, interrupting these thoughts with a touch of scorn about ripeness turning rotten, he imagines vast geological ages passing in moments that lift the enriched sea floor and sink the exhausted fields. Enthralled by the apparent ease of the coming transformation, he sees himself busy where the sea floor will have risen into new fields, starting fresh cultivation with the aid of his old tools, which will be none the worse for being petrified. As if he has not carried this fantasy far enough, he goes on to see the process as an endless cycle whose possibility of depressing him with its repetitions he will have to resist. The long view here is symbolic, and the speaker – since he does not seem to think of himself as a universal figure, such as Walt Whitman's self as a timeless everyman – is either designing a metaphor for the usefulness of persistence and faith in simpler compensations than he describes, or is allowing himself some bitterness about the agony of persistence in face of disaster and making fun of hopes for universal compensation, a view supported by Reuben Brower (27:115-17).

"A Roadside Stand" ["On Being Put Out of Our Misery"] is a somewhat cloudy political satire rooted in the Great Depression. The speaker describes a phenomenon he has observed and then expresses his irritation at it and his anger at prospective cures. The roadside stand (perhaps punning on *stand* as structure and defensive stance) features a farmer's produce, displayed to attract passing motorists. Everything about it is pathetic and contrasts with the wealth of city people, who rarely stop to buy. The farmers who erect such stands ask not charity but just a little overflow of "city money." But the motorists have other concerns and are annoyed with the stand's marring of the landscape, and the farmers seem irritated by the motorist's uncharitable neglect.

Identifying himself briefly with the sellers, the speaker grieves that they must grub for money to help them imitate the city's way of life. The farmers are just "pitiful kin" to the city dwellers, who are associated with proposers of New Deal social programs that would strip the land of its inhabitants and give them enforced work or doles, which in "sooth[ing] them out of their wits" will deprive them of intelligence and put their minds and spirits to sleep. Still regretful of the self-abasement of the farmers, the speaker resentfully blasts the city dwellers who pass them by or scornfully misuse their hospitality. With tricky shifts of tone, he concludes that the country people accomplish nothing through their effort and that it would perhaps be best to put them "out of their pain" more directly than with social programs – that is, to kill them off. But he recovers a sane view of things by reflecting that he himself would not like to be thus put out of his pain. The poem makes its scorn for social planners and city dwellers plain but leaves obscure its view of how the farmers should help their own plight.

"Departmental" ["The End of My Ant Jerry"] may be the most popular of Frost's social satires, though it is less esteemed than "Provide, Provide." Its kindly humor has spared it the criticism that other Frost attacks on regimentation often receive. The alternate title, rather than specifying a moral, merely highlights the pretended comparison between ants and human beings by referring to the dead ant as if it were a relative of the speaker. This animal fable rushes through its tale of a food-gathering ant who runs into a dead fellow ant and, rather than respond emotionally and help with its removal and burial, waits to give a signal to an ant designated to perform such tasks. Concern with religion and science is exclusively the province of the burial squad, for "ants are a curious race" – that is, they are strange; they do not have any real curiosity or religious sense.

The ants are earnestly devoted to their tasks but quite without emotion, at least until the queen issues a funeral directive with just the right sentiments, but in a mock-serious manner that contrasts with, rather than compares to, proper human responses. After a message is sent in "Formic" (formic acid, which is found in ants, may function in their communication by feelers), the Queen's speech, as John R. Doyle points out (29:97-98), contrasts the formality of "state," "shroud," and "embalm" with the tiny dimensions of "sepal," "petal," and "nettle" to satirize the pretended dignity. The solemnity of the "mortician" is undercut by his "feelers calmly atwiddle" and his "seiz[ing] the dead by the middle," a gesture that combines dignity with a crude impersonality reinforced by the other ants' unconcern. The conclusion is amusedly understated, for the lack of "ungentle[ness]" guarantees no feeling at all, and the ants' "thoroughly departmental" performance shows that all their connections with each other are governed by instinct, not by any individual or group feeling. Frost implies that twentieth-century life makes most of us similarly departmental, going about our delegated tasks, feeling little about them, and engaging in thoughtless rituals.

"The Old Barn at the Bottom of the Fogs" ["Class Prejudice Afoot"] may be the most thematically difficult of the poems in the "Taken Doubly" section, though its alternate title's meanings seem clear. "Class prejudice" refers to the higher classes' supposed hostility against the tramps who sleep in their barns and to the prejudice of the speaker's cultivated tramp friend against the rich for owning houses and lacking generosity. "Afoot" puns on prejudice running rampant and occurring in people who tramp around. The poem begins with the speaker's questioning reminiscence about a barn that never had a house but was used as an "outpost" gathering place. A hunter closes up the barn and closes the hunting season, frightening creatures sympathetically described as "fur-thing" and "muff-thing."

He closes the barn by placing against its double doors a set of props that formerly held the door open while the barn was being filled and then kept it shut to protect its contents from the weather. These doors have an "advantage-disadvantage," depending on one's social class: their being locked only from the outside makes them reveal tramps' invasions (the advantage) but robs the tramps of privacy (the disadvantage). The speaker remembers a man he had known, an earth-wanderer who had shared with him a detailed memory of this barn; the implication is that both men had slept there uninvited. They had remembered the place with a charmed fondness centering on how its crevices let in the only light. That its locks had been props had aroused this man's anger against the rich and conservative, whose security he had seemed to perceive in exaggerated terms. The wanderer had been clever and educated enough to suggest that the rich ought to place the prop-locks in museums as relics of vanished architecture and wood. He had hated these devices because they had kept him from a secure use of the barn, though the chief threat to him had come from fellow tramps, who might have locked him in. The prejudice here afoot radiates back and forth indiscriminately between the classes and subclasses, disturbing the speaker's idyllic memories of a barn whose obscuring fogs may affect more things than the landscape.

In "On the Heart's Beginning to Cloud the Mind" ["From Sight to Insight"], the speaker is a warmhearted observer who reconstructs his first vision of a desolate scene. Traveling by rail in a Pullman (sleeper) compartment across desolate Utah, he sees from his window "a single light" that makes him think the dwellers where it burns must feel a lonely despair soon to be worsened by the light's extinguishment. But thirteen lines into the poem, his thoughts take a sharp turn as his "heart begin[s] to cloud [his] mind." Marjorie Cook declares that this transition may be taken to refer to both his first vision and his subsequent thoughts, as if heart had been clouding mind and will now stop, or as if heart will cloud mind in what follows (72:82). The first view seems less likely, as heart is usually the agency of warm feelings and (for Frost) of insight as opposed to sight. In any case, the speaker now reconstructs all he sees.

The light, he decides, flickers because of interfering trees as the train speeds by. The people can keep it burning or put it out as they wish, and it will long go on marking their dwelling. The couple he is imagining get on so well that they always agree about the light, and when they decide to put it out, they will look at the surrounding dark woods not as threatening forces (like the trees in *Macbeth* that will bring Birnam wood to Dunsinane) but just as trees. The woman can think of less lonely places without renouncing their own, for the mutuality of husband and wife helps them face everything bravely. Their environment isn't as forsaken as it may look, for they know of lights in several neighboring dwellings, though these had been put out earlier this particular night and so are not seen by the speaker. At last he moves back from his speculation, recalling the late hour and the train's speed. He realizes that his far-groping insight had been wreathed by the smoke of fancy, which gives his happier thoughts a tentativeness where the clouding of mind by heart had brought visions that were encouraging but not necessarily reliable. In a 1952 interview Frost said of this poem, "It was a sort of reflection on myself and the New Deal," suggesting that the poem rejects liberals' views about human isolation that requires formal intervention, and takes a more cheerful view of human friendliness and self-reliance—a reading of his own poem that seems allegorically forced (15:135).

"The Figure in the Doorway" ["On Being Looked at in a Train"] presents a scene resembling that in "On the Heart's Beginning to Cloud the Mind." Again, the speaker is riding on a train through desolate country and wondering how the dwellers there (or at least one of them) put up with such circumstances. But in this poem it is daylight, and the person about whom the speaker thinks is seen rather than imagined. The landscape is monotonous—nothing but undernourished oak trees—and suggests poor circumstances for any form of life. Thus, the appearance of "a living man" in a cabin comes as a surprise. The man's great size emphasizes his cabin's tininess, humorously recorded through the observation that were he to "fall inward on the floor," his body would measure the cabin's length. He lives in isolation, but this is not too much for him. His "gaunt" appearance does not mean that he is deprived, for he is surrounded by necessities: wood for fuel, ready water, animals, and a garden for food. If he needs any companionship, here suggested by "entertainment," he can greet the train's passengers. That he is not shown doing so suggests an independence poised at the point of action, which adds to the speaker's reassurance about the man's self-sufficiency. As the alternate title suggests, the tables can be turned, leaving open who is the spectator and who really has the problem.

"At Woodward's Gardens" ["Resourcefulness Is More than Understanding"] is set in a large amusement park in San Francisco, where Frost lived as a child. In this poem an incident is reported in the third person by a speaker who interrupts and concludes the narrative with brief generalizations. Once a boy visiting the zoo had demonstrated to two monkeys the effect of a burning-glass by focusing the sun's rays on them until one got burned. The boy, amused by his superior knowledge, had been sure that the monkeys, being way down on the evolutionary scale, were terribly ignorant, and had been pleased that the burned monkey's reaction proved what the boy already knew about the effect of the glass. The boy would have learned nothing more, except that one of the monkeys had seized the glass. After having studied it without learning anything, the two monkeys had hidden it in their straw and confronted the boy with questions that the speaker assigns to them but mostly expresses himself. Under these circumstances, everyone's understanding of the glass, or lack of it, does not seem essential. What counts is knowing what to do with things, and on this score the boy had been wrong and the monkeys right. He had used the glass to torment them and they had been clever enough to get it away from him and then to hide it from view, though they could not understand its function. Therefore, their knowledge of what to do with it was better than his. Evolution without a corresponding moral sense had not helped the boy enough.

Frost ends the "Taken Doubly" section with genial cheerfulness in "A Record Stride" ["The United States Stated"], an apparently autobiographical poem expressing pride in family, self, and nation. This balladlike first-person narrative starts by establishing a concrete setting that quickly expands across time and space. The speaker thinks of his worn Vermont closet, inside of which is a pair of worn shoes, pointing toward the back wall. He jokes about their once having "surpass[ed] each other" as his stride shifted them alternately forward, and seems satisfied that they are now even in position and accomplishment. He thinks of the shoes as listening for him and asking whether they or, more likely, he is too old for walking. This reflection leads to a family-related reminiscence. He recalls that he had wet one of the shoes at Montauk, on the far tip of Long Island, and the other on the California coast. The "extra-vagant wave," as John R. Doyle points out, combines "extra," for distance, with "vagrant," for wandering, and also puns on *extravagant* (29:150).

The speaker sounds proud to have "two entirely different grandchildren" at the continent's edges. He wants to assure them of his pleasure, rather than anger, about the adventures they had led him into, which have left the wonderful memorial of a pair of shoes, each of which carries the salt of a different ocean. His fancy of recognizing these oceans by their different-tasting salts suggests the "record stride" made by the shoes; it is so impressive that they deserve to be preserved in a museum or, as here, through his poems. He puns on the thick skins of their leather keeping them from the thin skin of oversensitivity about their being retired from active service, and concludes with a mild apology for his joy in thinking that this fancied record stride was like a walk across the country, forming the nation or confirming its state and size – perhaps thereby, as John Doyle suggests, rehearsing Frost's pride in the breadth of his own movement from California to New England (29:153).

## "Taken Singly"

Most of the twenty poems originally grouped under this title are personal lyrics on familiar Frost themes, though the aging poet gives increased attention to questions of mortality and suffering, some of this hidden from immediate view. But social themes are not missing. At least two of these poems, "There Are Roughly Zones" and "Provide, Provide," might easily have been given alternate titles and placed in the "Taken Doubly" section; also, perhaps, might have the more lyric "On Taking from the Top to Broaden the Base" and "Sand Dunes" – in which case Frost might have supplied useful hints about his intentions.

"Lost in Heaven" expresses the speaker's exultation in opening himself to a dizzyingly uncertain union with nature and the universe, a transcendental theme presented with modern reserve. The speaker reflects on the emotions he experiences one night, when rain clouds disperse and open the sky (the atmosphere whose moisture gathers into dew) to view. He is delighted to orient himself by familiar stars. However, the stars are too scarce to permit him to place their positions or his, so he remains lost. But he celebrates this state as both desperate and creative, for though he first asks where he is, he then quickly pleads with the clouds not to tell him, so that he can let his "heavenly lostness overwhelm" him. More than making the best of a poor situation, he celebrates the rush of emotion that finds him loose in the universe (rather than safely anchored) and forced to intuit his position and moorings. His emotions parallel loss of self through the risks of passion and possibly also the biblical idea of losing oneself to find oneself.

The speaker of "Desert Places" also feels lost and tries to orient himself by the stars, but his circumstances and tone are very different. He goes rapidly past a field, awed by the swift descent of snow and night and disheartened by the smooth white cover over the last traces of vegetation, which presents a temptation to yield, as does much else in the scene, for everything seems gathered in. He participates as he yields the snowy field to the woods, envies the animals in their protective burrows, and feels so absent that he does not even count as part of the scene. "Unawares," used as an adverb to modify "includes," shows that the loneliness acts without thought. The speaker generalizes about the scene: its loneliness will intensify long before any relief arrives. The snow cover will thicken and be covered by night, and will lack physical expression and anything to say; "benighted," describing the snow, puns on both the fall of night and spiritual ignorance. In a slyly abrupt transition, the speaker scorns an unspecified "They" who might wish to scare him by pointing to empty spaces even more frightening than this field – the far reaches of the universe, presumably empty of consciousness. This passage may allude to Blaise Pascal's famous description of his fear when contemplating the infinite spaces between the stars, an emotion that helped restore his lagging religious faith. The "They" who would make such efforts to scare people must be scientists and ministers, the latter anxious to demonstrate God's power and potential refuge. The "nearer home," where the speaker has successfully faced such terrors, is the inner self, as in the phrase *to strike home;* its "desert places" are moral and spiritual wildernesses. As many critics have noted, "scare," usually applied to children's casual distress, is an understatement emphasizing the speaker's deeply experienced stoicism.

The dark mood of "Leaves Compared with Flowers" remains mysterious in scene and emotion. Richard Foster describes it as "a quiet, cryptic, rather self-hidden lyric" that yields its meaning in the context of Frost's life and work (86:422). For two stanzas, the speaker contrasts trees that bear well because of good nourishment and those whose smooth leaves and rough bark give more of what he wants – tactile experience in the darkness. Once he had delighted in large trees with very small blooms, but now he prefers small plants such as fern and lichens, whose blooms are almost too small to see – a mysterious combination of impressions. He is curious about the comparative beauty of leaf and flower, or at least likes to think about "which is fairer." He finds that people in general, unlike himself, do not know that "leaves [are fairest] by night and flowers by day," suggesting that the grief of night requires leaf and bark to be stroked for their smoothness and roughness, while the cheerfulness of day enjoys the beauty of flowers. At the end, he falls into a self-addressed chant, celebrating the leaves and bark that he feels and hears in his newly dark mood rather than the flowers he had found cheering when he was young. The darkness represents tragic life experiences, and the bark and leaf stand for alternating self-abrasion and self-steadying, though what is heard in the dark must be the rustling of leaves – perhaps a combination of soothing and questioning sounds. Foster speculates that "this strangely affecting poem, with its hovering atmosphere of loss, its rapt intoning of some inexplicit but profound grief or disillusion," was an elegy for Frost's beloved daughter Marjorie, who died shortly after childbirth in 1935 (86:423).

Frost may have placed "A Leaf-Treader" after "Leaves Compared with Flowers" for the sake of its variant symbolic use of leaves, here representing the cycle of life come to a temporarily satisfying end that the speaker knows he must resist. He speaks of his combined exhaustion, delight, and fear in treading down the autumn leaves, which have safely ended a season. During summer's fullness, the leaves overhead had represented life's fullness but could almost be heard speaking of the end that the life process inflicts on everyone. The last stanza focuses on at least two emotions – the speaker's "fugitive" tendency to be always on the move and his grief over loss – perhaps like those suggested in "Leaves Compared with Flowers." In the last two lines the tone shifts: with a strong counter-assertion, the speaker realizes that his feelings were not reason enough to join the leaves' enforced flight. In the freestanding sentence of the last line, he turns from his subject and addresses himself, bidding his knee rise up from the ground so that he can walk on the winter snow rather than yield to the freezing earth.

In "On Taking from the Top to Broaden the Base" Frost shifts from personal to general human concerns. The speaker represents the people who are no longer left alive at the end. He challenges a "squat old" mountain, suggesting that it has already spread too much to create yet another avalanche. But the mountain accepts the challenge and shoots down stones at a house whose roof and glass windows had been foolish enough to demand "proof" of its power. The dwellers try to keep the mud out, but it pours in and kills everyone, so no one is left to continue the foolish challenge with which the poem begins. Here Frost may be playing with the idea of social leveling by redistribution of wealth, an idea he disliked. With such an intention, an alternate title might have joined this poem to those in the "Taken Doubly" group.

"They Were Welcome to Their Belief," though written in the third person, renews Frost's challenges to time and grief. It denies that grief is especially powerful and, though acknowledging time's transformations of the aging protagonist, insists that those transformations constituted a difficult and cumulative task. Grief and care are personified, only to be casually dismissed for their self-importance. The man's snowy hair came not from them but from time, as signaled by yearly snowfalls. The speaking voice remains almost amused as it chants about what seem to be the slow, steady renewals of winter and the equally slow whitening of the man's head. The final stanza sings acceptance as the poem again grants the existence of grief and care but denies that they aged the man. The perspective is happily stoical without sentimentality, suggesting emotional liberation for the man, who holds off his griefs while submitting gracefully to time's effects.

Mortality remains in question in "The Strong Are Saying Nothing," in which courage takes a different tone. In this poem's pictures of desolation, planting, and hope, all details apply to the rural scene and the human spirit. During early spring planting, farmers work with lonely determination. Their approval of "selected seed[s]" suggests that only the deserving among both plants and people profit from cultivation. The second stanza's combination of human isolation, frailty, and persistence is reminiscent of Hardy's "In the Time of 'The Breaking of Nations.'" "A chain of seed [sown] in an open crease" combines realistic description with a metaphor for human lovemaking and the continuity of the race. The contrast of a man who sows with one who stumbles "after a halting cart" compares the more and the less ambitious. The natural scene grows vivid with the stabbing image of white plum blossoms that stand out all the more for their lack of leaves, and both doubt and fertility are blended in the anticipation that the weather may not allow the bees to pollinate the plums. The "wind [that] goes from farm to farm" also bears fertilizing agents, but it cannot predict where the pollens will catch and create blooms, just as people cannot tell what future awaits their spirits after death. Thus, just as the determined farmers must wait to see what harvest their efforts bear, strong people will not talk about what may lie beyond death until their spirits are put to the actual test.

"The Master Speed" was written to celebrate the marriage (which ended in divorce) of Frost's daughter Irma to John Cone, whom Frost much admired. It is a metaphysical celebration of love, using images and concepts familiar from "West-Running Brook." The "master speed" is a spiritual essence of the universe that moves through matter and time, and inhabits deserving human spirits. The first nine lines of this sonnet address the master speed itself, and the last five address a loving couple who possess it. The master speed can challenge the awesomely dissipating (though also fruitful) processes of nature and can go back in time through all the ranges of experience, but it was not given this power to enjoy its own mastery of time and space. Where description of its real purpose is expected, the thought breaks; the master speed is attributed to a couple to whom it gives unity with each other and, thereby, with the universe, which will be permanent once they realize the fullness of their love. The final image of "wing to wing and oar to oar" recalls the "wind [and] water" whose speed was both promise and threat as the poem opened. The couple's wings and oars, then, with the help of the master speed, will carry them with a power greater than that of wind to disperse or water to drown. Love's power is the universe's principle of triumph, guaranteeing resistance to decay, though the final emphasis is on a joyful and free-floating continuity.

Love is associated with nature differently in the compact metaphor of "Moon Compasses," in which the speaker steps out into a rain-drenched evening – possibly after having made love – to see in the moon's measuring and contemplative embrace of a mountain a parallel to a tender human embrace. The moon's power of measuring and the mountain's exaltation may connote the bestowal of worshipful status a female figure by a dominating male one. Seeing a personal statement here, Lawrence Thompson suggested that Frost's use of four dots instead of a period at the end show the poet's reticence to complete his thought (46:75-76). Radcliffe Squires's suggestion that Frost is trying to pull down the heavens to elevate man gives the poem a philosophic dimension (45:32).

The once-neglected but now much-admired "Neither Out Far nor In Deep" focuses its nature symbolism so sharply on human concerns that its haunting picture tends to dissolve into a contemplation paralleling that of the people described. The initially detached speaker observes people by the sea who make a uniform mass as they gaze away from the commonplace shore toward the depth and mystery of the ocean. Few sights are visible; a ship rising on the horizon and a gull standing on the soaked beach provide contrasting images of hypnotic motion and uneasy stasis. Implied commentary having begun with "They turn their back on the land," the speaker now philosophizes consistently. The people turn from the varying sights of land towards the distances of water, representing mysteries they hope to grasp, though the water may not really possess any more such truth than does the land. But the people continue to prefer this attempt at further vision, just as they do at the poem's opening. Despite their determination and persistence, they cannot achieve a penetrating vision of reality – nature and human nature – or what lies behind it. But they will not stop looking. In the last two lines, the speaker calmly withdraws, balancing admiration and skepticism, glad to see human speculation continuing but confident that it will not achieve much. The poem has been seen as a harsh commentary on human limitations, a charge Laurence Perrine answers by stressing Frost's insistence on the truly impenetrable depths that challenge human knowledge and the demonstrated capacity of the people to see part of the way as they strive to see farther (212). Similarly, Elizabeth Isaacs thinks the poet "joins forces with the rest of the human race when he climaxes the deceptively flat, calm poem with a grandiose, dignified ascent at its end" (34:150). Randall Jarrell takes a middle position, granting the poem a certain unpleasantness but insisting that the conclusion shows "careful suspension between several tones," making "a recognition of the essential limitations of man, without denial or protest or rhetoric or palliation" (98:43). In an elaborate comment on the poem, Daniel Pearlman boldly asserts that it is a covert allegory expressing Frost's anger at the conformism of 1930s American radicals, who turned away from the solidity and complexity of their native shores to the monistic simplicities of foreign socialist ideologies. Thus, the people Frost attacks do indeed fear to look out far and in deep. Pearlman supports this view with a close analysis of details and by citing parallels between the poem's message and conservative views evident elsewhere in Frost's writings (211).

The nature symbols in "Voice Ways" are part of a brief, gentle communication between the speaker and the woman he addresses. He starts with a contrast between how the rain has beautifully cleared the night's weather and the fact that "some things," meaning perspectives on life, are never clear. As the two of them enjoy the sights around them, he reflects on her amusing way of contrasting physical things with ideas, as in her admission that at least the weather is clear, though things of more importance are not. This mocking affirmation is a cynical denial that anything deeply important has cleared.

Interrupting the pattern of poems in which nature is gently ambiguous, "Design" suggests nature's terrifying potential for evil. Perhaps the most often initially misunderstood of Frost's poems, "Design" fools some readers because of its apparent matter-of-factness and mock cheerfulness. Such interpretation sometimes persists in face of Frost's claim that he wrote the poem as an answer to William Cullen Bryant's famous nineteenth-century poem "To a Waterfowl," in which the speaker assures himself that both the perilous and distant flight of a bird and his own steps will be carefully guided by God. The poem rehearses the speaker's contemplative observation of an outdoor scene. On a white specimen of a normally blue flower, he sees an albino spider, whose fatness and whiteness parody the innocence of a baby, holding a dead moth. The moth is given falsely esthetic qualities by being likened to a rigid piece of soft satin. Although these are indeed "Assorted characters of death and blight," they are immediately described as something cheerful – from the perspective of witches, for whom evil and horrifying brews of the normal are a delight. Randall Jarrell sees here a parody of breakfast-cereal advertisements (98:47).

With the seventh line, the tone starts to change. The speaker's normal, heartbroken response comes out almost straightforwardly in a condensed description, in which "snow-drop," "froth," and "paper kite" continue to mock and horrify. This voice that sinks toward despair takes a sharper descent with the second stanza's agonized questions. What, he asks, was appropriate about the color of purity and innocence as a backdrop for this small-scale murder? And why should a normally blue flower called the "heal-all" become a white camouflage for such an act? The questioning grows more sinister as he wonders what force had brought spider and moth together in the darkness. Toward the end, his questioning becomes rhetorical: he suggests that this tiny "design" might really be one of darkly evil forces. At the very end, he seems to pull back from his seriousness and suggest that perhaps there is no design on this unimportant level – that it governs only things closer to the human. Here he plays on the reader's self-concern, trickily contrasting it to the Bible's idea that God's eye is on the fall of the sparrow. Thus, if there is no design for small things, there can be none for larger ones. The poem alludes to the "argument from design," which says that if there is a design there must be a designer. The implication is that given such a terrifying and unjust example of design, the designer may be equally evil, or (as the very end of the poem suggests) nonexistent – for if there is no design for small things, perhaps there is none for anything. David Perkins argues that interpretations such as this are mistaken and that the poem is a "parody directed against a mock opponent," such as those who believe in the argument from design, a view Frost can't take seriously. Rather than arguing for the existence of demonic evil, then, Frost is just playing with the idea (119:36-37). This minority view may help explain why many readers of the poem do not share the speaker's apparent horror at the scene.

Nature better protects its own in the sonnet in couplets "On a Bird Singing in Its Sleep," whose form follows the tender build-up of confidence. Again, Frost celebrates the miraculous continuity of life amid dangers, this time choosing a bird whose lucky survival delights the speaker. Briefly half-awakening during intense moonlight, the bird risks destruction, but the speaker reassuringly recognizes that it sings only half its "inborn tune." He then explains why the bird is in no real danger, emphasizing that instinct makes it stop. Seven lines of adverbial modification precede the statement "It ventured less in peril than appears," which structure rehearses the speaker's breathless apprehensiveness. After eight lines, he switches to generalization about the bird's survival, sharing his pleasure in this with his readers as representative humans. "The interstices of things ajar" are mistakes of the creature and the creation (elsewhere Frost is less kindly about biological errors). The "long bead chain of repeated birth," which comes right before the reference to the difference between birds and men, reminds us of the miraculous survival of all frail creatures through eons of time. Still, the speaker implies congratulations to humans for surviving by less instinctive means, though his tender regard for the small bird and his pleasure in its survival reveal some envy like that in "Acceptance," in which the birds' resignation provides a model of self-protection for people.

In "Afterflakes" the speaker struggles with an intellectual riddle perceived in the nature scene. At first he looks to the heavens for an explanation of his shadow's appearance during a heavy snowfall, not indicating why this needs clarification. Next he reveals that he takes his shadow metaphorically, sure that its dark shape reveals in him a firmly defined dark spirit, unlike the storm's shapeless shadow, which apparently stands for nature's mindlessly raw force. But rather than demonstrate a connection between shadow and spirit, he turns an experience into a metaphoric reflection about human nature. At the end he is reassured by a look at the whole sky, whose pervasive blueness answers his first questioning of the heavens, though not very clearly for the reader. Now that the storm is past, the suspended afterflakes make the air look like a sheet of "gauze"; each flake is a "knot" on it, and the sunlight "shin[es] through." If the shadow of the storm was undifferentiated evil and the speaker's shadow the threat of a more precise one, the afterflakes are something different. The sun that shines through defines a slight obscuration, as if evil or difficulties of perception interfered only slightly with the clarifying and life-giving sunlight. He implies that his own shadow was just such an interruption and that with the proper determination he can go on seeing the sun and perhaps deriving insight from it. Thus, the man's shadow and nature's, when more clearly defined, seem less an obscuration than a help in perceiving overall patterns and the source of brightness.

Frankly delighting in changing weather, "Clear and Colder" chants praise for summer's turn into autumn's stormy exhilaration. The poem reports a recipe for making fall weather, dictated by the dominating wind, which also serves as chief cook preparing an "elixir" – a brew that extends life or improves health – here, the life of the spirit. This wind lets summer simmer to a thick consistency and then adds leftover wind from the direction of Canada. The speaker enjoys the thought of how it strips leaves, splinters branches, and brings sudden cold rain. As the mood grows glorious with vigorous action, the speaker directs (or reports the wind's direction of) more changes, cleverly asking for just a "dash" of snow. Delighting in thoughts that this is a witches' brew, he yet mocks the idea by prefacing those thoughts with "if" and by ambiguously suggesting that his eye and Cotton Mather's (a notorious Puritan pursuer and punisher of witches) enjoy discovering witchcraft. He takes pleasure in drinking this concoction as if it really were a witches' brew, but a noble and not an evil one, for "Gods above" share human love for it and, in coming to earth for it, seem to bring a bit of heaven.

"Unharvested" takes a differently sensuous pleasure in a phenomenon of autumn, with tantalizing philosophical hints. The experience strikes the speaker almost faster than one can recognize and evaluate it, giving the poem an aura of successive gentle surprises until one stops to reflect on the total picture. An unseen smell of ripeness takes the speaker from a routine route into a quick vision of a special Eden. Beyond the concealing wall, the apple tree has achieved a kind of delighted freedom and ease, its dropped "summer load" echoing the "summer load" of "The Need of Being Versed in Country

Things," which suggested sexual release. Its breathing "as light as a lady's fan" contributes to the sense of innocence in an Eden represented by an "apple fall / As complete as the apple had given man," which is identified by its "circle of solid red" fruit, hardly a scene of sin and death in any traditional sense. Any figure of Eve concealed here seems unjustly accused of sin; she has just acted naturally. Richard Poirier suggests that this is an Eden of the fortunate fall that made humans able to take control of their destiny (42:262), a workable idea if one sees the fallen fruit as essential to processes of nature. But the fact that the speaker is not stealing the sweet scent of the apples (in their casual decay, they are no one's possession) is an inversion of the stealing of the biblical apple. Natural process here looks like all there is to the Fall of Man. Furthermore, such process, enjoyed spontaneously, with a minimum of "stated plan," minimizes human sin and helps preserve earth as Eden. The main impetus of the poem seems to be to show delight in a surprising experience that demonstrates how unplanned things have their own sweet radiance and warn us against the dangers of too much planning, which is perhaps the real sin. The biblical allusions remain puzzlingly subtle, as if the poem means several things in several ways.

The people in "There Are Roughly Zones" have done much planning about a fruit tree, which leads to apprehension and grief. Its poignancy, however, lies less in any mistake they have made than in the necessity of living on borderlines between right and wrong and of facing oppositions between aspiration and limitation. Addressing his family and a wider audience who shares his dilemmas, the speaker sits indoors on a bitter winter night and broods about the fate of a peach tree brought northward past its zone of probable survival. Feeling the outdoor threat, he shares his apprehensions with his companions as he restively broods about the meaning of their act. Emotions surge and sway and turn as he contrasts the house's safety from such weather to the painful vulnerability of the peach tree. His voice rises in childlike protest when he says "It is very far north, we admit," and then thrusts toward puzzled self-accusation with "What comes over a man . . .?" He indecisively feels both admiration for aspiration and criticism for ambition. When he speaks of there being "no fixed line between wrong and right," which turns the question of practical judgment into a moral dilemma, he tries to see his overreaching as unacceptable arrogance, but never quite manages to do so, for he still feels betrayed. His efforts had deserved success, and circumstances still seem to be the chief villain. His thoughts return to the tree as if it were a child over whose fate he patiently agonizes. The poem ends with surging affirmation, for the "limitless trait in the hearts of men" is what he really admires, and his thoughts' linking "blame" to "limitless" and "hearts" in resentment against fate shows his continued dedication to aspiration. The poem fuses a concrete memory with a fiercely persistent attitude toward life—regretful but aware of the difficulty of recognizing zones, yet not cramped by them. This subtlety of processes that baffle humans may be for Frost another version of the Fall of Man.

"A Trial Run," a novelty for Frost, is a riddle describing an electric fan. The speaker is afraid of it and puns on "hair-raising" for its physical and emotional force. He describes electric current as "metal-sap" to contrast it with the sap of plants. He anticipates that the fan will run so fast that it will shake the floor, even though the floor seems steady as a "stone reef." But he adopts a warlike determination and takes extra comfort from assurances that the machine is well built and that since his fingers on the switch stop it as well as start it, he remains in control.

In "Not Quite Social," an oblique but perhaps less puzzling poem, Frost himself seems to talk familiarly with people who have criticized his flight from society to rural life, where personal concerns outweigh social ones. These people seem fairly forgiving, for some will admire what he did, probably having wanted to do it themselves. Others will think his punishment should be mild, for they too recognize the universal impulse to escape, symbolized by the city, as the speaker compares himself to the builders of Babel, who wanted to escape earth. Although he acknowledges some arrogance in his stance, his desire to flee the earth still suggests a quest for the ideal. In granting some guilt by saying "You have me there, but loosely, as I would be held," he also affectionately suggests that his critics' hold does not get at all the truth. Still, he offers some apology, explaining that he needs his own distancing humor and that he never really denied social bonds. He is, then, willing to accept punishment for his sins, even the severest punishment – death – as long as it comes naturally. This suggests that the fate of all people is punishment enough for their basically innocent, though not quite social, choices. The last two lines indicate that the speaker will add some repayment by not only giving back what we all give back but also making an apology as mild as this statement.

Frost remains not quite social in "Provide, Provide" – one of his harshest and most tonally complex poems, reportedly inspired by a strike of charwomen at Harvard University (21:437). Frost is said to have sometimes finished reading it by saying "Or someone else will provide for you," surely a warning against the encroaching paternalistic state. The speaker remarks on a former movie queen who had become a charwoman because her beauty had faded and she had not provided for herself, to illustrate "the fate" that all should carefully avoid. He cynically specifies two basic strategies: either die young or take the most elaborate precautions possible. The impracticality and arrogance of dominating the stock exchange or becoming royalty to achieve security, and the need for such protection against harsh epithets, show anger against the pain of such necessities and the prospect of such insults. At the poem's most difficult point, the speaker seems to acknowledge a different possible path: reliance on what one has accomplished and being true to oneself. But the poem provides no transition between this and the continued cynicism of "No memory of having starred," which would normally be introduced by at least a "But" to say that states of mind will not make up for cruel circumstances. Still mock-cynical, the speaker concludes that dignity comes mostly from possessions and comfort, and again advises everyone to prepare to buy what cannot otherwise be secured. The use of the poem's title in the final line echoes its snarling syllables, pointing toward necessary but nasty action. Recognizing the harshness here, David Perkins yet finds ethical sensitivity in Frost's driving us "to a shocked recollection of the minimal lives, the limited and dismaying choices, men and women may be brought to. If it comes to a choice between 'boughten' friendship and 'none at all,' the first must be preferred" (118:240). After having surveyed critics who consider the poem a cynical defense of monetary self-concern and those who take it to be a sarcastic rejection of that view, Laurence Perrine concludes that Frost's emphasis on the possibility of being "simply true" to oneself – among other details in the poem – suggests that this is Frost's real choice (240).

## "Ten Mills"

Slightly altered from its appearance in *Poetry* magazine (and less so from the original single-volume *A Further Range*), this group of ten small poems, each numbered with a roman numeral, is offhandedly downgraded by its title, as though each is worth about a tenth of a cent. Joined perhaps by a certain skepticism and self-defensiveness, the poems otherwise show little connection. "Precaution" is a condensed witticism that takes an ironic view of youth's proud daring, which scorns the conservative values of the old but proves its own falseness by leading at last to that same conservatism. Instead of boasting of radical courage, the speaker acknowledges his lack of daring, but makes an at least moderate suggestion that his stance may save him from that decay which the young radical fears. "The Span of Life" continues contrast of youth and age, this time both of the dog and the speaker. The dog once jumped up happily at its owner's approach, but now all it can do is turn its head and bark, reminding the speaker of his own more slowly approaching but equally assured mortality. "The Wrights' Biplane" combines admiration for a lasting achievement and acknowledgment of its initial frailty. The Wrights' first airplane was a model for later human flight, but its frail, boxlike structure made it resemble a kite. It will never be forgotten, however; this accomplishment of two brothers named Wright takes added permanence from their name and its doubling. "Evil Tendencies Cancel" uses a single example from tree cultivation to express social conservatism. A wise farmer seems to know that one disease on his chestnut tree will be ended by a parasite that attacks another disease. If evil tendencies cancel each other, perhaps all is well and it is best not to act hastily. "Pertinax" (Latin for tenacious) shows the speaker's boastful determination. He can face all kinds of chaos and not hastily accept tentative solutions in the vague shape of clouds. He wants something to really count on – the firmness of form, presumably in social ideas as well as in art. The speaker's determination is echoed by the rhyme sound's half-snarling thrust from the back of the mouth toward the clenched lips.

"Waspish" looks like a witty description of a wasp, but the title suggests that it is an overlapping portrait of a proudly and narcissistically defensive person and a wasp. The creature or person assumes an energetically wiry stance, ready to sting anyone who challenges him – but, the speaker declares, he does not need to worry about his pride and status, for he is "as good as" other creatures or people. The waspishness looks like a waste. The insect in "One Guess," a tiny riddle poem, seems less allegorical and less troubled. He is a grasshopper, his eyes full of color spots, his leg bent to rub against his body and produce song, and his mouth puffy with a chemical. "The Hardship of Accounting" pretends to issue instructions about overconcern for how money is spent, but it looks more like an irritated reply to people who have called the speaker to accounting. The wearily regular meter and continued single rhyme echo the speaker's defensive disgust.

In the last two poems of *Ten Mills* the speaker turns more explicitly to questions of his own limited understanding and fate. The speaker in "Not All There" wittily remarks that he cannot be sure of God's existence – or at least, he cannot communicate with him. But he is willing to take some of the blame, for when God tries to talk to him (or is God mostly an inner voice?), communication fails because he isn't mentally or spiritually keen enough to get the message. The joke of his being there "not over half" suggests a crippled failing, perhaps on both sides. "In Divés' Dive" alludes to the rich man in Luke 16.19-31, who finds himself in hell with the beggar Lazarus and begs Abraham to send Lazarus back to earth to warn the rich man's family of the torments that await them. The allusion seems to be Frost's declaration that he does not need warnings about his fate but will continue to take his chances. Life is compared to a poker game that the speaker continues to lose, but he will feel unfairly treated as long as his chances for life, liberty, and the pursuit of happiness, which the Declaration of Independence claims for all people, remain open. "It is nothing to me who runs the Dive," which may express his skepticism about the nature of God, is followed by his assertion that he will continue to take his chances on what he can make out of whatever hand is dealt him.

## "The Outlands"

The three poems originally grouped under this title venture out from Frost's home territory into early South American history, biblical times, and the England that Frost visited early in the century. "The Vindictives," as J. M. Linebarger has shown, is based on material from William H. Prescott's *The Conquest of Peru* and *The Conquest of Mexico;* Frost conflated and changed details with historical inaccuracy of which Linebarger disapproves (284). Addressing his readers as if they are close at hand, with a grim ferocity suggesting an unexpected lesson, the speaker identifies himself with the exploited and betrayed Inca Indians of seventeenth-century Peru, from whom the Spanish conquistadores, led by Francisco Pizarro, wanted nothing but all the gold they could obtain – something for which they did not hesitate to murder and betray. Frost's voice pulses on in anger, interrupting the narrative to describe the Indians' feelings and to make his own judgments on the Spaniards' cruelty and fanatical pursuit of gold, and of the Incas' humility that finally turns to lust for revenge. The first stanza shows the conqueror's boundless greed running away with itself and destroying all principle. As the Incas plan their revenge by hiding the one thing the invaders want, the earth and water in which they hide the gold becomes a symbol for the spiritual emptiness the conquerors pursue, which contrasts with the Incas' "self-sack and self-overthrow" as they hide or discard possessions precious to them for their artistic and religious values in order to answer their oppressors and teach them a lesson. The Spaniards' self-dehumanization is explicitly denounced, and the Indians are given their own special dignity despite the primitiveness of their culture, as shown by a cave's "cracked bones, human and beast." The "great . . . gold chain" that serves as a palace gate contrasts the Incas' everyday cultural and decorative use of gold with the Spaniards' lust for it, implying that the Indians have an innocence that the invaders have not corrupted, symbolized by the buried gold chain lying "bright in the filth." The strange placing of quotation marks around the concluding stanza implies that it is a speech by the Incas, or the speaker's summary of what they had to say. The pleasure they take in hating is grim, but their attempt to show their enemies how their love of gold denies reality counterposes the Incas' values and the Spaniards'. To the Incas the decorative gold is beautiful and life-illuminating; to the Spaniards its "trappings" are the body of power exhibited in their conquests and their culture. To die "of being brought down to the real" seems a just punishment for the Spaniards, especially if they can be made to see what is happening.

Belshazzar, king of Babylon and son of Nebuchadnezzar, was destroyed by practicing false worship – a parallel of the deserved or real fate of the conquistadores. He is the figure far in the background of "The Bearer of Evil

Tidings," a story of escape from a corrupt world into a backland of innocence. Belshazzar (Daniel 5.2) is famous for having seen strange handwriting on the wall, which only Daniel dares to interpret. The words say that Belshazzar has been laid in the scales and found wanting. Doom follows promptly, after which the Persians take over his empire. Frost has imagined an innocent messenger carrying a more specific warning to Belshazzar, but deciding to steer clear of civilization's dangers and make for the backlands of southern Asia, where one delightful thing after another happens to him. A local girl gives him love, a permanent home, and the comfort of her people's religion, which is based on the legend of a princess who bore a god's child. The naiveté of her people connects to their isolation from the centers of population and power. They are tucked away among the Himalayas, partly to protect the questionable story of their royal line. That the messenger and these people "both ... had their reasons / For stopping where they had stopped" is a lightheartedly sardonic comment on the threats of the great world and the innocence of spirit that sometimes must protect itself with myths. This other world is unlike Belshazzar's, and the messenger does best to save himself and not bother with what cannot save itself.

"Iris by Night," the last of Frost's poems about his close friend Edward Thomas, is set among the Malvern Hills of England, where they had joyously wandered before Thomas's departure for the Western Front, where he was killed in 1917. Laurence Perrine has searchingly illuminated the poem's details and sources [182]. Frost describes their shared vision and walk as a near-religious experience, guaranteeing the permanence of comradeship. "Iris" means rainbow and also names the Roman rainbow goddess. The evening of this special walk across the hills, with its miraculous vision of a rainbow wrapped around them and sealing their friendship for eternity, is so drenchingly moist that its extraordinary creation of an atmosphere close to hallucination seems largely but not wholly possible. Perrine suggests that the "confusing lights," compared to those at Memphis which finally made a fresh unity, allude to the myth of Osiris (partly a sun god) being dismembered but restored by Isis so that he could newly arise as the sun (182:37). The image of light that is "a paste of pigment in our eyes" represents colors dispersed by mist and then run together. In such moisture-laden air, a rainbow might appear close up and look "like a trellis gate." Perrine describes the "bow and rainbow" that seem to surround the men as a double rainbow, usually called the pairing of a primary and secondary rainbow, with the second one behind the first and dimmer, its spectrum reversed. Such phenomena, however, remain vertical and cannot become horizontal, and to be seen must remain ahead of the spectator. That the rainbow does not move ahead of the men but becomes a unit encircling them must be a fantasy or an illusion expressing the close bond between them. It does not try to carry away the proverbial "pots of gold" but marks out the great treasure of their friendship.

As Perrine remarks, their being "elected friends" combines an election from heaven and a choice passionately made. Perrine further suggests that the circle is a symbol of perfection and that the relation of the men returns to their being "one another's guide" (182:38).

## "Build Soil"

Frost chose this as a heading for two topical poems, each aimed at Roosevelt's New Deal. "Build Soil," subtitled *"A political pastoral,"* was read in May 1932 at Columbia University before the occurrence of the political conventions of both political parties. The poem has been much criticized as a thoughtless attack on all political planning and a defense of unthinking individualism. Laurence Perrine, who seems not to share its political view, defends the poem as expressing a considered conservatism whose praise of individualism is balanced by an acknowledgement of the necessity of social controls (151). Roughly modeled on Virgil's first eclogue, "Build Soil" is a dialogue between the failed potato farmer Meliboeus and the poet-farmer Tityrus, in which Tityrus responds to Meliboeus's suggestion that he write some useful advice for the crisis-ridden country. Tityrus replies that the situation calls for a calm response and then sketches out his social views. Though hardly a proponent of socialism, he admits that some forms of government control have always been needed, but he does not like pure socialism because it compels people to love one another and thereby flattens out all real love. He notes that ambition has been socialized and then pretends to oppose the socialization of ingenuity, which can threaten stability.

Several critics excoriated Frost for this view, but Perrine sensibly argues that at this point Frost is sarcastic and really believes in the necessity of ingenuity. Tityrus continues, a bit less tongue in cheek, that if he were dictator he would let things take their course and then take credit for the outcome. Again, critics have criticized Frost for praising irresponsibility, but Perrine thinks Frost here just shows more faith in the efforts and judgments of individuals than in those of dictators (151:233). Starting at line 131, Tityrus-Frost examines the conflict between individualism and excessive socialization, or unity among nations and between people, seeing internationalism and loss of individuality as a great danger, which view prepares for his central metaphor: build soil. Tityrus defends the function of markets as testing grounds (as mentioned in "Christmas Trees") and then argues rather abstractly that country and city should maintain their distinctions (he may be referring to Roosevelt's proposed farm program), for the right kind of cultivation of the soil is the best model for human development and progress. "Build Soil" then becomes a metaphor for individual, artistic, political, and especially intellectual development. Tityrus asks that ideas be considered carefully before being put into action, which he links back to his great fear of "unseparateness," which he in turn connects to loss of self-reliance, as experienced by apprentice poets who will not continue without encouragement and people who join too many groups. At the end, he has partly won Meliboeus over, for the sheep farmer joins Tityrus in his criticism of unseparateness. He plans to go home and think things over for himself; "coming to our senses" puns on becoming sane and feeling for oneself.

"To a Thinker," first published in January 1936 as "To a Thinker in Office," is a follow-up to "Build Soil," and – in light of Frost's views – seems so thoroughly applicable to President Franklin Roosevelt that Frost's switch from affirming that it was indeed about Roosevelt to claiming he had written it three years before Roosevelt's term began and that it was about liberal thinkers in general makes one doubt the poet's memory. This change of views is recounted in *Interviews with Robert Frost* within the space of a few pages (15:83-88). Viewed as a comment on Roosevelt's first years in office, the poem is easy to interpret. Seemingly, Frost denounces Roosevelt's various and shifting social programs designed to pull the country out of the Great Depression. The poem mockingly accuses Roosevelt of too much rationality in his frequently changing social programs, but it also mocks these changes as an alternation of desperate and unthinking sallies. The speaker concludes that this thinker should trust his own instincts more, as does the bardlike poet.

In fact, Roosevelt had begun by favoring continued experimentation in pursuit of workable measures and had developed his initial program with the help of a brain trust of economic and political thinkers – probably another source for Frost's satire on thinking. In any case, the president seems to be accused of shifting back and forth from radical to conservative programs, alternatively emphasizing persuasive rhetoric and specific measures, and sometimes acting the dictator. The poet-speaker advises the president to return to democracy – to accept the poet's advice. When he calls him a "A reasoner and good as such," he seems to be mocking him for his persuasive abilities (which made him the object of teasing) rather than for real rationality. The "gift you do possess" is probably this ability rather than true reasoning. Partly apologizing for his own views by granting that he "never really warmed / To the reformer or reformed" and granting some grace to conversions, Frost quickly shifts his position by describing the president's movement "from side to side in argument" as a process of repenting for the mistakes he has just made; thus, his conversions are an annoying part of his inconsistent programs rather than a real attempt to reform himself. The advice that the president not use his mind too hard is slightly mocking for Frost's praise of his own bardish instincts implies that his are better than those of the politician he attacks.

## "Afterthought"

Originally singled out as an afterthought to this collection, "A Missive Missile" is a genially wry comment on the difficulty of communication between the ages, implying a similar future impasse for Frost's own poems. Mas d'Azil – in France, near the Pyrenees – is the site of ancient cave dwellings with many wall paintings and well-preserved artifacts. These dwellings, however, date not from the million years ago Frost grandiosely specifies, but from the paleolithic era (about 15,000 years ago), and their inhabitants belonged to modern humanity. Frost's speaker first assumes a cozy relationship with these people by asserting that the beautiful artifact he examines had been designed for his pleasure and as a message to him. Examining this pebble painted with a jagged line and two red dots, he struggles to interpret its message. A spade-bearing archaeologist suggests that perhaps it describes the sender's being doomed to sacrifice, but the speaker cannot be sure that the cave dwellers needed motives, as others do, or really intended any meaning in their design. The archaeologist must now idly wait for a reply to the ancient artist, whom the speaker imagines to be standing by. He still wonders why he can't see what the design meant – a frustration, he realizes, perhaps paralleled by some readers' reactions to his own writings. Continuing his self-criticism for failing to read the spirit of things, including this painted pebble, he laments that he tends to interpret things too much in the spirit of his own age and sadly resigns himself to not comprehending messages from such a distance – as if the souls of the ancients were still alive in their artifacts and in the "river beach" on which they lived.

# CHAPTER 10

## A Witness Tree
## (1942)

Six years after the death of his wife, Elinor, and four after the suicide of his son Carol, Frost published *A Witness Tree,* his seventh collection of poems. Several of the poems were written shortly after Elinor's death, and a few of them date back to the beginning of the century. Using "Beech" and its ancillary "Sycamore" (an unaltered quotation from *The New England Primer*) as an introduction, Frost followed with five unnumbered sections whose titles are sparer and more enigmatic than those in earlier volumes.

### "One or More" (and Introductory Poem)

In 1975 William H. Pritchard declared that this book's "opening sequence of ten poems is the most impressive one found anywhere in the *Complete Poems*" (290:130) – a view moderated, by 1984, to "as weighty and sustained an expression of Frost's 'inner weather' as is to be found anywhere in his poetry" (18:227). Pritchard further observes that these poems differ from Frost's earlier performances because of the sparseness of particular settings and the infrequency of dramatic situations and a commenting speaker, and he implies that the pain in them is related to Frost's recent losses (18:227-228). Anthologists and critics have agreed with this estimation of the work. "The Most of It" has been praised by several of Frost's harsher critics, and "All Revelation" is recognized as a remarkable and novel performance. The widely anthologized "The Subverted Flower" has been admiringly discussed as one of Frost's few direct treatments of sexuality. "The Silken Tent" remains a favorite among anthologists.

Lawrance Thompson noted that the territorial markers in "Beech" resemble those on Frost's Homer Noble farm in Ripton, Vermont (22:92). Louise Bogan observed that early American surveyors marked the corner of each square mile by axe blazes in trees and that these scars remain underneath restored bark (67:655). These observations cast doubt on the imaginary line being just the projection of a territorial marker, for such lines, though not physical, are not purely imaginary. Frost's line is imaginary in lacking line markers but also, more importantly, in symbolizing borders in the speaker's mind. Thus, the poem resonates between real scene and inner world. "Iron spine / And pile of real rocks" look both real and symbolic, showing a combination of erect strength and painful penetration and weight (almost a crucifixion image). The deeply wounded tree is a real border marker, but the mental realm is represented by pain moderated by formal dignity in "impressed" and "commit to memory." "My proof of being not unbounded," with its cleverly restrained double negative, suggests that the speaker has had to accept limits – as everyone must.

The truth that is established lies within the boundaries; it is the factuality and universality of what the speaker has suffered. The last two lines add a penetrating complexity: the dark and doubt of circumstances lie within and without his painful but controlled territory. Thus, the outside world can offer little fresh assurance and requires the same control as the inside world. The poem implies a ceaseless struggle for endurance and wisdom in both worlds. With playful grimness, the poem is signed "The Moodie Forester," Moodie being Frost's mother's maiden name.

"Sycamore" refers to the tree that the short man Zaccheus climbed in Luke 19.2-8 to get a better look at Jesus. John Lynen thinks this sycamore parallels Frost's witness tree as an aid to achieving reliable vision (38:187), an idea that may apply to other poems of this collection. The first section of *A Witness Tree* is called "One or More" because the poems in it refer to people relating to others, present and past, or because they show people struggling with isolation. Being more than one sometimes honors figures of love for their giving, or criticizes reluctant love, as in "The Subverted Flower," or desperation, as in "Willful Homecoming."

"The Silken Tent" is a virtuoso sonnet performance in which a single sentence and a comprehensive metaphor are maintained in imitation of the breathless effort of the woman portrayed and of the admiring speaker. The woman is compared to a tent on a mild summer day, when winds come and go. Every detail characterizes her and her human relationships. The silk suggests softness, smoothness, delicacy, and femininity. The drying of the dew on the retaining lines allows them to relax so that the tent-woman's central pole remains almost independently erect but is actually held loosely by silken ties that stand for thoughtfulness and love. This central pole points toward the heavens (both sky and realm of the ideal), showing her soul's self-confidence. The ties to "everything ... the compass round" reveal her awareness and concern for all people and the whole scope of experience. When the summer air produces a slight stir, one of the guys goes taut, making the tent-woman aware that she is bound rather than completely free. The tautening represents tensions in relationships, and the slightness of the bondage shows that the woman's tender dutifulness responds not to compulsion but to loving necessity. Although Frost presented the poem to Kathleen Morrison, evidence suggests that he originally wrote it for his wife, Elinor (18:229).

"All Revelation," as Reuben Brower noted (27:139), "is Frost's most symbolist poem," radiating overlapping meanings. It connects to the poems grouped with it by its central concern with human love as what gives meaning to the universe and takes meaning from it. The speaker, generalizing about human life, contemplates a series of difficult metaphors. The "head that thrust[s] in" is a child being born, a person looking into a cave or a geode, and a person trying to decipher existence; it also suggests phallic penetration as the start of life and a means of love. This head enters the "Cyb'laean" avenue of earth (Cybele is a sensual earth goddess), but it does not know where it comes from or where it goes when it dies. These are the mysteries about which we, as participants and witnesses, wonder during our brief instant of life. The mind with which we question is as apparitional as what it tries to grasp.

Still, we have our precious experiences and successes in understanding. Our heads thrust into existence the way a cathode ray penetrates a sealed geode (a hollowed limestone formation with crystals projecting into its interior), here symbolizing earth and experience. Such rays, used in early scientific experiments, create luminescence in the crystals, revealing their color and pattern (27:141). This experience is visionary, as the third stanza abruptly illustrates, because of the illumination of human eyes looking into others. This is the basic pattern of love, and also the first step in a child's gaining its sense of identity as its eyes catch those of parental figures. These eyes looking into each other create a bond with the farthest and closest portions of the universe – the stars and the flowers – which are given their significance by love. The process is interactive. Our eyes give and take meaning from stellar fires and biological nature. Thus, earth and skies are concentrated into our eyes, and love reveals to us all that is to be known – or at least all that we are allowed to know. We need not be afraid of the overwhelming size and distances of the universe (as in "Desert Places"), because they have been brought down to a dimension we can grasp. This is Frost's version of God as love, a view partly qualified by his apparent insistence that all revelation is a product of our own minds.

Like the two poems that precede it, "Happiness Makes Up in Height for What It Lacks in Length" balances joy in earthly love against possible diminishment or bafflement. The lengthy, abstract title prepares us for more statement than the poem offers and thus increases the surprisingness of the poem's blended concreteness and generalization. As the speaker addresses the "stormy, stormy world," he seems to be talking about life. But immediately thereafter, images of mist, cloud, and sun create a real scene, which again becomes general with the elevated diction of "Obscured from mortal view" and the ambiguously physical and spiritual "lasting sense / Of so much warmth and light." The speaker rapturously combines memory and contemplation, and with "If my mistrust is right" shows himself wrapped up in thought. After the curious mention of his "mistrust," meaning uneasy suspicion, his attention focuses on a specific scene in which the sun shone unfailingly all day long; the sense of the day's sweeping on blends with the rapidity of movement that started the poem. In a formal declaration of enraptured contemplation that blends scene and general emotion, the speaker declares "I verily believe." The "verily" contains a carefully considered affirmation that answers the earlier "mistrust," but the "fair impression" of the next line keeps it in a realm so mental that it may be self-created. Now he addresses his beloved, and the shadowlessness of this remembered day becomes a symbol for the perfection of their shared solitude. Their walk through "blazing flowers" seems both a high point of life and a reminder of mortality. Their shared solitude is enriched by a change of scene, as if they need to share a complex vision of reality, to face the changes that gave this moment such perfection.

For the poem "Come In," "One or Two"—this section's original heading—might be changed to "One or Two?" The speaker is clearly but not quite happily one, unless he makes two with the thrush whose invitation into the dark woods he refuses, just as he refuses to become one with the darkness itself, which may represent death. First published early in 1941, this poem may be spoken from the vantage of the widowed poet and may have been placed here to show—to himself or whoever takes the hint—that alone as he is, he will continue to watch the stars for his remaining time rather than enter the dark woods of paralyzing grief. The poem has affinities with "Stopping by Woods on a Snowy Evening," but here responsibilities to others go unmentioned, and the speaker cheers himself up with a final humorous twist, suggesting that messages from nature are more products of the imagination than of nature's wisdom. Standing at the border of field and wood, he enjoys the dusk but notices the greater darkness of the woods. He imagines the bird on its tree, unable to move in the darkness (as in "Acceptance"), but expressing its love of life through song. The sun casts enough remembered light to make a scene for his hearing, though there is also a suggestion that the sun has placed its vitality in the bird. The dark woods are "pillared" like a temple, but the bird's music is more like lamentation than celebration, though the speaker has acknowledged a life-impulse in it. Can the beauty of the stars represent the final stages of life? Frost may be variously playing with images of sun, stars, and birdsong. The simplicity of this poem is deceptive.

The speaker of "I Could Give All to Time" seems relatively alone in the world and keenly aware of time's annihilations, but he dwells with the riches of his past, which help him challenge time. Looming over the poem and the world in a special personification, Time is gravely dominant but calm and unboastful, as if fulfilling an assigned task. This combined personification and impersonality adds to Time's dimensions, but centrally offers an attitude the speaker rejects: it is an impersonal process that swallows up everything and denies its meaning. The first two stanzas describe vast geologic changes; details of sea and land are also personified. The eddies of ocean that play "like the curl at the corner of a smile" fuse the semi-indifference of Time to a similar feeling in what it affects, since the smile comes from the sea but expresses Time's controlled emotion. In the last stanza the speaker is almost willing to accept this attitude toward Time, but he makes an exception with a calmness that echoes Time's; the repetition of "except" shows hesitation flowing into determination. He will not yield what he has held, which may be a great deal, but the conclusion indicates that he is thinking of all that was most precious. Luckily for him, the customs officers at the border of Time (or the border between life and death) have slept often enough for him to carry across his most precious memories into the Safety of his spirit – a realm that has become what it is because of what he has transported there. The last line is calmly and determinedly understated, its monosyllables and echoing consonants underlining its quiet firmness.

In "Carpe Diem" (Latin for "seize the day," a famous formula from Horace), time is again the focus. The poem's two quiet children are apparently the speaker of "I Could Give All to Time" and his now physically absent lover. Time remains problematic, but here the speaker is less sure of triumphs over it. Again, a personified figure dominates: Age, a mysterious and kindly manifestation of the atmosphere, who watches over two young lovers. The twilight hour, the church bells, the children's being strangers to Age – all show the young people's undetermined future and the speaker's partial sadness toward what he now knows awaited them. Easily enough, Age had tried to make them conscious of the preciousness they would soon lose – which reflects an attitude only age can understand. Life ceaselessly awaits the future and evaluates what has occurred. Only the distance of anticipation and memory sharpen things, and at least for the young, what is close up floods the senses and blocks an organizing shape. That the present is "Too present to imagine" gives imagination the final say about reality and value. The poem, however, does not reject "carpe diem" as advice. It merely explores the universal poignancy of transience as it relates to hope and memory, and leaves more gently open and insubstantial the triumph of memories celebrated in "I Could Give All to Time."

Resisted ravages of the past are also the central subject of "The Wind and the Rain," which takes its title from the clown's final song in Shakespeare's *Twelfth Night,* a song about life's transience and foolishness. The poem's scene is relatively undefined, but the two numbered parts correspond first to the days of the speaker's youth and then to his present desolation. In Part I he walks through an autumn landscape, exhilarated by fierce wind and rain, which energize him into song filled with seasonal anticipations of death as a release. Looking back, he warns himself that he would have felt differently had he known "The many deaths he must have died / Before he came to meet his own," echoing in a sadder key the anticipations of "Carpe Diem." Next a rhetorical question implies that the young should know that prophecy of grief leads to its fulfillment. The speaker's emotions swing back and forth as he reflects on life's complexity. He reasons that it was only right to sing of ill as well as good, but he cannot escape his attitude of having tempted fate. "Happy sadness" summarizes this section's dominant tone, and the last line looks forward to the second part's unspecified griefs.

Part II is mysteriously set in the summer, probably representing both the fullness of the speaker's life when grief had overtaken him and the present from which he looks back in pain. The scene is more indefinite and symbolic than that of Part I. The fullness of his symbolic flowers comes from the grief of water, representing suffering or tears. But he warns himself not to estimate too highly flowers that have thrived on and absorbed such a limited abundance of water. In an extravagant metaphor, he challenges flowers to accept gigantic floods, for even flowers past their prime need such a testing, just as buds need concern for their future. Shifting to personal application as in Part I, he says he needs his share of the water and that only drouth-breaking rains will bring him to life or maintain his life. "More than should be said" refers to the mysterious relationship between pain and creativity, leading to rain and sunlight as wine and magic lead to soul and body. He is outside in a fullness different from that of Part I. At the end, the landscape alters again as he walks through a rainy dusk. The downpour expresses the grief for which he can no longer produce tears; the "stay" in "none left to stay" is used in the archaic sense of "prevent." He has become one with the atmosphere, as at the poem's beginning, but this now makes him one with the world's intertwined grief and creation.

The protagonist of "The Most of It" wonders in several ways if he is one or two. The poem is typical of Frost's treatments of what John Lynen calls "The struggle between the human imagination and the meaningless void man confronts" (38:148). The central symbol, the great buck, contrasts with the paired doe and buck in "Two Look at Two," suggesting that this poem may deliberately look back to that poem's human companionship and more successful yearning for a bond with nature. Here, the harsh third-person voice overlaps with the protagonist's point of view but also, by its inflections, adds to the mockery that he experiences. The protagonist has been living alone by a lake across from a cliff. After four lines of generalization, the phrase "Some morning ... he would cry out" switches the narrative from the general to the specific. To "ke[ep] the universe" is to both attend to it and give it what meaning one can, and he is convinced that his role in doing so is painfully limited when he succeeds at waking only a "mocking echo" of his voice. One particular morning his complaint about life makes his query more specific with the familiar human demand for responding love. The "And nothing ever came of what he cried" does not indicate when the jarring answer following "Unless" came, but that answer was imposing enough to create a vivid memory. The great buck embodies nature's meaning but at first looks to the protagonist as if it might be human – a foolish hope sardonically cancelled by "Instead of proving human when it neared." He is as alone as ever, though the buck's splendor and strength radiate from its actions as it creates a waterfall and penetrates the brush. It goes back into its own wilderness and the man is left as he was, alone and aware of nature only as an uncaring power. Whatever company he needs he must find within himself or among humanity. The universe or nature has no reply for our basic questions – at least not most of the time, or not until our imaginations shape things nearer to the heart's desire. John Lynen thinks the poem shows "man's true stature in that he cannot ever be satisfied with nature" and that the speaker sees the buck's remoteness and inhumanity but also admires its magnificent strength (38:148) – a view that perhaps too much separates speaker and protagonist.

In the sonnet "Never Again Would Birds' Song Be the Same" there are two characters, not one. The man remembers and believes the woman's miraculous accomplishment: her loving voice had entered the voice of birds and forged a bond with nature – permanent for him and perhaps for the world. The speaker looks back at the life of his protagonist-self in this Eden of his love. That "He would declare and could himself believe" what her voice had accomplished suggests that his loving imagination has made the transformation. "The daylong voice of Eve" shows the woman's lasting innocence, which had permeated the atmosphere. The call or laughter that "admittedly" gave her voice its influence suggests that its power had been excited by his demands, to which she had responded with the eloquent softness that had entered the atmosphere and the birds' song. Although "Be that as may be" grants that the transformation was made in response to him, it also goes on to insist on the reality of the change, for the woman's voice survives in the birds' now that she is gone – or at least this is "probably" so. But certainly for him, "never again would birds' song be the same." He switches from the psychological to the mythic by making her an uncorrupted Eve who had come to teach birds the music of love and had thereby transformed the world.

Frost intimated to Lawrance Thompson that "The Subverted Flower" was based on an incident from his courtship of Elinor (20:512), probably Frost's reason for withholding it from publication until after her death. Narrated in the third person, the poem begins in the middle of an action, after the young man has begun passionate advances that the woman rejects. The flower that he "lashe[s]" in his hand and then casts down is the dominant symbol, complexly developed. Initially it stands for the phallus and later also symbolizes the passionate center of the man's rejected feelings; on another level, it stands for the woman, who has subverted her feelings as well as the man's. He handles the flower to demonstrate an impulse he is asking her to share and not reject, but as her rejection persists, he grows cynical and animal-like, and her frightened view of him exaggerates both traits. The beautiful flowers bring out her radiant femininity, but she evades his embrace. He can grasp only her arms; the strange idiom in "He stretched her either arm" probably means that he held both of them. As he tries to persuade her of a shared feeling, she cannot be sure she has heard correctly. Her fear makes him seem increasingly animal-like and paralyzes her.

The momentum of his threat is briefly interrupted when the woman's mother calls her toward the protecting garden wall, but she continues to see him as an animal, a view perhaps justified by a sexual gesture more obvious than his handling of the flower: "An arm worked like a saw / As if to be persuasive," an imitation of masturbatory movements designed to invite her to sexual satisfaction. Not surprisingly, the man is now slightly hysterical, and rather than being a "tiger," he now has a "snout," like that of a pig. His "evasive" eye shows that he also feels shame. Here the narrative voice begins to comment, noting with dismay that the girl saw the phallic flower and the sexual organ behind it as corrupt and was blind to the beauty it might lend to a man. The phallic impulse began the man's threatening behavior, but his gross transformation came partly from her inability to respond with some warmth. At this point he is overcome by shame and begins his retreat, having changed, metaphorically, from tiger to pig to degraded and disoriented dog, retreating in cowardice and with a desperation paralleling that shown by the woman's foaming at the mouth. The image of words in her mouth like a "bit" combines self-disgust and regret for her action—feelings reinforced by her looking backward as her mother draws her home, as if she cannot let go of this puzzling experience. Though the poem is much anthologized and commented on, critics have been hesitant to specify the details of the flower symbolism. Few consider the possibility that the man has actually exposed himself, which would make the flower initially more specific than a symbol, connecting to the arm working like a saw—though such an interpretation increases sympathy for the girl's hesitance and disgust. An unusually daring poem for Frost, it explores powerfully ambivalent feelings in both man and woman.

"The Subverted Flower" ends the sequence of lyrics admired by William Pritchard and others, but four additional poems were originally grouped under "One or Two." "Willful Homing" is reminiscent of "Snow" and may present an autobiographical figure in a similarly ambiguous light. The strangely sardonic third-person voice reinforces the detached self-criticism. Again beginning in the middle of an action, Frost writes of a "he" who represents a typical stubbornness, proud of his self-reliance but at last acknowledging the need of others. He has been out in a blizzard until later than is wise. Though the storm is nasty enough to be disorienting, he sits on a snowdrift as if it were a horse to control, and makes clever plans. Though proud of his independence, he is resigned to accepting an invitation into a door, but in wanting to seek it in his own way, he compromises his ideals and makes himself likely to fumble at the entrance. The last line, viewing the man's plight from the outside, is emphatically sardonic. Those awaiting him or aware of his plight will think he has tried too long to remain independent, but apparently they will give him a wry welcome to home or to the human community.

"A Cloud Shadow" also deals with isolation, though more lightheartedly. Reading a book during the depths of winter, the speaker fancies that the breeze fluttering the pages is looking for a poem on spring as a sign of an arrival for which he has almost given up hope. The atmosphere is so wintry that he cannot believe anyone could ever have written about spring – or at least that such thoughts could now be counted. The breeze is displeased by his thoughts, for she has been busy looking for the pages he denies, and her irritation that he may make her miss the poem on spring reprimands him and seems to leave him feeling properly put down.

"The Quest of the Purple-Fringed" was first published in 1901 as "The Quest of the Orchis." George Monteiro argues convincingly that Frost had mistaken the early-blooming gentian for the late-seasons orchis and that he had later covered his mistake by using the phrase "Purple-Fringed," which applies to both flowers (108:89). This poem treats the speaker's isolation tenderly. He is tramping across the countryside in early spring, looking for the first bloom of a much-loved purple flower. The details build up a hushed anxiety as he feels the combination of warmth and coolness and is haunted by landscape details that charm but are not what he wants. Still, the weather is just right, and even the fox seems to go in anticipation, but the flower he seeks has not appeared. As the middle stanza begins, he finds and bows to the long-sought flower in worship of its fullness. The flowers' stillness (for he has found a clump) and their paleness create a moment of ghostlike perfection that deprives everything else of significance and reminds him of imminent decline. But his concentration yields to languid wandering and resignation. Any fullness past this moment will be no more to him than the decay of fall. Frank Lentricchia finds in this poem "the purest celebratory moment in Frost's poetry," that "for the lonely man who haunts Frost's poems . . . almost makes everything else seem bearable" (37:86).

"The Discovery of the Madeiras" subtitled *"A rhyme of Hakluyt,"* elaborates on a brief episode from Richard Hakluyt's *The English Voyages,* which tells of an Englishman named Macham who, "with a woman he had stolen," had been tempest-cast on the island of Madeira, where "the woman [had] died for thought." As in the poem, he had built a memorial for her and sailed to Africa, where the local king sent him on to Castile. The psychological elaborations and the story of the slave couple are Frost's inventions. The poem ends the group *One or Two* with a treatment of two contrasting couples: first, the English gentleman and lady who have run off together, she possibly fleeing her husband, and second, the slave-couple whose mutual burial at sea is narrated to the Englishman by the ship's captain. Throughout, the English lady is hesitant and remorseful, more lonely than accompanied, and regretful of leaving stability behind in the hope of a "vague Paphian bourn," referring to the illicit love sponsored by Aphrodite. Matters are made worse by a stormy sea, whose filling the sailors with guilt parallels the woman's unease. A hull that looks like barrel staves and a mast like a stick suggest the ship's frailty. With her distress increased by the storm, the woman cannot respond to her lover's implication that she had wanted him to carry her off; his passion may have fooled him into thinking women want to be forced. In any case, the two of them acknowledge a mutual confusion of motives.

The captain may be dimly aware of the relevance to these lovers of the story he tells the man about the disease-ridden slave whose lover had begged to be thrown into the sea with him. The grim suggestion of a "funeral-wedding" for the slaves contrasts to the love-death theme as it applies to the lady and gentleman. The slave woman had gone willingly to her love-death, whereas the lady shrinks from both life and death shared with her lover. When the gentleman relays to her (probably vindictively and self-justifyingly) the story of the slave lovers, she sinks into sickly despondency as her guilt feelings intensify. Her lover asks that they be put ashore in hope of saving her, probably feeling that "an untossed place" will contrast with the sea as the arena of her conflicts. After her death on the island where they were cast, he tries to build a memorial for her, even though their love was unsuccessful–but he fails, as shown by the bay's eventually being named for him rather than her. That the African Moors who imprisoned him are swayed to give him his freedom suggests a masculine sentimentality, and the misnaming of the bay suggests that the world ignores plights like the lady's, though the speaker's final reflection implies that everything is vanity. George

Nitchie, who compares the lady to T. S. Eliot's Prufrock (41:213-14), thinks that the slave lovers, unlike the lady and gentleman, achieved self-mastery (41:03) and that the woman seeks expiation for herself and punishment for her lover (41:108).

## "Two or More"

The title for this grouping suggests either humans joined together in society or one individual standing in opposition to society. The group begins with Frost's best-known patriotic poem, "The Gift Outright," which is printed a second time in the 1969 edition after Frost's poem written for John F. Kennedy's inauguration, for it had been his intention to read both poems on that occasion. Here Frost presents himself as spokesperson for Americans and adopts a tone of grieving and longing desperation that slowly yields to love and triumph. The poem opens by describing the American people's first possession of their land merely as land – before they also belonged to the land – partly because the people were subservient to their English masters. With "Possessing what we still were unpossessed by," a partly sexual metaphor is extensively punned on. We were unpossessed because ownership of the land was denied us by England and because we did not give ourselves to the land in the spiritual and physical union love demands. A variation of this idea is in the next line, "Possessed by what we now no more possessed," which means that as we began a deep involvement, it was denied by the foreigners who still ruled. These limitations were overcome when Americans realized they had to give themselves in an act of passionate surrender, for to give oneself "outright" means to do so immediately and totally, as lovers do. Again Frost puns: "deed of gift" as "deeds of war" refers to certificates of possession and sacrificial acts of possession. The land "vaguely realiz[ed itself] westward" because the action proceeded spontaneously over a long period but led to a crystallization resembling the nation's birth. This vagueness is shown by the country's being "still unstoried, artless, unenhanced" as its development continued, which echoes the earlier unpossession and creates a sense of unformed spaces that have not yet achieved their myths. John Doyle points out that "artless" means simple and sincere as well as without works of art (29:49). In the high sense of convincing story and belief, these myths are projected forward in the last line, with its curious perspective from the past: looking at the present and the still-hoped-for future and asserting that they will become reality.

"Triple Bronze" stands not quite at the opposite pole from "The Gift Outright," Frost having turned from joy in the creation of his national community to a defense of his individuality, which includes the protecting power of his country. The title is adapted from Horace's *aes triplex* (triple bronze), the shield for which he had wished to protect Virgil on the elder poet's voyage to Greece. Such a shield would have one layer of hardened metal deposited on top of another, providing an almost impenetrable protection. In this poem, threat and protection seem supernaturally created, one as compensation for the other. The Infinite that threatens is everything outside the speaker's skin, and the Powers that create his shield are internalized divine forces. His skin, marking individuality, provides the first shield. Next comes a dwelling, which protects him from marauders. Last, he must share another protection with his national community, which shuts out foreign states and adds to his identity. The "too much" of the last line is cautiously understated, offhandedly echoing the everyday phrase "that's too much for me" – recalling Frost's frequent statements of endurance in the face of emptiness, but here suggesting that he exercises a normal privilege.

"Our Hold on the Planet" returns to the mood of poems like "Riders," "The Census Taker," and "The Times Table," with their varying affirmations of or longing for human survival. As in "There Are Roughly Zones," the speaker starts with a concrete scene involving the weather and moves on to generalizations about human nature, again with a childishly yearning voice that seems to both apologize and plead for its claims. The scene concerns a lucky situation: farmers had needed rain and it had come in just the right quantity, promising good growth of the grain, and the "natal wet" soil promises more for the future. Suddenly philosophical, the speaker acknowledges nature's frequent opposition to people, but the present instance shows, however scantily, enough luck to guarantee human survival – proved by the proliferation of humanity. Although there is "much" against us, still nature "must" be a little more for than against "man." The playing off of these words against each other shows the speaker yearning toward the heart's desire rather than affirming the practical or emotional claims of his stance, as in "The Census Taker" and "The Times Table." The statement that nature must be "a fraction of one percent at the very least" in humanity's favor has become a famous signature for Frost's cautious affirmations.

In "To a Young Wretch *(Boethian),*" Frost takes a jocular look at "two or more" as it bears on his relationship to a young man who has robbed his woods of a Christmas tree and thereby made the poet-speaker reflect on how social good and ill balance each other. The poem is "Boethian" in following ideas of the late Roman philosopher Boethius (480?-524), who taught that the divine purpose is good, that our human perspective is too limited to see this, and that evil is really good because it protects us from mistaking partial good for the whole. Frost's speaker considers the pleasure this young marauder has taken in stealing his tree, though he could have honestly purchased one and saved the speaker discomfort. In Boethian manner, instead of seeing the young man's Christmas joy as an offense, he prefers to class it with acts in which two good things oppose each other – as must be the case (he cynically remarks) in war when each side claims the gods' favor. In conclusion, as he sadly contemplates the decorated tree deprived of its natural setting, including the stars overhead, he thinks about the artificial star now on the tree, thus illustrating opposing goods, and he tries to accept the situation with proper Christmastime forgiveness.

"The Lesson for Today" concentrates on social issues in its attack on the notion held by T. S. Eliot and earlier poets that they lived in the worst era and needed to adjust their writings to it (for example, Eliot maintained that only chaotic poems can adequately reflect chaos). Frost had already declared himself on this subject in his famous "A Letter to *The Amherst Student*" (13:105-7). The poem has many difficult aspects, especially its allusions to the medieval British Latin poet and schoolmaster Alcuin (735-804), who became a tutor at the court of Charlemagne (742-814), and its quick transitions between the voices in its imaginary dialogue with Alcuin. Reuben Brower pointed out the poem's imitation of Alexander Pope's style and the conversational manner of Horace's satires (27:105-7), and Betty S. Sutton provides both the text of the Alcuin poem Frost alludes to and a detailed analysis of various passages and allusions (187:81-96). The speaker begins with doubts that his age is really the worst, but offers to go back in time to discuss that possibility with a medieval Latin poet who might have complained about living in a time unfavorable for poetic greatness – a time when the classic period was finished and the modern scarcely started. Back then, Latin quantitative verse had been abandoned for the meter and rhyme of medieval Latin, and the poets sang mostly of Pagan delights, as in the Goliardic song in which the quoted *"ver aspergit terram floribus"* means "the spring sprinkles the ground with flowers."

By calling this poet the "Master of the Palace School," Frost identifies him as Alcuin, and he then describes his age as too chaotic and inimical to learning to allow for great poetry, though Alcuin would not have thought of that excuse. In the poem's most difficult passage, the speaker alludes to his own contemporaries thinking their time is "out of joint" (as Hamlet complained his was) and writing verse to match its disorganization. However, he and Alcuin would not have done this; they would have been afraid that if they had embraced or swallowed the statistics that show a bad age, they would have distorted themselves out of "human shape." He then delivers a lecture about all times being equally difficult, playing on the notion of both himself and Alcuin as teachers (though not really scholastic philosophers) who know that "the groundwork of all faith is human woe" – that is, that suffering motivates faith and creativity. This is an allusion to Alcuin's famous epitaph, beginning *"Hic rogo, pauxillum veniens subsiste viator,"* (187:85), which addresses the passerby with traditional warnings that he too will become ashes and food for worms, which should teach him to care less for things of this world and more for the spirit. Alcuin's poem does not use the familiar medieval phrase *"memento mori"* (remember [your] death), but subsequent uses of it summarize Alcuin's epitaph. The speaker and Alcuin hold similar views: the ancient poet believed that religion showed man as a lowly worm, and the modern poet believes that science sees him as a meaningless dot. "The cloister and the observatory saint" are the monk and the scientist; times have been very bad for both of them. Frost's speaker imagines Alcuin addressing his pupils at Charlemagne's court, among them the possibly imaginary Roland and Olivier (famous in *The Song of Roland*), instructing them to "be happy but polite" in a miserable age. The result "at the summons" would be for these students to sit down to write Horatian satires featuring the doctrine of *memento mori*. Switching to his own era but still generalizing, the speaker declares that all times are difficult and takes a sideswipe at political liberals' idea that state control will bring heaven on earth.

The speaker stresses that the difficulties of this life belong to all times, and he compromises with ancient views by seeing mankind as "either nothing or a God's regret" – that is, insignificant or deeply flawed. He grants that philosophers of all times can only see the "universal Whole," into which we all vanish, as rabbits do into holes. Again addressing Alcuin, he admits that he has put arguments into his mouth and jokes that his own seeing all ages as equally dark makes him a "liberal" – someone who argues against his own side, in this case against the notion that the modern age is triumphantly dark. The address to Alcuin stops suddenly with the speaker's declaration that he would put his hand on the monk's staff and tell him that he had read his epitaph, which (as the final section shows) had led him to visit a local modern graveyard. There the speaker had read various tombstones and given much thought to his own approaching death, which had led him to reflect on the incompleteness and imperfectability of everything – an idea responsible for much literary gloom. But he is determined to take his "incompleteness with the rest" – that is, to accept the human condition with all its limits. In conclusion, he tells Alcuin that he accepts the doctrine of *memento mori* but has a different epitaph for himself: "I had a lover's quarrel with the world," meaning that though he found much wrong with the world (and perhaps hoped to see some changes), he did not denounce or renounce it but instead addressed his life to it in love.

## "Time Out"

Many of the eight poems originally grouped under this heading look at small events and sights in the landscape. In the sonnet "Time Out" the speaker takes time out in various ways: he pauses from his climb up the mountain, changes his usual reading from books to the "book" of nature, and tries to look differently at accepted ideas. The mountainside forms the pages and the flowers its words. "It took that pause" shows the breathless hurry he now interrupts. The plants that he reads with his fingers as well as with his eyes are close to the ground, suggesting an intimacy his hurried ascent had blurred. That the flowers are "fading on the seed to come" shows nature in endless transition. The slope given his head by his new gesture forms the basis of a moral. Rather than staring at the world in opposition or analysis, he has become gently reflective, having adopted a way of seeing that "may be clamored at by cause and sect" because some people view things in set ways and would disapprove of his open-mindedness. "But it will have its moment to reflect" emphatically but gently shows his resistance to the world's hasty prejudices and implies that pauses like his can make their claim on everyone.

Dated about 1901 in *A Witness Tree*, "To a Moth Seen in Winter" is the second of this volume's three poems tenderly regarding small natural things. Seeing a moth desolated externally, as he is internally, the speaker offers it protection from the winter, but it declines his warm, sheltering hand. Seeing the moth desperately pursue the absent love of its own kind, he finds touchingly human its "incurable untimeliness" – that is, its search for what the time cannot offer. He calls this trait the "only begetter of all ills that are," echoing Shakespeare's dedication of his sonnets and thereby reversing precious inspiration into inevitable despair. Our lives, he suggests, pursue what the moment cannot offer. The moth is right in flying from him. He knows that he can't influence its life, let alone save it, and he ends with the sadly comprehensive reflection that he is sufficiently burdened with trying to save his own life, showing that his task is as difficult as the moth's. Although his own plight intensifies his sympathy for the moth, his delicate tenderness minimizes the tendency toward self-pity and creates an atmosphere of fragility and loss.

The insect in "A Considerable Speck *(Microscopic)*" lends its size, situation, and panic to a sardonic but not uncompassionate treatment. The speaker is indoors, concentrating on the task of writing, and the tininess of the creature moving across his sheet of paper calls his attention first to the curious fact of its vitality and then to its semblance of intelligence. He studies it closely, surprised that something so small can have a will and intentions, and amused by its dislike of his wet ink, which perhaps indicates that it shares some of his own doubts about his writing. "Plainly with an intelligence I dealt" puns on the insect's simplicity, but its desperately evasive movements reveal to the speaker that he is a threat to it and lead him to feel a bond with it. As if to show he doesn't need to dominate, he explains his lack of the "regimenting love" of social meddlers. He can be harsh or detached when he must, but since the creature is doing no harm, he has no need to destroy it. The situation is thus comfortably resolved, but the speaker cannot resist drawing another mild self-congratulation from it: he sardonically implies that he reads far too many sheets on which the writing displays very little mind – perhaps even less than is shown by a microscopic insect's maneuvers to keep itself alive. The criticism may apply to some of his own attempts at writing.

The title of "The Lost Follower" is a parodic reversal of Browning's "The Lost Leader," about a poet who became a lackey of the reigning powers – often thought to refer to William Wordsworth's acceptance in old age of the British Poet Laureateship. Both sardonic and tenderly resigned, the speaker says that all the good poets he knows who desert the art do so not for money but only because of their utopian political intentions, though their "Shelleyan dejection" often shows them to be desperate for success. The poem plays with the idea of song as golden and with the ancient idea of a Golden Age, which still stands for perfection in society. Losing hope in their political goals, the defecting poets settle for living with the poor; one has now embraced poverty in the company of his wife. The speaker declares that it is dangerous to argue with these people that progress will not bring the society they expect to be created by government redistribution of money or by warring political factions. He illustrates this contention by recalling the archetypal Ghibellines and Guelphs, contending political groups of medieval Germany and Italy who created violently divided loyalties. At the end, the speaker is relieved to recognize that the former poet counts on his continued friendship and will not argue – but he cannot help noticing the friend's persistent and desperate hope to create an earthly paradise.

A note in *A Witness Tree* dates "November" at 1938, suggesting the context of rising European wartides – the Spanish Civil War, the Munich Pact, the German takeover of Czechoslovakia – all portents of worse to come. Yet the poem expresses a typical autumn theme: the year has gone down to a splendid yet disheartening death, and the observers realize that another season has passed with less accomplished than hoped and less to look forward to. But the details are richly descriptive. The leaves scatter in glorious colors until their shifting in the wind ends as they become a rain-beaten sheet. With a pun on "wasted" as implying destruction and loss of time, the speaker laments that we boast of our accomplishments but forget how much we let our spirits remain asleep, and grieve instead of enjoying life, all of which becomes more poignant in face of the increasing "waste of nations warring," a threat to all life.

Destruction remains a central theme in "The Rabbit-Hunter," in which the speaker seems painfully both outside and inside the situation, empathizing with the hated hunter as well as the miserable rabbit. He sees the rabbit-hunter as "Careless and still," but if the "gun depressed" describes both the slant of the hunter's gun and the speaker's mood, the hunter's aloneness in the "ghastly snow-white" swamps implies that the hunter shares some of the speaker's terror and depression. The yelping hound, more aggressive and unthinking than either of the humans, is reminiscent of the dogs in "Mending Wall"; its noisy delight places it halfway between the speaker's and the hunter's engagements. The rabbit is shadowy in its quickness, and also in the sense that the hunter denies its individuality and right to live. The poem ends in desperation as the speaker reflects that killer, victim, and spectator cannot understand the nature of death and, by implication, the rightness or wrongness of what goes on here. The situation thus serves as a tiny paradigm of the human condition.

Mixing general, historical, and topical allusions, "A Loose Mountain *(Telescopic)*" takes a more sardonic view of destruction. The poem was probably evoked by the appearance of the asteroid Hermes, the "loose mountain" of the title, which in 1937 came within 480,000 miles of the earth, a record closeness. Its half-mile diameter and the gravitational pull between it and the sun created apprehensions that it might crash into the earth. However, the poem begins by describing a familiar yearly meteor shower (usually occurring in November), the Leonid. If any of the meteorites were to land on earth, they would produce a dust almost too fine for humans to feel. Frost's speaker declares sarcastically that only starwatchers like the Magi would look out for such a phenomenon, which he views as a heavenly reprimand to humanity for daring to confront the darkness of outer space with artificial lights – a hint of Promethean arrogance. This yearly (but greatly varying and much-observed) phenomenon reminds him of the recently noticed asteroid that seemed to threaten earth, as if the asteroid were something that the personified Outer Black of the universe might hurl toward us the way the famous ancient slingers of the Balearic islands (Majorica, Minora, and others off the eastern coast of Spain) hurled murderous stones from their slings. (Hannibal used thousands of these slingers as mercenaries in the Punic wars.) The Outer Black, he concludes, is probably just holding back so he can bombard the earth when it will do the most damage. Typically for Frost, something small predicts a larger threat, but the concluding implication that the universe may have some perhaps deserved damage in store for our planet differs from Frost's usual hopes for its future.

Threats of astronomical disaster are greater but more genially contemplated in "It Is Almost the Year Two Thousand." Frost starts with an allusion to the myth of an ancient Golden Age, but instead of satirizing "the true Millennium" expected by political radicals, he almost takes pleasure in accepting scientific predictions of a final catastrophe for the earth or humanity. The "golden glow" of destruction looks like the earth suddenly burning up. He takes a calm stance toward this eventuality, apparently amused by the idea that it will not distract people from placidly tending gardens and engaging in small acts of scholarship, although it would at least be a spectacle worth watching, an "end deluxe." The diction and rhyme mock our fears and ordinary pursuits, but the tone is delicately balanced between regret for lost simplicities and criticism of seeming trivialities.

## Quantula"

This section consists of nine short poems, like the "Ten Mills" section of *A Further Range,* and it has a similar balance of geniality and sarcasm. "In a Poem" is a happy exposition of Frost's theory of interaction between poetic form, momentum, and insight. The speaker declares that poems generate their own joyful continuity, and though some people may object to rhymes, he sees them as objects that solidify a poem. The stroke and time of meter help the writer's momentum discover means to express what he must say. This idea resembles Frost's prose formula that like a piece of ice on a hot stove, the poem must ride on its own melting (13:20).

"On Our Sympathy with the Under Dog" looks like a satire on the ins and outs of minor politicians who claim to represent the underdog and on the various complaints of underdogs themselves. First, the politicians come to power or get attention. Then they lose power or renew their complaints of affliction. The highest politicians, shown as Roman senators dressed in togas, which expose their legs, are afraid to defy lest they be attacked by underdogs in office and by those who can only make public complaints.

The writer of these poems knows what suffering is, as he tells us in "A Question," perhaps placed here to contrast with the public complaint of the preceding poem. The questioning voice addresses humanity from the unknown vastness of the universe and focuses narrowly on the souls and bodies of humans who wonder if the mysterious gift of life was worth the mystery of their afflictions. But the pain is personal, and everything goes unexplained. The poem is a stoic sigh of pain, perhaps intended to both praise and express a lonely stance of endurance.

Frost's speaker plays with ideas of location in "Boeotian," probably placed after "A Question" to show his ability to stay more happily in conditions of doubt. He praises the notion that wisdom is not native to one region – in this case Attica, the birthplace of Platonic wisdom – but may also come from other regions, including Laconia, which gives its name to pithy expressions of doubt, and Boeotia. In any case, he is pleased to accept wisdom where he finds it and to make his own synthesis.

Probably the most famous of these short pieces, "The Secret Sits" also seems carefully placed, as if to declare the failure of the wisdom just cautiously boasted of, and perhaps also the failure of the prescience claimed in one or two other poems in the "Quantula" section. Critics occasionally find Frost here warily and wearily commenting on God's elusiveness. More likely, he is writing about the true meaning and structure of all the things and events around which we weave our dances of speculation. The Secret is personified, as if its enjoyment of and knowledge of its own nature were essential to the structure of reality. The speaker seems to divide his feelings between frustration at being outside and satisfaction that he knows how problematic everything really is.

"An Equalizer" angrily attacks the views of economists who wish to redistribute wealth by what Frost considers unnatural means. The sarcastic remark that he will show something "as true as [that] Caesar's name was Kaiser" suggests that he is going to describe a falsehood after playing with the names of rulers whom he compares to the equalizer. Such a person wastes money, despises those who accumulate it productively, and attacks those who, unlike himself, use resources thriftily. But when the equalizer sees inequalities of wealth, he offers his own prescription to improve public health (a pun on "equalizer" as a dose of medicine, such as a laxative or a headache pill).

Perhaps trying to moderate his harshness, Frost places "A Semi-Revolution" next, suggesting his willingness to favor or at least to accept gradual changes. Alluding to such failures as the Russian Communist Revolution, he notes that complete revolutions have a way of continuing rigid class structures. His suggestion that a Rosicrucian can confirm this idea may appeal to the moderate mysticism and humanism of this Renaissance-era and modern quasi-religious sect. The difficulty faced by "executives of skillful execution" in slowing the momentum of revolutions quietly mocks them, for they really cannot be revolutionaries. Recalling the concluding metaphor of "An Equalizer," Frost jokes about "salves" (undercutting them by the rhyme with "halves") to suggest a gentle application of everyday medication.

"Assurance" asserts the self-reliance of the person who scorns equalizers and wants his revolutions carefully executed. Its metaphor sarcastically comments on the persistence of chaos and threat from nature and society, even though humans fancy that they have set up solid protection. The danger of the sea doubtless does not care how people defy it and will continue to threaten and demand as much as ever. This looks like a tangential warning against too much social control and confidence—unless Frost is thinking more in the terms of the next little poem, "An Answer," whose metaphor partly continues from that of "Assurance." In "An Answer" The Islands of the Blessèd (an image of an earthly paradise from Greek mythology, as old a myth as that of the Golden Age) stand in the middle of the sea of universal discord. The speaker addresses a young man curious and hopeful about such places of safety and retreat. Looking back tolerantly and warmly across his own experience, the speaker declares that he has never seen "a blessèd one," the joke turning on this phrase's curious ambiguity. Acting as a mild curse, it regrets the failure of such hopes but preserves a nostalgic longing for them.

## "Over Back"

Frost's original title for the group of six poems concluding *A Witness Tree* comes from "The Investment" in *West-Running Brook,* in which the phrase describes sparsely populated rural areas. These poems are reflections on some subtle feelings amid such regions, though they are not linked by any striking continuities. The speaker of "Trespass" shows Frost's typical concern with boundaries—his desire that they be respected but not harshly imposed. The speaker here grasps his subject with a conversational emphasis, as if rehearsing the experience for someone who might not sympathize, or as if he were holding an inward conversation with the trespasser and crankily displaying the emotions his politeness makes him keep to himself. Thus, "No, I had set no prohibiting sign" is a combined assertion and apology for his possessiveness. This quietly growling mood continues in his description of the intruder's "surly freedom" and his "busying" himself in "my woods," though the speaker's tone may seem more surly than the intrusion. Then he apologizes for the other person, noting the innocence of his looking for fossils inside rocks, valueless to the speaker and yet part of his property. He notes how very long the intruder remained. Relief comes suddenly and cordially, producing a quiet glee in the speaker's reassertion of "my property" after the intruder's "little acknowledgment" of debt and boundaries of ownership. Life may be simple "back over," but it has its proprieties and its restraints.

In "A Nature Note" the speaker's rural isolation makes the autumn farewell of a flock of whippoorwills occasion for puzzled nostalgia. The "piece of their bills" the birds give him and his family is a scolding for their remaining behind as the season ends. The birds sing noisily and with broken rhythms, making their "mock farewell" a self-congratulation for their flight and a ridicule of those who stay behind. The speaker looks for a special meaning in such a formal and fortuitous event and just manages to find one. It is "September the twenty-third" (usually two days after the end of summer), suggesting that the birds had stayed as long as they could and were issuing a warning about autumn. The repetition of the date shows quietly hesitant meditation on the part of the speaker, as if he were mocking himself for his effort and his discovery.

"Of the Stones of the Place" makes a strong reference to being "over back," for its speaker addresses a specific person who no longer lives near him on the rocky New England soil but has moved out toward the Great Plains, where the "wind soil," or loess, goes down thirty feet, unobstructed by rock, and is so rich it seems "good enough to eat." On the other hand, the speaker's pasture is crowded with boulders, like "a basketful of eggs," and he amusingly suggests sending a boulder to his friend, who "could slap and chafe" it into a statuelike shape (reminiscent of the speaker's desire to hold a meteorite in "A Star in a Stoneboat"). As such it would make an "eolith palladium" – that is, a Stone Age version of Pallas Athena's statue, specifically the one at Troy that supposedly guarded the city. The idea here is that it would guard the American West, though the traditions it would guard might (as the conclusion hints) be those of the New England the speaker's friend has left behind. This friend need not carve a face or inscription on it, but if people ask him what it means, all he need do is identify it as "The portrait of the soul of my Gransir Ira" (comically and regionally rhymed with "inquiry"), for his grandfather – so cozily and antiquely referred to – would represent the hard New England spirit, which faces the adversities of stony fields and hard-bitten existence. The probable pun on "ire" reflects anger in the old ancestor's expression. The last line is a witty throwaway; if the boulder isn't really the portrait of his forefather's soul, at least it came from his rocky regions and is a good memorial to his character. Thus the speaker mildly twits his friend on having deserted New England and recalls him to a bit of native pride.

In "Not of School Age" the speaker is literally "over back," where a pre-school-age child has painfully little companionship and thus quickly becomes the "one friend" the speaker makes as he finds his way through the noise of wind-whipped woods toward a single house, where the apparently lone child must shout to be heard. The child's mother wants to know what is going on between the boy and the speaker, who must struggle to understand the boy's speech but manages to learn that he longs to be at the nearest school, where the adult could go but not he. The child has seen the flag there, identifying the place and its communal nature, and since he cannot go, he has asked the speaker to verify the flag's presence. The child's loneliness parallels the man's but is more poignant because he can do little about the limits of his world, which remind the speaker of how lonely it is "over back."

As if arranging a strategic withdrawal from "over back," Frost moves toward this collection's end with "A Serious Step Lightly Taken," another of his patriotic celebrations of the pioneer spirit, New England endurance, and the country's future. The speaker and his family had plotted their way on a map whose graphic details they had read with metaphorically daring enthusiasm, pleased to accept the challenge of "burrs," "snake," and "hollow head," representing hills, stream, and lake, and ready to face the prospect of a dotlike town for civilization. Their car had just about given out, but the door they tried admitted them into a house in which they settled solidly enough to assure their contribution to the long continuance of the nation on this side of the Atlantic, aided by their being "aloof yet not aloof" – that is, independent but friendly and making their own contribution to the soil and civilization. Since the nation has been maintained for three hundred years, he declares, they will help make it at least three hundred more, joyously anticipated as "A hundred thousand days" of impressive history, which is likely to include "half a dozen major wars" (not so frightening in prenuclear days) and rather more presidents than the thirty-two the nation had (up to Franklin Roosevelt) when this poem was published.

Frost's speaker is wittily "over back" in the satirical dialogue of "The Literate Farmer and the Planet Venus," in which a farmer voices pseudo-sophisticated views like those Frost usually attributes to city dwellers. The farmer is "literate" about science, technology, and evolution. The time is summer or fall 1926, when Alfred Smith and Herbert Hoover began looking forward to the presidency, and when Venus probably shone with an unusual brightness in the evenings. The characters joke about the latter; the farmer suggests that the illumination of the nights may eliminate the need for sleep. The traveler prefers to see the mysterious light as a star, and the farmer jokes that it cannot be "Serious" (Sirius) but is probably an electric light improved by Thomas Edison (then still active in his Menlo Park, New Jersey, laboratory). As a modernist, the farmer makes fun of the Bible, agrees with Darwinian evolutionism, and sees humanity achieving a new stage. The traveler mildly agrees to accept some evolutionary ideas but is annoyed at a liberal friend who regrets the whites' takeover and wants to return the country to the Indians. He remains sure that the light is a star, but the farmer insists the heavens are plotting an all-night brightness like "one big blob / Of electricity." The traveler argues that night is needed to refresh and question the human spirit, but the farmer will not yield his liberal stance and is angry at people who won't let science free them. Sure that the light is a new Edison invention, he looks forward to spending sleepless nights helping to perfect humanity, comically alluding to Edison's preoccupied neglect of sleep as though it is an advantage rather than a deprivation that hurts people's appearance and spirit. He thinks getting up on the wrong side of bed causes wars and thus hopes that freedom from sleep will end wars. Edison, he claims, knows that "a bed has no right side" and hopes to see beds eliminated, an idea linked to Edison's supposed faith that improved light will end our difficulties. The traveler's concluding "Marvelous world in nineteen-twenty-six" may be a weary attempt to end the conversation, but it also playfully acknowledges the wonders of science. The literate farmer's views are fantastical, but the traveler's conclusion seems generous-spirited. It is all good fun with a touch of seriousness.

# CHAPTER 11

## Steeple Bush
### (1947)

Frost's eighth collection, *Steeple Bush,* published when he was 73, was received more coolly than his earlier volumes. Reviewers showed respect for the poet's talent, triumphs, and persistence, but their praise for the poems was sparse and often forced. Randall Jarrell found only one poem, "Directive," worthy of Frost, and thought the bulk of the poems sounded like the work of someone who had once been a great poet but now had only the mannerisms of one (57:209). Frost's friend George Whicher implied that there was no falling off and expressed sympathy for Frost's new and drier approach (57:210-11). Reviewers tended to see the mocking poems about the atom bomb and recent international tensions as smug, but a few praised them for fresh daring. In subsequent years, anthologists have rarely chosen poems from this collection, with the exception of "Directive," and the sparing critical comments on these poems show more interest in their continuities with Frost's established themes than in any of their intrinsic merits.

The title and organization of the book remain puzzling. It was originally divided into five sections, the first apparently untitled. However, since the first seven poems were preceded by a page titled "Steeple Bush," paralleling the part-title pages, some critics took that to be the name of the first section; however, that page is simply like an additional title page for the volume. The word "steeple" is paralleled in the title of the third section, "A Spire and a Belfry," and the poem "A Steeple on the House" features the phrase "the steeple on our house of life," suggesting that the steeple chiefly represents aspiration toward ideality. However, the "steeple bush" of the book's title is central to the collection's second poem, "Something for Hope," in which it describes a hardy bush significant more for its part in a cycle than for its own endurance. Thus, Frost's use of "steeple" remains ambiguous. Still, it is difficult not to see the collection's title as representing the poet's advancing age, a career in its last stages, and complex hopes for the future.

## Section One (Untitled)

The seven poems of this untitled grouping all deal with persistence and discovery, common themes in Frost and probably intended as organizing principles here. "A Young Birch," an affectionate celebration of a tree courageously achieving its maturity, resembles several early poems about flowers spared by mowing and small creatures struggling for survival. The birch, however, takes a more active part in its growth and persistence. The way it cracks its sheath and shows its coming whiteness makes it youthfully feminine and prepares for that brilliant whiteness that can "double day and cut in half the dark" – that is, fill the night with a daylike brightness. Unlike other native trees, it seems to lean its trunk at a trusting angle, an image that leads naturally into the recollection that people clearing out brush are so taken by the charm of the birch's shoots that they spare them until stage by stage they develop into trunks. In a manner recalling Frost's praise of the mowers in "The Tuft of Flowers" and "Rose Pogonias," the speaker cozily tells other rural people that their hired help would not cut down such a birch but would realize that their employers want it spared – even though the employers are not there to give instructions but rather are "reading books or out of town," suggesting pursuits less essential than admiring and fostering the young birch. The concluding lines allude to the opening of Keats's "Endymion" ("A thing of beauty is a joy forever: / Its loveliness increases; it will never / Pass into nothingness"), implying a double triumph: the birch's growth and its being admiringly spared for the sake of its intrinsic beauty.

Persistence is treated differently in "Something for Hope," in which the perspective is less lovingly esthetic and more philosophically agricultural. The "hope" of the title is in the slow natural cycle that will restore destroyed grasslands and, by nourishing cow and horse, keep humanity flourishing. Meadowsweet and steeple bush are among some seventy kinds of spirea, hardy flowering bushes that usually grow wild but often grace gardens. Frost's speaker classifies them as weeds because they are not edible and crowd out the useful grass. The poem's voice is patiently familiar as it delights in everything it sees and lectures to itself and fellow mortals who may be slow to see how things work out for the best. The idea of waiting for natural cycles to restore fertility echoes "In Time of Cloudburst," but the vision and tone here are less extravagant.

The speaker delights to think of "maple, birch, and spruce" springing up and forcing out the meadowsweet and steeple bush – as if everything desirable happens in good time – and reminds his rural audience that their rocky soil is not promising in any case. He makes puns as he sees trees putting on "wooden rings" and letting "long-sleeved branches hold their sway." The wooden rings of yearly growth also represent marriage to time and nature; the branches hold sway in the wind and royally display their rule. He looks forward to the cutting down of these trees, pleased to think of their usefulness as lumber and of the freshening of the soil for new grass, and glancing regretfully at the "lovely blooming but wasteful weed" that will be displaced. The hundred-year cycle does not bother him, and he thinks that freedom from government interference ensures such processes in general – forgetting, perhaps, that he had to give instructions on cutting down the trees. His emphasis is on patience and letting things take their own course, and he raises the practical aspects by referring to the cow and horse that will eat the grass rather than survive on the hope that, as Horace puts it in *"spes alit agricolam,"* sustains the farmer.

Rescue and survival are crucial in the quite different "One Step Backward Taken." The speaker here sounds, perhaps, like a lonely and threatened old man, glad to have been spared by a sweeping disaster and getting ready to face the world again. According to this large-scale metaphor, he has just been where a gigantic mud slide and avalanche disrupted and broke down much of the world, but his declaring that he "felt my standpoint shaken" shows that he is referring to his view of the world's disasters – which might include Frost's personal losses and the recent upheaval of World War II. However, he had saved himself by the simple gesture of "one step backward taken," which might refer to a slight shifting of his viewpoint toward the sweep of years or to a simple and courageous recovery of perspective after being spared a widespread doom. In any case, he has not been struck by the "world torn loose," and the change in weather may symbolize external changes, a recovery of his spirits, or both. Seeing the poem as primarily philosophical, Marjorie Cook suggests that "the universal crisis" of the poem is both cosmic and "involv[es] universally accepted concepts" toward which Frost declines to take a rigid position but continues to pragmatically accommodate (71:229).

"Directive" is probably Frost's most anthologized poem, after "Stopping By Woods," "Mending Wall," and "After Apple-Picking," and quite possibly his most lengthily discussed; it is analyzed in many articles and most critical books about him. It is certainly his most admired poem from the period after the publication of *A Witness Tree.* Randall Jarrell declared it "one of the strangest, and most characteristic, most dismaying and most gratifying, poems any poet has ever written" and found it "hard to understand but easy to love" (98:50-54). The poem is thick with allusions, some more covert than others. The time different from "this now too much for us" alludes to Wordsworth's sonnet "The World Is Too Much with Us." The "story in a book" about the place where a town was worn away may, as S. P. C. Duvall argues (164:482-88), alude to the description in Thoreau's *Walden* of a place of ruined dwellings, which may also be the source of "the two village cultures [that] faded / Into each other," though Frost's early biographer Elizabeth Sergeant thought it described Concord Corners, Vermont, and Franconia, New Hampshire (19:351-52). The concept of being "lost enough to find yourself" alludes to Luke 9.24, in which Jesus preaches "For whosoever will save his life shall lose it; but whosoever will lose his life for my sake, the same shall save it." The necessity of protecting the drinking goblet with a spell like one St. Mark prescribes refers to Mark 4.11-12, in which Jesus declares that he speaks in parables so that outsiders will not understand, be converted, and so gain entrance to heaven. The dominating allusion is that made to the medieval myth of the Holy Grail, made famous by T. S. Eliot's use of it in "The Waste Land." This legend tells of the cup Jesus used at the Last Supper, which was taken to Britain by Joseph of Arimathea, where, after being lost, it was pursued by various knights in the hope of purifying their society. Only Galahad, the knight of perfect purity, was permitted sight of it, after which he died. The legend made the Holy Grail a symbol of spiritual wholeness. Frost's invitation to the reader to drink of a cup "like the Grail" may be his down-to-earth answer to Eliot's quest for a highly formal tradition.

Hard to classify, "Directive" may be called a philosophical monologue combining narrative, description, and instruction addressed to the reader as someone sharing in a quest that the speaker himself labors through and concludes. The imaginative action recommended is set in Frost's own New England, whose real and mythic past becomes a symbol for the past of humanity (at least in the Western world). The tone is intimate yet gently sardonic, implying that the speaker's plight parallels the reader's. At first the reader is indirectly advised to think back toward a deep past in a place profoundly changed from the present but still seemingly in the same locale. There he will see a simplicity of life and environment that the poem shows bearing the effects of time. Ancient house, farm, road, and countryside reveal their coming decay but also carry signs of their former vitality, as if the reader could simultaneously experience their change and their former existence. Sardonically imitating a country person deliberately misdirecting a city person, the speaker wishes to guide the reader toward a helpful lostness. Cultural and geologic changes that open chasms in ways of thinking and living are symbolized by the quarrylike road, worn as if by wagon wheels and a glacier.

The researches of David R. Clark have failed to turn up any Panther Mountain in Vermont or New Hampshire (161:257, n. 4). Frost seems to have made up the name, and Clark suggests that it sounds like "a monster in our path" (161:114). He also posits that "the serial ordeal / Of being watched from forty cellar holes" is appropriate for a quest and shows people from the past appearing as phantoms to the traveler's apprehensions. The ghostlike eyes looking out from "firkins" (old-style quarter casks) suggest an ancient culture dubious of newcomers. With the excited woods rustling in triumph over the traveler's head, the symbolic method changes. At the poem's opening, apparently real landscape, slightly personified, showed the wear of culture and environment; here and later, natural details edge closer to personification, mysteriously representing human attitudes or emotions, as if the younger trees were enacting the boastfulness of replacements for older generations or symbolizing endurance amid decay. At this point, human figures from the past enter explicitly, and the reader is mockingly asked to take cheer from the thought that this worn-out road once carried the vitality of a person walking home or conducting a "buggy load of grain," implying that the life of the past mysteriously defies dissolution, or at least remains in memory as a sign of indestructible human vitality. David Clark suggests that this person represents the dead whom we must all soon join (161:112). Speaker and reader are immersed in a past brought to life in front of them, and so the speaker can talk of the trip as an adventure backward in time to the drama of dissolutions reenacted by the imagination. The reality of these changes is made vivid by recalling the fading of two cultures into each other, representing the decay of New England towns and possibly symbolizing the decline of orthodox religions into superficial faiths. That "both of them are lost" seems a tragic inevitability that may yet be defied by the advice offered here.

Reminding the reader that one must lose one's life to find it, the speaker recommends spiritual withdrawal into this recovered world and exclusion of everything else. To make oneself at home there is to reexperience the past in a way that recovers the best of a simpler era and then moves beyond it. Becoming at home there, the reader must temporarily accept terrible diminutions: fertile fields exhausted, a children's playhouse whose oversimplifications must be accepted as part of the past, and then a real house gone to ruin. The "shattered dishes" from the playhouse may represent the apparatus – including communion cups – of conventional Western religion, and one would "weep for what little things could make them glad" out of poignant envy of once-sustaining faiths that no longer seem viable. The house is no more a dwelling: the foundation is gone, and lilacs line the cellar opening, but it is just a "hole," now closing as impersonally as dough folds over. "This was no playhouse but a house in earnest," because it once was a human dwelling where the values represented by the children's playthings were truly sustaining. The speaker is reaching the culmination of his directive as he sends the reader to the brook that supplied water for this house. Its cold water was close to the primal energy of the universe, the very stuff of God expressing itself through life's persistence. The "valley streams that when aroused / Will leave their tatters hung on barb and thorn" personify human energy turned back on itself with the vindictive destructiveness of those who will not endure their fate and who hurl themselves self-destructively against a supposedly cruel cosmos. They have lost old faiths and cannot replace them. Perhaps the spring's cold water represents not only reality but also the courageous lifeblood that helps humanity accept responsibility for itself rather than seek a savior.

Finally emerging in first person, the speaker reveals that he has already gone this way himself and has hidden a drinking cup–"a broken drinking goblet like the Grail"–which the reader is free to take and use. David Clark suggests that this represents Frost's own poems, which the reader must struggle to plumb for their saving meanings (161:116). If so, the citation of the biblical defense of parables is Frost's playful boast and apology for his subtleties. The waters and the watering places are the deepest reaches of the human imagination, the substance or equivalent of God, perhaps no longer available through revelation, but apparent in experience as the only viable path to acceptance of a painful life that leads toward death's uncertainties. This basic faith insists that life is purposeful, is not to be wasted, and must be renewed by courageous acceptance. The task of being "whole beyond confusion," paralleling (as many have noted) but also going beyond Frost's poetic pursuit of "a momentary stay against confusion," cannot utterly dispense with confusion, but it asserts an affirmation beyond it and a commonality of faith and purpose with those from the past whose formal faiths we may not be able to share.

In "Too Anxious for Rivers," the speaker again offers advice about facing human destiny, but here concern with death becomes central and the allegorical details have little scenic base. The title refers to excessive anxiety about where life goes after death. The reader is asked to consider a mountain as the end of the world or of life, but the idea of a mountain as an obstruction or an impossibly high goal raises the question of how the river of life will find its resting place if everything ends in a mountain. The enigmatic "I never saw so much swift water run cloudless" probably means that such water is always cloudy, standing for life's obscure destiny. This river flows into another enigma: "the canyon / Of Ceasing-to-Question-What-Doesn't-Concern-Us," which may mean that much as we are concerned with our fate after death, we ought to just accept the fact that we "have to cease somewhere." Or it may imply that once we are dead we will cease our concern with, and questioning of, our destiny. Or the phrase may express the indifference of death's realm itself.

The poem shifts abruptly to a gently mocking rehearsal of a Bengal creation myth, which offers nothing convincing or comforting about our origins and destination, and which the speaker declares is not really inferior to scientific explanations. All such accounts are like bedtime stories designed to comfort children before the light goes out, and science must leave the continuation of its explanations to our dreams, which seem to be the source of all our knowledge. Frost implies that existence is dreamlike, though the conclusion of the poem returns to a more realistic view of creation, in which the initially molten and vaporous earth and atmosphere that created life are explanation enough for life's meaning. However, we do not need science or myth to explain this. Long ago the Roman poet Lucretius, in his *De Rerum Naturae (On the Nature of Things)*, long a favorite of Frost's, attributed creation and being to the great goddess of love. Lucretius thought we could take this knowledge for granted without exploring the universe in the spirit of the philosopher Epicurus, who had been Lucretius's great teacher. The word "essay" in the concluding "essay of love" means "attempt" and emphasizes love voyaging forth into the universe to do what it can. The implication is that this is the best humanity can accomplish and is sufficient protection from the fear of death.

"An Unstamped Letter in Our Rural Letter Box" satirizes philosophical pretensions. The title casts the poem as a missive left to the author of these poems, and the poem itself is spoken (or, rather, written) by a "tramp astrologer" who has just spent the night sleeping in the author's pasture. Concerned that his presence might have caused a disturbance, he writes to explain and apologize. He enjoyed this night out because of the terrain and trees, one of which helped keep him warm as he slept, but his reminiscence of a city park and his electing "to demur" once more from ordinary society show that he likes this kind of life. In the night he had an unusual experience: feeling a rock underneath him, he woke up and saw, or thought he saw, the unlikely sight of two meteorites plunging in "the largest firedrop ever formed." This, he claims, sent two memories plunging into a similar fiery unity, "and for a moment all was plain / That men have thought about in vain." Thus, he got quick and convincing answers to the kinds of ultimate questions Frost's speaker had struggled with in "Directive" and "Too Anxious for Rivers." However, he does not remember what he learned well enough to relay any of it, and he concludes with a combined apology and compliment to his host, who—since we all know our "own discernment best"—will have picked out his own revealing sights from the heavens and will have reaped other spiritual advantages from his successful farming. In conclusion, the "tramp astrologer" says he has left this message to enforce the notion that as someone *"in forma pauperis"* (in the shape of a pauper), he has had insights that deserve respect. The poem satirizes pretensions partly shared by Frost and expressed in some of the surrounding poems, though Rachel Hadas thinks the tramp declines to explain his cosmic insights because of decorous concern for "his own mysterious experience and . . . the separateness of another person's experience" (31:174-75).

In "To an Ancient" concern with achievement and permanence persists in a partly self-satirical mode. Slightly reminiscent of "A Missive Missile," this poem is less concerned with communication from the prehistoric past and more with the speaker's own response to time's obliterations. The address to the ancient as "You" (the word is several times repeated and rhymed) emphasizes the impersonality of the prehistoric person addressed, whose claims to immortality are limited to the bone from his skeleton left in the sandy bed of a brook and the eolith (primitive stone implement) he left in a cavern where he did his cooking. This impersonality, however, is briefly put aside by the speaker's sense that such elemental but convincing evidence of human life is like meeting a person "face to face." But the personal touch fades quickly as the speaker reflects on the archaeologist's dating of the evidence and discussion of the ancient's brute nature. The omission of a period or semicolon after the line "We date you by your depth in silt and dust" appears to be an error by Frost. We moderns are presumably "nonplussed" (not taken aback) by the ancient's brute nature because we take a hard-headed view of change (which may not promise well for our reputation in the future). The ancient's bone was singular enough to stamp him as a distinct type and so to make humanity remember him. This leads the speaker to reflect on his own claims to immortality, including his poetry. The evidence he is looking at suggests that leaving one's bones behind lets them accumulate the hardening lime of endurance, which creates a sufficiently firm memorial. The poem may take a gloomy view of artistic creation, but it takes an unsentimental view of art and memory as the road to immortality.

## "Five Nocturnes"

This small group of poems, numbered and titled in the text, all deal with the speaker's confronting a spiritual night and coming off with a limited triumph. "The Night Light" tells of a woman who kept a light burning while she slept, presumably to quiet her fears – a goal it did not achieve, for the light gave her bad dreams and made her wake up, but at least she thought it helped God keep her alive. The allusion to the prayer that asks God to keep one's soul unless it must be taken suggests childishness. The speaker is annoyed that "Good gloom on her was thrown away," for she made no constructive use of the darkness that he endures "night and day" as he looks ahead in fear to even worse darkness. The last two lines bespeak his combined acceptance of and spell against that darkness, whose stoic productivity he has hinted at.

In "Were I in Trouble" the speaker lies alone in a dark room and witnesses a light from which he does not expect any real help and that is not of his own making. Rather, it comes from the headlight of a car bouncing down a mountain road (emphasizing his isolation) and has almost, but not quite, nothing to do with him. He is "touched by that unintimate light" – physically, as it enters his room, and emotionally, as it speaks of fellow human beings. But he realizes that it offers nothing to him and that if he were in trouble that night, a mere traveler in the neighborhood would "do [him] no good." It also looks as if no one but a traveler could appear at the edge of this nocturnal scene.

In "Bravado" the speaker boasts of having made his way through a lifetime of nights without looking to the stars – not so much for illumination as for warnings of fate's dangers. The stars are thus pure symbols of evil possibilities that he has had to disregard in order to find his own way. And as he says in conclusion, he "had to take" the risk; if he had not, he would have been held back and confused by fears. Having taken the risk, he has evidently gone a good distance with some safety, or at least success.

In "On Making Certain Anything Has Happened" the speaker, as nocturnal witness, is comparatively detached. He has been a self-appointed observer of falling stars, as if a missing star were a "seed-pearl sun" – that is, the fallen-away beginner of a new world. Frost's use of this image is a curiously positive way to express the sense of lost potential. However, the speaker seems dubious about the significance of his observations when he reports his hesitance to tell the church that a star is missing from the Southern Cross, or the state that one is missing from the Seven Sisters, or Pleiades (called "the Crown of Rule" in "The Peaceful Shepherd"). If he were to make such an announcement he would need to be sure it was accurate; this seems to be a spoof on humanity's belief that the stars rule one's fate. Here, as in "On Looking Up by Chance at the Constellations," order in the heavens seems sure to last the night, but if it does not, the affairs of mankind do not seem likely to suffer.

Jocularity and serious personal assertion converge in "In the Long Night." Frost's speaker imagines himself living "with a solitary friend" in an Eskimo igloo, so close to the North Pole that the compass needle "stands on end" (in fact, at the true magnetic North Pole, a compass needle dips down). He amuses himself with thoughts of appropriate arctic entertainment, nourishment, and socializing: he and his companion would substitute gazing at the Northern Light (presumably the singular indicates a mist-enshrouded sun, not the Northern Lights) for reading, and drink oil and eat fish with their visitors, called Etookashoo and Couldlooktoo in honor of their footwear and sky-gazing. Together, they would all make the best of the cold situation. He would be a "rankly warm insider" because he would hold a high rank here and because conditions would make him smell rank. Their activities would occupy them through the six months of arctic night, but they would get enough rest on their eider-filled mattresses to be prepared for the arctic summer, or day, which lasts another six months. Thus, the situation becomes an allegory for the speaker's ability to endure cold and darkness in the assurance that compensating warmth and light will follow.

### "A Spire and a Belfry"

Frost's section title for these seven poems, drawn from a line of one of its poems, would seem to predict treatments of religion or spiritual values, but at least two of the poems require some forcing to fit into such a category. The speaker in "A Mood Apart" is in a posture of prayer, which makes him feel that his spiritual privacy is assaulted when some schoolboys merely look at him through a fence. His posture "on [his] knees to growing plants" is a gesture of worship (in an age before some people systematically communed with plants), and his "lazy tool" and low-voiced chants are close to religious ceremony. Not surprisingly, what he takes to be spying makes him stop singing, but that his heart almost stops suggests that he experiences a shock deep enough to make him question his essential self, which was allowing itself full expression in his "mood apart." The poem expresses a kind of antithesis to "Revelation" from *A Boy's Will,* in which the speaker regrets the way humans are closed off from one another, and it helps dramatize Frost's conflicts and alternations between privacy and community.

"The Fear of God" is no apology for the stance in "A Mood Apart," but Frost may have placed it here as compensation for traces of arrogance in the other poem, which it turns out to echo, but in a different tone. Addressed to those readers who may share his dilemma, the poem seems mostly the speaker's lecture to himself about the dangers of impressive success destroying one's humility. He warns himself and his readers that such success comes largely by chance. Presumably even if based on great talent, it is given by "an arbitrary god" who must deny it to innumerable people who desperately want it. The position is shaky enough to tempt one to complex arrogances. "Lack of license / To wear the uniform of who you are" may refer both to a buried sense that chance, not the license of intrinsic value, has bestowed high standing, and to the likelihood that some people will deny one's right to a position. These inner feelings and outer responses can make one adopt a "subordinating tone" – that is, a stance that puts others in their lowly places. But such behavior is a betrayal of one's own deepest spirituality and, on top of that, a misuse of one's character strengths, which should be used to protect one's privacy, not to make showy display.

"The Fear of Man," which stood opposite "The Fear of God" in earlier editions, was – if not planned as a companion piece – clearly placed as such by Frost. It too offers an apology, but for excessive shyness and timidity rather than for possible arrogance. "The Fear of Man" is largely argumentive exposition clothed in personification and metaphor. This poem creates a convincing picture of a half-brave and somewhat neglected girl making her way home alone through a city and a night perhaps less threatening than those of contemporary America. She is more frightened of "being spoken by the rude / And having her exposure misconstrued"—always real possibilities, as boors abound—than of encountering actual dangers. After this delicate portrait, with its frequent suggestions that the imagination offers more threats than does reality, Frost's speaker—surely the shyly defensive poet himself—takes cognizance of the puzzle his complex personality has made for many people and quietly apologizes for combining personal defensiveness and artistic subtlety in his life and works.

Concern with the purpose and perhaps the destiny of the soul returns explicitly in "A Steeple on the House," which Radcliffe Squires classifies with numerous poems in which ladders, trees, and other ascending shapes symbolize "the urge toward heaven" (45:54). However, as Laurence Perrine has argued, this urge need not assert faith in immortality, which the poem presents tentatively enough to support the notion that aspiration toward heaven may merely be an impetus to moral and loving behavior (120:87-88). The poem says that we do not need to live in the steeple of eternity or perhaps even to fill our thoughts with it, but the spire and belfry "coming on the roof"—as if effort or some kind of grace bring them out—are symbols of the body taking on spirituality.

"Innate Helium," which faced "A Steeple on the House" in earlier editions, seems placed to balance or complement it. Religious faith is treated sarcastically, as "a most filling vapor," which probably alludes to "hot air"—that is, foolishly unconsidered speech. "It swirls occluded . . . under tight / Compression to uplift us out of weight" describes such faith as a response to fear and misery. The bird bones similarly filled for buoyancy may appear to be an affirmative image, but they are frail structures and come from a realm that does not share people's need for serious thought. Helium, which is more useful and safer than hot air (or hydrogen) for balloons, represents that intrinsic rather than forced faith which deserves our respect.

The aspirations treated sarcastically in "The Courage to Be New" are political rather than religious, but Frost probably placed the poem here as an additional comment on the limitations of spires and belfries. The poem is a post-World War II commentary on the hopes for universal peace through organizations like the United Nations—hopes that had flourished after World War I, when the League of Nations was founded. The speaker expresses both admiration and weariness toward the views he describes. He sees people asserting supposedly changed attitudes and promising to end warfare; the "Federation of Mankind" alludes to Tennyson's famous phrase from "Locksley Hall" ("In the Parliament of man, the federation of the world"), a nineteenth-century prediction of modern quests for world government. The concise third stanza says that people are intelligent enough to suspect, as the speaker does, that their warlike impulse is not the basest human trait. Implying some inconsistency in these people, the speaker may sympathize with their "ever breaking newness," but he sarcastically implies that they can implement their plans for change only when others give them workable suggestions.

With "Iota Subscript," Frost concludes this group of poems about aspects of ideality with a work whose full comprehension is helped by some knowledge of classical Greek. Addressing his beloved, the speaker compares himself, in his relationship to her, first with a capital "I," then with a lower case "i," and last, with an iota subscript, a small ligature attached to certain Greek letters to make them form diphthongs. Thus, he first denies a looming ego, or perhaps even any independent existence. Then he denies that he has even a small ego, and finally he makes his existence wholly dependent on his beloved's by asserting that if anything in him resembles the Greek letter that is the equivalent of our "I" it is the iota subscript, which can appear under alpha, eta, and omega. The iota subscript, however, is rarely contracted into the upsilon; rather, it is usually completely absorbed into it. This implies that the speaker's self has its meaning only insofar as it becomes a part of the beloved. Ward Allen makes a similar explication of the poem, with the elaborated explanation that the lover becomes like an undersong below his beloved, which enhances not the melody but the lover's apprehension of it (181).

## "Out and Away"

The twelve poems grouped under this heading do not depart strikingly from those headed *A Spire and a Belfry*. The sense of farewells to life and struggles for ideality is equally strong, though there are more outdoor scenes. In "The Middleness of the Road," which returns to earlier Frost modes, a convincing outdoor scene is pervasively symbolic. The speaker drives along a road, jauntily pleased with the scene and his reflections, which balance between the limits of the beautiful things he sees and the ideal realms they suggest but cannot really represent or explain. The road ahead seems to enter the sky where the road rises and to enter a quiet wood where it bends. But though he may fancy that the fuel powering his car resembles thrusts into the unknown, this process is limited to the physical world. It has "almost nothing to do" with the different dimensions of "flight and rest," representing death as a climb into heaven or as rest in the seemingly static woods. But the "universal blue" of sky and the "local green" of earth only suggest meanings, and the physical properties of the exploding gasoline have "almost nothing to do" with these other meanings, so perhaps this kind of physical order may say something about spiritual realms, just as the already accepted symbolism of blue sky and green earth are merely suggestions. The speaker is sticking to the middleness of the road not only between heaven and earth and life and death but also between the suggestions of natural symbols and perhaps even scientific paradigms. Robert Fleissner relates this poem to Frost's praise of the golden mean, while cautioning against seeing an apology for middle-of-the-road politics or muddling through, and he compares it to the praise of temperate choices in "Stopping by Woods" and "The Road Not Taken" (85:214-15). This view, however, slights the poem's tough-mindedness about painful philosophical dilemmas.

In "Astrometaphysical" Frost speculates in ways he cautions about in "The Middleness of the Road." The speaker's direct addresses to God allow a combination of playful desperation and fancy. He has loved the sky and its astronomical sights, contemplation of which has dizzied him into humility (much looking at the sky does create dizziness and strain). Suddenly treating these sky sights as symbols for Heaven, he boasts that he deserves rewards for having loved everything heavenly – presumably the universe's beauties and life's goodness. Thus, although he cannot quite allow himself the boastful hope that death will put stars in his crown, according to the old formula for great deservings, he still hopes that his love of the sky will send him more in the direction of heaven than of hell.

The speaker of "Skeptic" expresses more skepticism about science than about the kinds of religious faith Frost intermittently plays with and questions in *Steeple Bush*. The speaker claims not to believe the evidence recorded on the back of his eyes and on camera film, both of which respond to light with changing impressions. He seems to be examining a supernova, or exploding star, and denying that it vanishes and leaves no traces, as if that might be evidence for a disappearing universe and the mere materiality of everything. Having refused the evidence of one set of senses, he retreats into his deepest feelings. At times, different senses feel the universe so close that he can only compare it to a birth covering that still surrounds him. Frost expresses a playful but determined semipantheism in which the self insists on its unity with the cosmos as a fact of experience and thereby takes it as a proof that nothing, including the self, will ever end. Troubled by the poem's denial of realities, Radcliffe Squires finds the bulk of it "organically impossible and freakish" (45:34). Perhaps the poem needs special tolerance for its intransigent rejections and deliberate arrogance.

"Two Leading Lights" makes a joking comparison between the personified Sun and Moon, the former a sensible and unpretentious male and the latter a silly and flirtatious female. The Sun is satisfied to shine just during the day, though his enormous power would seem to entitle him to shine when he pleases "by right of eminent domain" – that is, by the right of a sovereign to take what he wishes. The Moon, on the other hand, though she has been assigned the realm of night by "the notedest astronomers" (ironically described, for viewing the moon at night is a commonplace, nontechnical observation), sometimes doesn't bother to shine at night and at other times comes out during the day. (The speaker does not say so, but these are ordinary occurrences, determined by the moon's cycle and by the relationship of the earth's orbit to the sun, referred to in "his wishing ring.") The Moon places herself flirtatiously next to the Sun "as Sheba came to Solomon." At the end her presumption is slightly undercut by an apology for feminine whim. The poem lacks the kind of philosophical implications other astronomical poems in this collection would lead one to expect.

"A Rogers Group" takes its name from the American sculptor John Rogers (1829-1904), whose sentimental statuette groups, often of families, were popular during Frost's youth. The poem describes a young family frustrated by a trolley's not stopping for them in a strange city because they did not know where the corner stops were. Passers-by were not enough moved by their picturesque plight to offer them help.

The speaker of "On Being Idolized" views a commonplace situation from an unusual perspective. Feeling the undertow sweep sand out from under his feet as he stands in the surf, he must shift his steps to maintain his balance and not fall. This situation reminds him of human precariousness, exemplified in idealized lovers who can suddenly prove to be false and topple over in the estimation of their admirers. The poem attempts a playful integration of both the idealized and the idolizing persons losing balance and ground.

"A Wish to Comply" forms a companion piece to "Skeptic," in which the speaker questions what his eye perceives. In "A Wish to Comply" he cannot manage to see what science wants him to. The poem is based on a famous experiment by the American physicist Robert Millikan (1868-1953), in which oil droplets were blown into a chamber where the tiny electrical charges of electrons and protons were measured by observation through a telescope. The speaker in Frost's poem is asked if he saw what happened inside such a chamber (or in a situation symbolized by it), and he embarrassedly must admit that he probably saw nothing more than the reflection of his eyelid. He combines an uneasy admission that he was yielding to social pressure, and most particularly his desire to agree with science, with a defensive explanation that he had tried his best.

"A Cliff Dwelling" is set in the American Southwest amid the ancient pueblos of vanished tribes. The speaker gazes through a sundrenched atmosphere in which sky and earth merge, trying to make out the forms of ancient dwellings. Everything is on the edge of illusion or disappearance. At last he thinks he sees the entrance to a cavern in which someone lived, and a human figure forms in his imagination as if it were present. It is crouched in the cave, a refuge from his fears. As the figure comes into focus, it starts to disappear. The speaker sees its underfoot as it vanishes, representing the fading of its race. At last the speaker recalls the fact that this happened very long ago. Two critics make interestingly contrasting interpretations. Richard Poirier stresses the way in which the poem uses negatives to desperately make vivid a vision that it then suddenly denies. He thinks that the focusing of "years ago" to "ten thousand years" deliberately destroys the whole vision, as if the speaker at last acknowledges the vanity of his imaginative recovery (42:85). Rachel Hadas thinks the tiny figure is another Frostian symbol of the human need for shelter and that Frost creates a sympathetic observer to recover the meaning of the past (31:68). Not mutually exclusive, these views point up the speaker's ambivalence: his yearning for human persistence and his uncertain faith that he makes a contribution to it.

"It Bids Pretty Fair" uses a single metaphor to echo the themes of such poems as "Our Hold on the Planet" and "Riders." The speaker looks around himself with seemingly casual wisdom and sees human life on the planet as a drama about whose indefinite run he can be confident – almost as if he were contemplating the aspects for decent weather. Wars seem a small and perhaps commonplace difficulty; the only potential problem he sees is with the sun, represented metaphorically by the electrical system that keeps a theater illuminated. Thus, he falls back on confidence in nature's energy as an almost, but certainly not a reliable, source for humanity's continuance.

"Beyond Words" expresses a moment of frustration. Its title indicates that the speaker's feelings, soon to be revealed as intense hatred, cannot be put into words. He sees a row of icicles hanging down from the roof gutter, and their swordlike shapes and iciness represent his hatred and the weapons he would like to use against his adversary. But he is not going to use such weapons, and as he struggles for words, he hesitates between finding adequate ones and finding a threat that he ought to hurl.

In "A Case for Jefferson" Frost lashes out at Marxist extremists, making one of them a "case" to be approached with the wit and democratic faith of a Thomas Jefferson. "Harrison" is a fashionable and shallow intellectual, at night arguing for the sexual freedom Freud is often thought to have supported, but by day promoting Marxian revolution. The speaker grants that Harrison also loves America but – his outrage increased because the man is a fellow Yankee – thinks his political position can only lead to the foolishness of blowing the country apart in an attempt to make it perfect. The speaker implies that this would only bring ruin. The poem offers no detailed arguments but ridicules by showing impulsiveness, self-satisfaction, and simple-mindedness.

The speaker of "Lucretius Versus the Lake Poets" sounds like a college professor, which Frost was for many years. He addresses satirical professional talk to his dean, reflecting on their previous evening's conversation, which had contributed to his own education but left him frustrated. As a student of the Roman philosopher Epicurus and his poet-disciple Lucretius, he thought their idea of "Nature" encompassed the entire cosmos, which he sarcastically calls "the Whole Goddam Machinery" to express his frustration with the scope of, and some solutions to, the problem.

But he and the dean had been discussing the four-line poem "Dying Speech of an Old Philosopher," by Walter Savage Landor (1775-1864), whose second line provides this poem's epigraph. The dean must have been comparing Landor to the English Lake Poets (primarily Wordsworth and Coleridge). Their philosophical nature worship focused on the beauties of the English countryside and influenced other poets. Thus, the Lake Poets defined nature differently than did Lucretius, and the dean had argued that Landor took their view. The speaker agrees with the dean that it is silly to see nature as the opposite of art, and though he may not be certain the dean has the definitions right, he explodes into good-humored praise of the dean's wisdom, affirming that the dean's power ought to be "plenary"–that is, dominant. The speaker is like a student good-humoredly yielding to his teacher's superior but annoyingly confident wisdom.

Frost makes a different kind of fun of superior wisdom in "Haec Fabula Docet," Latin for "these things the story teaches." The poem's external form–but not its method–resembles that of the famous beast fables of the French poet Jean de La Fontaine (1621-1695), which were good-humored verse adaptations from the acerbic fables of Aesop and other earlier writers. La Fontaine's characters are always animals, and though he attaches labeled morals to many of his fables, their judgments point up human foibles with a minimum of harshness. It is hard to see why Frost's Blindman is called La Fontaine, except perhaps to contrast profound human weaknesses with the shallower ones that troubled La Fontaine, implying blindness in some moralists. In Frost's poem, though the Blindman's extreme conceit starts his trouble, the arrogance and presumption of all the characters turn back on them and lead to destruction. The Blindman is too proud of his independence, and the man who wishes to warn him is ostentatiously loud and then physically aggressive with his "staying hand." This exacerbates the Blindman's pride and makes him so angry that he throws his back out of order and tumbles into a ditch. Instead of rescuing him, the workmen are so outraged by his rejection of a charitable act that they bury him. The "Moral" is deliberately partial and ironic, for though the speaker criticizes the Blindman's ostentatious independence, he is equally harsh about the man who offers help and about the workmen. Frost's conservative view is that help should be offered with polite caution and rejected without savagery or retaliation on anyone's part. A page of notes for *Steeple Bush* offers an alternative last two lines for the moral: "Or with the independence of Vermont / Are absolutely sure to come to want." In these lines the irony is different and more explicit, for Frost would not have criticized the independence of any state, especially a beloved New England one, or have seen it as producing harm. This variant also suggests that Frost was playing with his material, perhaps trying to focus an ugly mood.

An irritated tone persists in the sonnet "Etherealizing," in which Frost centrally satirizes intellectualism while taking a sideswipe at theories of evolution. The theory turned into creed looks rather like the intellectualism of a T. S. Eliot, some of whose characters resemble the beach-dwellers whose "atrophied" bodies and dominant brains are satirized by Frost (though Eliot himself did not admire such characters). Reinforcing his ridicule by rhyming the formal "atrophied" with the down-to-earth "seaweed," Frost goes on to compare these superintellectuals to jellyfish who lie toward the beginning of the evolutionary chain – so unconvincing an image of brainpower that it seems intended to show degeneration, not development. Frost might have in mind the intellectual ruminations of some theologians, though his conclusion focuses on overly intellectual poets who, as they lie by the sea, will have to pray that the tides of reality do not wet down their self-satisfyingly dry verse.

In "Why Wait for Science" Frost turns his satirical ire against both the assumed presumption of science and the foolishness of humanity for depending on it. Personified Science controls means that terrify humanity, toward which she is sarcastic because, having called on her for destructive means which may succeed completely, it now seems ready to call on her for salvation through flight to another solar system. Frost's astronomy errs here, for the star closest to us is four years (not "a half light-year") distant. Rather than wait for a reply from Science, the speaker suggests, humans should get away by the same means by which "fifty million years [the time it took human beings to evolve] ago we came." The amateur who can explain likely means of salvation resembles the speaker, who soon declares that he has an explanation but deliberately fails to say what it is. "If anyone remembers how that was" sarcastically comments on the enigma of evolution and seems to contradict the possibility of reliable explanations, amateur or otherwise. But once the speaker declares that he has a theory, he is quick to admit that it will not really explain or help. This may be a theory of reverse evolution, a notion that a return to a primitive state will save humanity from the dangers it has let science create, though such a process would not get us off the planet. Rachel Hadas seems to think the other choice is some mode of spiritual existence (31:161).

Uneasiness with his stance may have led Frost to the third-person detachment of "Any Size We Please," whose voice speaks about a person hugging himself. Rachel Hadas compares this person to the animal-as-human figure in "The Bear," in which she finds Frost sympathizing with the human conflicts represented by the perspectives of microscope and telescope (31:160). In this poem the figure is torn between making a melodramatic gesture toward embracing the universe and asking explanation of it and angrily rejecting such a gesture as worthless. Eventually he embraces himself as all of the universe that can befriend him, almost as if his being is the universe. The Einsteinian view of space as curved describes his sense of self-containment. The man had felt himself "too out," a phrase used in "Build Soil" to criticize social involvement as distinguished from self-reliance. When the man slaps his breast, he imitates the gesture of a person checking against the robbery of a wallet or purse, but he is checking for his essential self, further verified by his "hugg[ing] himself for all his universe." Rachel Hadas suggests that this phrase means that he hugged himself both for the sake of the universe and as its replacement (31:161), a workable idea if the final stress on self-containment isn't weakened – though the poem's title does imply that the universe can be any size we will it or imagine it to be.

"An Importer" is a satire on people who delight in the supposed novelty of exotic Asian artifacts and manners. A secondary satire on American mass production, which these same people consider beneath them, is doubtful. The ridicule of imported things is focused on a prayer machine, which automatically asks for pardon. "Mass-producing with a vengeance" plays on the idea of inhumanly produced religious ceremony outstripping industrial mass production, which shows the pretentious worshipers of such devices honoring something worse than American products could be. The homey comparison of egg-sucking grandmothers to the duplicitously clever Asians is a put-down of their admirers' aristocratic pretensions.

At least five of the last seven poems in *Steeple Bush* deal with the atom bomb, already alluded to in "Why Wait for Science." In "The Planners" Frost's speaker considers the effects of atomic annihilation on three groups: the unborn, who will never know what they missed; the dead, who will remain ignorant of the devastating change; and the social planners, some of whom will be arrogant enough to think they can still save the situation. In fact, such people would count for nothing, but they would not lose their arrogant assumption that they could "change our manners" and save us – a mocking reference to their superficial view of human nature. The speaker's irritation that they would still consider their attempts important after such destruction shows him thoroughly disheartened by a spectacle that humanity seems to deserve.

"No Holy Wars for Them" is a satirical jibe at the nations that had an early exclusive hold on atomic weapons. They seem to have the power to do good by destructive means, whereas the small states without these weapons can only be good – which means that they must make meaningless alliances or perhaps exercise neutrality. Thus, "Holy Wars," echoing the Islamic notion of jihad, are ironically reduced to their opposite. The powerful states might do some kind of good for themselves, but certainly not much for humanity, and the weak states might create annoyances that could be easily put down. The poem echoes the sneering voice of the powerful but fuses it with a most unpolitic irony.

"Bursting Rapture" combines sexual, agricultural, and medical metaphors in an angry pretense that atomic destruction will cure mankind of its ills. The speaker complains that farming's new demands for technology have strained his nerves to the point of disease. Thus he goes to the doctor (who may represent science or philosophy in a cynical mood) for a cure and gets the supposedly cheerful reassurance that the tensions he suffers from afflict nations and are mounting toward an ecstatically orgasmic climax. The doctor's reference to "a certain bomb" coyly implies that it will give both less and more than we will have hoped for, the two somehow combined in the relief of utter destruction.

America's initial, jealous monopoly on atomic weapons is concisely satirized in "U.S. 1946 King's X," which alludes to the early British sign for a truce territory – a sign that made its way from British children's games into American ones and here marks atomic weapons like the safe or forbidden territory in children's games. The poem mocks a childish position in a slightly childish manner. The "fingers crossed" suggest a petulant adoption of game rules, and the "no fairs" create a whining voice, with the help of a colloquial twist.

"The Ingenuities of Debt," which Randall Jarrell considered the second most impressive poem in *Steeple Bush* (57:209), resembles Shelley's "Ozymandias" in its icily ironic treatment of a pretentious culture that could not save itself. Ctesiphon was an ancient Parthian city famous for a great vaulted hall, thought to have been a palace. After its occupation under the Roman emperor Trajan, its Greek culture was destroyed, and the place soon became a ruin. The speaker attributes to this city a snickeringly clever and self-serving motto: "TAKE CARE TO SELL YOUR HORSE BEFORE HE DIES / THE ART OF LIFE IS PASSING LOSSES ON." Its haunting of the human brow suggests that it expressed both arrogance and self-doubt. This advice, he admits, may have delayed ruin, but the delay appears simply to have been a normal one in human affairs. Looking at the ruin, he scornfully notes that "the ingenuities of debt" had not been able to save the city from its inevitable surrender to greater forces, a process promoted by the moral weakening revealed in its motto. Now sand, in the form of a serpent, seems to make its way through ruined grandeur into the great hall, where it will soon gather energy to attack the inscription – though actually the sand is blown by the wind and has no power or will. Thus, inevitable natural forces join moral weakness to ruin an arrogant realm.

"The Broken Drought" satirizes a different kind of cynicism. The speaker mocks a "prophet of disaster" who delights in the idea that civilizations crumble and relishes the notion of a barren earth. At a convention for the study of social stasis or decay, the prophet of doom is alarmed to hear that rain is breaking a drought, and he responds to the joy of those assembled through a gesture described by Rosalind in Shakespeare's *As You Like It* (4.1.71-72), when she declares that "very good orators when they are out [of matter], they will spit." This is a gesture of uneasy skepticism, but the prophet is (or pretends to be) unshaken because he knows that a tiny rainfall will not cure the earth's universal drought. The last six lines relentlessly continue his point of view. As he delights in the prospect of an utterly barren earth, his concluding rhetorical questions show that he thinks earth was always so and that men were foolish to occupy it. Frost bitterly mocks social thinkers who revel in a universal rottenness they criticize but really do not want to see ended.

Frost concludes *Steeple Bush* with a sort of indirect prayer for humanity's salvation, in which he takes a humble and desperate stand against the prophet of disaster. The title of "To the Right Person" refers not to someone addressed but to the person for whom a closed schoolhouse may open. The poem's central image is a schoolhouse in New Hampshire whose physical position high above sea level provides for gentle mockery of its high status. At present it stands closed, or at least it looks so tightly closed that no one can be admitted and education there has apparently ceased. Its "tight-shut look," suggesting that "mere learning was the devil," implies that education amid the crises of modern life has shut down in despair before insoluble problems. The doors, however, may open to the right person, who can be penitent about human sin and thoughtlessness and make a school's doorstep the equivalent of the mercy seat – the place where the sinner begs for a forgiveness beyond his deserving. If he is admitted, learning and life will presumably continue. Perhaps he resembles the one just person for whose sake God will spare the cities of sin.

## "An Afterword" from *Complete Poems* (1949)

Of the three poems that originally comprised this section, two are reprinted in this subsection. The third, "Closed for Good," finds its final place (with slightly modified text) in *In the Clearing*. Like other poems, "Take Something Like a Star" uses stars to represent unattainable ideals that tease us out of thought but leave us with healthy aspirations. Frost's speaker addresses the fairest star from a gently self-deprecatory perspective, allowing it distance and reticence as part of the power of its beauty and mystery. But after six lines his tone turns bitter as he asks for some convincing and memorable expression of truth. The star stands for the mysteries of God and the universe, but it replies only in terms of the mere physical process of its burning. As if conducting a dialogue both humble and demanding, the speaker pretends that he can accept this if only the star will be more specific about its burning or will give hints about the structure of the universe. Getting little direct help, the speaker turns gently contemplative as he compares this star to the one represented as a steadfast hermit in Keats's "Bright Star" sonnet, in which a distant star becomes an analogue for the poet contemplating the condition of mortality and then moving toward love's joyful surrender. Frost's star asks us to emulate its own noble condition by rising above ordinary and destructive passions such as those that lead mobs to praise tyrants and destroy innocent victims. If the star cannot teach us metaphysical ultimates, at least it can provide a moral model of calm steadiness. If we fix our minds on it, they can remain attached to ideals and help us be "staid" – that is, unwild and thoughtful – in our behavior.

"From Plane to Plane" is a blank-verse dialogue with almost no plot, slightly reminiscent of the exchanges between Silas and Harold Wilson in "The Death of the Hired Man." In that poem, the more educated youth piques the pride of an old failure. Here Bill Pike, a wise old farmhand, and Dick, a clever young college student, fight "on an equality" and about equalities. The title refers to the social and educational distance between them and also to their contrasting ideas about rest from labor. Bill Pike insists that professionals like "the Doctor," whom they see crossing the landscape in his horsecart, do not really work for a living and do not have to accept much responsibility for their failures. Dick argues back that Pike's method of resting between hoeing rows of corn is just like what the Doctor does, but Pike rejects this argument. He insists that he merely fights "to keep his extrication"; that is, he resists an involvement that would destroy his individuality, whereas the upper classes avoid work out of sheer laziness. Pike illustrates his point by talking about the sun that sets the summer on fire but then rushes off for fear of melting everything into a sticky and sticking unity. Attempting some reconciliation, the men joke about the Doctor's business in wintertime, playing on it as the season of Sickness and (unspoken but thought by Dick) Cygnus or, rather, Cygnus's absence. At last Dick struggles to acknowledge Pike's viewpoint without completely giving in. Since Pike has praised the sun for its special independence, Dick compares Pike to the sun as something that bestows wisdom but does not want any thanks. Alluding to the association of the sun with God in Milton's *Paradise Lost* and to its worship in ancient cultures, Dick suggests that the sun does not want to be worshiped as a god. He is partly turning the tables on Pike by acknowledging some wisdom in his view of labor but assuming that Pike will not want special honor for this wisdom. Pike, who knows nothing of Milton's positioning the sun close to but a little lower than God, accepts Dick's hazy compliment but goes on to cite his own example of a mythologic figure that takes the blame for our weak wisdom: Santa Claus, whom he describes as "a scapegoat." Pike seems half-conscious that his use of the sun as an example of his own position about labor and extrication is a little strained. His insistence that there is a Santa Claus seems to be a reification of excuses for kinds of failures and parallels Dick's turning the sun into a scapegoat for Pike's insistence on extrication. Dick's quoting of "So I have heard and do in part believe it" (1.1.165), spoken by Horatio about miraculous peacefulness and calm stars at

Christmas time, shows Dick's wish to acknowledge that Pike's acceptance of Santa Claus resembles his own acceptance of the sun as a model for human wisdom. Working from plane to plane, Pike and Dick have managed to agree that people of all classes have difficulty telling the difference between laziness and a quest for independence and would probably be wise to accept each other's myths about the reasons for their stance and for their successes and failures.

# CHAPTER 12

## In the Clearing
## (1962)

Frost published his ninth and final collection of poetry, *In the Clearing,* less than a year before his death. Some of the poems had appeared in periodicals and pamphlets as early as 1951, but many had never seen print before; a few appear in expanded or corrected versions. As with *Steeple Bush,* the critical reception was quite mixed. Some critics expressed the view that Frost had little talent left; others offered kindly affirmations of his persisting and even experimental talent. Only rarely was the volume seen as at least partly a late-life triumph. Few of its poems have found much favor with anthologists or with later critics. One reviewer shrewdly noted that Frost placed the four strongest poems of the collection first (one of these, "Closed for Good," had been previously collected, in 1949).

"A Cabin in the Clearing" serves as the volume's title poem, though that title is also related to the quotation of "And wait to watch the water clear, I may" from "The Pasture" (1915) as an epigraph for the book. Both title and epigraph emphasize Frost's sense of a career rounded and completed and suggest that this collection is a farewell to his audience and to the world. The clearing represents final clarifications of his stance toward life, increased freedom from burdens and bounds, and his role in the pioneering life of the American people and humanity, as that life is treated in "A Cabin in the Clearing." Originally, the table of contents and several blank pages set off two groups of poems under the headings "Clusters of Faith" and "Quandary," while the other poems went ungrouped.

"Pod of the Milkweed," which Richard Wilbur declares charges an insect and flowers with vast implications of spirit in matter (57:248), resembles such animal fables as "The White-Tailed Hornet." Again, Frost takes a skeptical view of nature's creative potential. The poem contains some unusual grammar and word choices. The largest problem of interpretation lies in understanding the relationship between the title and the two objects of focus: milkweed and butterflies. This difficulty is clarified by Laurence Perrine's observation that both milkweed and butterflies have pods and that the single pod left hanging in line 45 is the chrysalis of the only surviving butterfly, not a seedpod of the milkweed itself (238). Thus, the "pod" of the title refers to both botanical and insect pods.

The poem's first sentence runs for seven lines. Its grammatical subject – "the milkweed," whose profusion of bitter milk and sweet honey demonstrates "the theme of wanton waste in peace and war" – appears at the opening of the fifth line, having been modified by the long adverbial phrase that opens the poem. Frost shows a struggle for survival as mobs of butterflies get drunk on milkweed honey and batter one another to a colorful death. On one day of overwhelming sweetness, many butterflies born that day have died in this struggle. Frost concludes by noting that the profusion of the weed, presumably there to propagate itself, has resulted only in the survival of one butterfly pod, whose future looks precarious. This survivor asks the unanswerable question of why such profusion seems to have come to nothing, which implies doubt of the usefulness of those evolutionary processes that science sees as creative. The poem sounds genial but, as Perrine notes, has much in common with Frost's frequent treatments of nature as uncaring and perhaps purposeless.

"Away" provides the first of several leave-takings of the world. As in "The Wood-Pile" and "Good Hours," the speaker walks through a landscape that urges thought, but here the scene's sketchy description reinforces its allegorical quality. Jaunty rhythms, grammatical inversions (as in "The world desert"), casual reference to Eden as "the Park," and near-cliches ("Good friends in town," "get well-wined") create an informal and slightly mocking stance. The speaker combines joy in his last day's earthly independence from the companions he is putting aside and delight in the inner companionship of his free mind. He is moving toward death, for his shoe and stocking no longer hurt, and he is leaving for "the outer dark," a departure he briefly pretends is like the expulsion of Adam and Eve. But he reduces them to myth and punningly jokes that he is "put out with" no one, meaning both that he has made a free choice and that he has no one to be angry at for forcing him to leave. Rather, he tentatively suggests, he obeys an urge to be finished with earthly things and to arrive at the next stage. He concludes with a wryly joking threat that if he does not like what he next finds, he may have the will to return.

As Joseph Kau has pointed out, the quotation "I'm – bound – away!" is from the nineteenth-century chantey "Shenandoah." By placing the quotation in its original context, Kau argues that it reveals a strong apprehension beneath the poem's "confident air" and "saucy tone" (146). In "Shenandoah" a white trader tells the Indian chief Shenandoah that the trader has returned to claim the chief's daughter, but he then declares that his wanderlust forbids him to stay and that he is "away, I'm bound away." Frost's punctuation of "bound," Kau maintains, emphasizes that his speaker is not really making a free choice but is bound to leave. The humor of the last stanza hides his apprehension and shows that "desire and volition are illusory." This is a strong argument, but it may underestimate a playful acceptance fused with the poem's implied resentments.

"A Cabin in the Clearing," this volume's title poem, provides a philosophical leave-taking of the world as an evening contemplation tentatively draws down the curtain on humanity. The clearing is the dwelling place first of the human race and then of its American specimens, but it also represents their difficult pursuit of the meaning of their existence and their courageous resignation to puzzlement about it. This is Frost's only short poem in the form of an intellectual-allegorical dialogue. Mist and Smoke, appropriate personifications of dwellers around a forest clearing, represent the difficulty of clear or stable perception. They contemplate a human couple asleep in a cabin in the clearing. Mist and Smoke begin with conflicting statements, Mist doubting humanity's understanding of its place and purpose, Smoke defending humanity's persistence and pursuit of civilization and self-clarification. Mist extends his doubts to neighboring people, and Smoke extends hope for all.

After each figure has spoken twice, Mist begins to compromise his view, playfully admitting that though these humans may not know where they are, he does not "give them up for lost." In seeing himself as part of their landscape and himself as "the damper counterpart of smoke," he admits that puzzlement is part of the human condition. His saying "I am no further from their fate than you are" implies a permanent limit to understanding. He has mollified Smoke, whose attention turns to the local situation, in which the humans are now seen as European Americans intruding on the realm of the Red Man—who perhaps has a better understanding of his earthly environment. Mist tacitly acknowledges that the protagonists are representative Americans, and he knows that with their curious and pragmatic bent, they have asked both the natives and learned people for explanations of the human place and condition—explanations that have not been forthcoming. Frost here thinks of Americans as the vanguard of the human race, a theme developed at greater length in "Kitty Hawk." Smoke's last speech refers to the puzzlement of Americans about their place and identity. "Who they are is too much to believe" because their practical accomplishments are remarkable. "They are too sudden to be credible" shows admiration for their sudden conquest of America. Mist's last speech shows that he too is now talking about Americans. The "daylong theme" that humans continue to discuss in the dark is what they will do next; the solemnity of their conversation suggests that their concerns are spiritual as well as material. Mist and Smoke are both literally and figuratively eavesdropping on the house. Their interest in "tell[ing] the bass from the soprano" may represent their desire to distinguish between male and female voices, or between age and youth. The concluding comment in italic reinforces the indefiniteness of knowledge and the mystery of the human spirit. The overlap between Mist and Smoke and humanity suggests the dreamlike nature of existence.

In "Closed for Good" Frost makes a low-key and personal leave-taking from the world and the human race. Figuratively approaching his last moments, but literally out for a walk on a well-cut road, his speaker inhabits a world represented by an autumn scene, from which those who have lived before him have fled, to leave him to final contemplations and to intimations of how his spirit may continue in the scene. In the first line, "own" means "admit." "The passers of the past" suggests both those who have gone the route he now walks and those who rush ahead into novelties he does not care for – possibly the same people. They have formed a civilization and leave him to his own perhaps old-fashioned ways, though he imagines them using conveyances of old times, as if they would make him relive the past. Now he walks his own solitary road, communing with the natural scene and fancying an address to a tree about its fallen leaves priming the roadway in preparation for a fresh coat of white paint from the coming winter snows, in an extended metaphor drawn from painting.

Like the speaker in "Directive," he seems to be deliberately leaving the modern world behind to get back to essentials, this time probably the world of eternity: the light coat of leaves showing below the brush of snow suggests both mortality and the persistence of spirit despite the absence of form. As he imagines himself walking on into winter, he realizes that he will be dead soon. The "slight beast," whose being "mousy" and "foxy" reveals its power to survive, suggests a kind of immortality through the continuity of life, but also a diminished personal existence for the speaker. Frost is dramatizing the inability of humans to imagine their known world existing without them and expressing a combined farewell and a wish for a lasting hold on it.

"America Is Hard to See" interrupts the sequence of farewell poems that continues with "One More Brevity" but connects to these poems through Frost's concern with America as the place he is leaving. This satirical poem rings many changes on Columbus's setting sail westward, not in pursuit of the New World but to find a route to the Indies, which he died mistakenly believing he had done. The first two stanzas emphasize Columbus's desire not to disappoint the investment of Queen Isabella of Spain, who had financed his initial voyage, but rather to find a route to the richest part of India. He was in competition with the Portuguese sailor Vasco de Gama, who soon found a sea route around Africa to Asia and came home laden with more riches than Columbus. Frost laments that Columbus did not know he was finding the New World and admits that as a boy he was ignorant of Columbus's ignorance and might have written a poem celebrating Columbus as the self-aware discoverer of America as more than the Promised Land – as a place for humanity to start over. Writing after World War II and painfully aware of growing geopolitical problems, Frost now says that Columbus's discovery turned out to pave the way for such imperialistic competitions as will plague mankind until, having run out of space, we are forced to live in crowded peacefulness if we are to survive.

Columbus got few rewards for his venturing, and now Frost imagines him still traveling, in a phantasmal guise, looking for a true passage to the Far East. Frost fancies the navy towing Columbus's phantom ship through a lock of the Panama Canal. The last four stanzas range across other American questions, moving from the problem of physically identifying America to that of recognizing its essence. He alludes to such European classics as Toqueville's *Democracy in America* and to such modern books as John Gunther's best-selling *Inside America,* but quickly switches to the idea that Columbus will make his way across barriers to the Far East but will attribute the opening not to our technological successes but to his will or an earthquake. Frost refers ironically to Columbus's "High purpose," feeling that this is just what Columbus lacked, and sarcastically tells the phantom explorer to be on his way to riches in China. But should Columbus get there, he will find the Chinese disgusted with foreign exploitation and religious missionaries. With a final twist of scorn, Frost recalls the successes of the conquistadores, who found easier prey among the Aztecs than Columbus would find among the Chinese. Helen Bacon suggests that this poem "stresses a missed opportunity for godhood and the inevitable weariness of trying to find the ideal" (220:9), and she uses this view to relate the poem to the three that follow it.

"One More Brevity" centers on the speaker's single night's entertainment of a lost dalmatian dog that has run away from the traffic speed of modern life and receives a royal entertainment until the next day, when it goes on its way. The "brevity" of the title refers to the speaker's quick look outside his door, to his attempt to understand the world, and to the dog's brief visit. His "last look" at the sky stands for contemplation before a sleep that resembles death. The narrative combines a convincing realistic surface with a series of allegorical suggestions. After the speaker looks out to see Sirius, the dog star and the greatest of the fixed stars – to Frost, a symbol of the material and spiritual combined – a dog arrives that is later described as an "avatar" of this star. The dog's weary puzzlement suggests Frost's combined flight from and engagement with the world, as well as the inability of nature to explain itself.

Bacon offers a detailed explanation of the dog's name, Dalmatian Gus, as a clue to the poem's total intention (220). The name, she argues, associates the dog with Augustus Caesar through allusions to several passages in Book 8 of Virgil's *Aeneid.* Gus is a shortened form of Augustus, and Augustus Caesar achieved a major victory at Dalmatia. Augustus, in turn, fought against various forces of darkness and was at last, along with his adopted father, Julius Caesar, elevated as a star god. Bacon maintains that this complex allusion explains the poem's concluding assertion that the dog's overnight descent has brought to Frost intimations of those profound meanings that he "wasn't disposed to speak" and throws light on all the poem's details: "Every commonplace detail of dog and human behavior proves to be related to the idea of election, or of the grief and exhaustion associated with the struggle to bring the spirit to earth, or of the poignant brevity of an encounter between god and man" (220:8). Bacon then notes that the next two poems deal with themes of struggle and pursuit of social order.

"Escapist–Never" is at least partly Frost's reply to those who accuse him of avoiding the dilemmas of the modern world and refusing to take a stand on crucial issues. The third-person stance shows a painful distancing of himself from the accusation and distress over a ruthless self-examination. The person dramatized here does not look back at failures but looks at the fears beside him, which lend his race a creative or necessary crookedness that is still a straightness because he proceeds as directly as courage and conditions allow. Midway in the poem he becomes a pursuer of figures that run on ahead of him, each pursuing a seeker yet further on; the whole process insists on the desperate elusiveness of the ideal and also on the continuity of the human spirit in the human race. "The future . . . creates his present" because only his pursuit of the ideal gives significance to what he is. That "all is an interminable chain of longing" poignantly associates him with both humanity and existence itself. The slight ghostliness here recalls poems of pursuit in *A Boy's Will,* but the association of the self with others shows an older person's awareness of his mortality and a longing for connection with what will follow him.

Having been invited to read a poem at John F. Kennedy's inauguration in January 1961, Frost composed "For John F. Kennedy His Inauguration" to read as a prelude to reciting "The Gift Outright" (first published in *A Witness Tree*). Sunlight and wind kept Frost from reading more than a few lines of the new poem, in an occasion poignantly recorded on film, but he rescued the situation by proceeding to recite "The Gift Outright" from memory, pausing to note that he was changing its final line to read "Such as she was, such as she *will* become" rather than "would become." At the opening and closing of the poem, Frost indicates that he is predicting for Kennedy a rule over a new Augustan age–that is, an age like the long, fruitful, peaceful rule of Augustus Caesar over Rome. Frost is pleased to be personally representing artists as part of this inauguration, and he sees Kennedy's novel invitation of a poet as a prediction of promising qualities in the new administration.

His main theme, however, is the way America's courageous struggle for independence has set a model for the rest of the world. He delights in recalling the English settlers' successful dominance of what became America and alludes to the motto E Pluribus Unum (Out of Many One), which describes the political structure of the United States and reminds him of the courage of the founding fathers. He sees America's struggle for independence as a model for the post-World War II struggle for independence by many formerly colonial nations, whose turbulence we are bound to admire because it resembles our own successful struggles. To counter gloomy predictions about America, he celebrates the Wright brothers as courageous innovators and suggests that the new administration will show daring like theirs in bringing about significant changes. He mentions the recent election, in which Kennedy won by a popular-vote margin of only 112,000 votes, and is delighted by the courage of Kennedy's challenge and the celebration of political courage in Kennedy's book *Profiles in Courage,* which he alludes to without naming. He hopes that Kennedy will bring such courage to his administration and will show less concern for our national limitations and more faith in our exertions. The atmosphere that enables him to say these things gives him faith that "a golden age" – a symbolic tag for an ideal society – may be dawning, which will honor the arts as well as political power.

"Accidentally on Purpose" begins a sequence of five poems originally grouped as "Clusters of Faith." All concern the mystery of the creation and Frost's insistence on some form of faith. The first poem thrusts satirically at pure materialists. Such people see the Universe as composed only of matter, in the large form of stars and planets and the tiny form of atoms. These scientists see the Universe as meaningless until humanity evolved and introduced thought processes. Frost jokes that Darwin, who tried to describe evolutionary processes, somehow created them, and then insists that materialists are wrong. The Universe at least had the purpose of creating humans who are aware of purpose; that this purpose came "to a head" in people indicates that humans are a major purpose and have the brain that realizes it. But Frost leaves the nature of the creator open, foreshadowing the antisexism of contemporary theologians by questioning the gender of the godhead. Frost wishes to be granted that intention exists, which idea he finds "near enough to the Divine" to serve as a religious faith. The last stanza, considering the balance between intellectual and emotional purpose, opts for the superiority of love over intellect.

"A Never Naught Song" again rehearses faith in creation as a purposeful occurrence rather than the accidental coming of universe and mind out of nothing, but here Frost hangs his argument on a scientific schema. Everything, he insists, began with thought, although it first manifested itself in matter in "a state / Of atomic One," which is the structure of the hydrogen atom, believed since the 1930s to be the building block of the universe. Hydrogen is formed from a single proton (its nucleus) and a single electron that revolves around it. Matter was then "complete" in that there was substance and process to allow for all developments. Matter was one, yet also had parts, which could conflict or join together, laying the basis for conflict and connection among human beings. Thus, being "is all the tree / It will ever be," meaning that the structure and material for growth have been here since thought created matter with all its potentialities. His atomic One is so small that the inherent coherence in the universe that it manifests is hidden from our eyes, and so we disbelieve in that coherence, which was only mythologically expressed in Yggdrasill, the great ash tree of Norse mythology, whose roots and branches hold the universe together. The puzzling two lines after "Yggdrasill"–"Out of coming-in / Into having been!"–suggest that the coherence of atomic One came into existence but is now thought of as having never existed because we cannot see it. Thus, our image of reality has almost nothing in it but the force of thought because we cannot see the coherence it created in matter.

The creator, who remains invisible in "A Never Naught Song," is given playful embodiment as "an Archer" in "Version," whose title suggests it is another creation myth and perhaps a variation on other Frost poems. Here everything begins with an Archer who shoots a shaft to create an eternally self-renewing universe. This process releases the comic tension of relief in the face of the fear of nothingness, for what he hunts is non-existent until his arrow strikes "the non-existence / of the Phoenix pullet" and itself becomes the matter it was trying to find in her. Non-existence appears to be an idea that must be countered by the Archer's creative force, an emptiness that must be turned into something as self-renewing as the Phoenix, which rises from its own ashes at fixed intervals. The Greek word *"me on,"* meaning "non-being," reveals the antiquity of the notion. Thus, the Archer's own substance, or at least his chief agency, becomes the body of being. "That's how matter mattered" playfully describes matter coming into being and being important.

"A Concept Self-Conceived," a caution against pantheism, may have been placed in this sequence to qualify the ideas Frost flirts with in the preceding three poems. Here he describes as "childish" the new belief that the universe, as an "All," somehow created itself, perhaps just by taking thought. Of course, pantheism is not a new belief, as Frost soon recognizes, but it can be a version of some new science-based and generalized faiths. As "good old Pantheism," this idea seems not much of an explanation. The great "reassurance of recall" is the recognition of pantheism as heresy and the return to more conventional faith. If we continue to give children the choice between pantheism and theism, we may leave them in confusion. The best alternative seems to be to raise them with one belief or the other and not to let them make a choice.

"Clusters of Faith" concludes with an untitled two-line epigram less concerned with creation than with the burdens existence creates. The use of "Forgive" as the first word creates an immediate sense of strong guilt, which is soon partially withdrawn. The effect parallels the sudden switch from asking God's forgiveness to accusing God of causing all the trouble. The speaker's "little jokes" may be his skeptical poems as well as his human flaws, which are part of the burden placed on him by the Lord's much bigger joke of having created his puzzlingly painful existence. The clash of diction between the conversational phrases "little jokes" and "great big one" and the elevated "Forgive," "Lord," and "Thee" contrasts earthly suffering to the distance of that God about whose nature Frost remains puzzled.

The long autobiographical reminiscence "Kitty Hawk," which has a complicated textual history discussed by Joan St. C. Crane (184), relates to "Clusters of Faith" through its making the Wright brothers' airplane a symbol for the descent of the spiritual into the material. The poem recounts Frost's trip to the Dismal Swamp and the Outer Banks of North Carolina from 6 to 30 November, 1894. He had gone to visit his future wife, Elinor White, at St. Lawrence University in Canton, New York, carrying two copies of his pamphlet of poems *Twilight*. Elinor received him coolly; he threw away his own copy and set off in a quasisuicidal mood for the Dismal Swamp. Frost's reasonably accurate account of his adventures relates his mood to the Wright brothers' invention. The description of the poem as "a skylark" suggests its wildly playful progression and also recalls the poet Shelley, whose "Alastor" it alludes to later.

Part One of the poem, entitled "Portents, Presentiments, and Premonitions" sketches Frost's bitter mood as he arrived at the northwest corner of North Carolina, not far from both the Dismal Swamp and the long sea reef known as the Outer Bank, the location of both Nag's Head and Kitty Hawk. Some nine years later, on 17 December, 1903, on the sands of Kitty Hawk, Wilbur (1867-1912) and Orville (1871-1948) Wright were to make the first piloted and powered heavier-than-air flight. Frost was angry about a letter from Elinor and exultingly anxious to express to the surrounding wild weather his frustrations about love. Now, in retrospect, he claims he was on the verge of creating a poem that might have rivaled in its sublimity the Wright brothers's flight. Both Lawrence Thompson (20:517-18) and Laurence Goldstein (185) think the subject of that poem was to have been the puzzling character of Elinor White. The "Master" whom Frost later met in "Kitty Hawk" is Orville Wright, who became Frost's friend not long before Orville's death. Shelley's Alastor, whom Frost resembles in this poem, is a demon-driven poet seeking a woman-spirit matching his soul. Frost claims to have boasted to Orville that he might have preceded him in making a significant flight here, and then rehearses with irritated sympathy the Wrights' struggle to have their accomplishment properly recognized, as it finally was when in

1927 President Hoover commissioned The Wright Brothers National Monument on Devil Hill near Kitty Hawk. Before this, to the chagrin of Orville Wright, the Smithsonian Institution had honored Samuel Langley as the inventor of the airplane.

Frost changes the theme of this unwritten poem from the frustrations of love to a celebration of Sir Walter Raleigh's doomed settlement at Roanoke (1585-1591). Returning to his North Carolina ventures, Frost recounts how he was taken in by a group of drunken and sentimental duck hunters from Elizabeth City. They were important because their friendliness aborted the "Götterdämmerung" his song-poem would have been. Their excessive concern for his innocence (presumably, they stopped telling off-color stories) led him to flee to the beaches, where he talked to an officer of the Life-Saving Service. Again Frost was embarrassed, for this man inquired about his religious commitments and rehearsed the story of Vice-President Aaron Burr's daughter Theodosia, who had been on a schooner headed from Georgetown, North Carolina, to New York City in late December 1812. The schooner was never heard from again, and rumors abounded about Theodosia's fate. Burr's intense devotion to his daughter perhaps reminded the poet of his own puzzlement about the nature of love. Walking with the officer, Frost quoted "And the Moon was full" from Tennyson's "Morte d'Arthur" and mentally compared himself to Theodosia Burr as the object of other people's concern for his soul and fate.

With Part Two of "Kitty Hawk," Frost moves from personal reminiscences to consider the Wrights' accomplishment, joyful at having been at its location when it was unthought of. He recalls an aerial celebration in the neighborhood and delights to think that Americans have not been willing to remain on earth. We are only "somewhat" Lilliputians (miniature humans) because we have had the strength of mind to achieve flight. Frost rushes ahead to rehearse a contrast between the significance of human flight as he understands it and as it was variously denigrated in the years just after the Wrights' first accomplishment. Religious people may criticize such inventions as parallels to humanity's sinful quest for knowledge in Eden; he agrees with the comparison but sees both as positive ventures into the unknown. For him the fall is "Our instinctive venture / Into what they call / The material," and he sees this innovation as a parallel to God's daring to take on flesh, which is also an analogy for poetic creation.

Celebrating the movement of civilization to America ("West-Northwest"), Frost notes the West's doubts of the spiritual value of its material progress. He rejects this view, however, backing himself up with reference to the East's rising "from its long stagnation" and embracing scientific innovation. He expands on the notion of spirit entering flesh through a subtle allusion to the Bible passage in which Jacob, making his way from Beersheba to Haran, near the Dead Sea, and doubtless passing through

Moab, slept with a stone for a pillow and saw a ladder from heaven. In his sleep, Jacob heard the Lord bless him and his people, and on waking he set up a stone pillar to be God's house (Genesis 28.10-22). This pillar is Frost's "slab / Of . . . basalt," and the "radio Voice" that speaks must be, as Richard Wilbur has noted (57:147), God addressing Jacob in an unaccustomed manner. Thus, Frost sees humanity's flight into air and space as the equivalent of Jacob's ladder, a bond between heaven and earth. This voice continues to answer the false-minded pulpiteers who see science as irreligious. Such scientific-religious pursuits came to a great head with the Wrights' flight, which the radio voice now celebrates as American and not Russian. Frost cautions against arrogance – "Earth is still our fate" – but this cannot keep him from celebrating Americans as people unwilling to just name things, insistent on accomplishing what they have named.

Part Two, after what has been an introduction, divides into three named subsections. "Talk Aloft" puns on speech coming from powered flight and talk so boastful it goes out into, and prospectively conquers, the universe. Citing a view like the Spinozan ethic that virtue is its own reward, Frost affirms that accomplishment rather than aspiration is most to be desired. If we did not have novel means of travel, we would remain "where we were," near familiar cities. Instead we must dare greater flights into the universe, surely space travel, through which humanity will bring intelligence to the rest of the universe, which would be just wasteland without us. Still, he acknowledges that humanity projects a "ray" not its own but rooted in some ideal – an ideal we have incorporated into our *"mens animi,"* (the mind of the spirit), which is the core of the only thinking race in the universe.

In "The Holiness of Wholeness" Frost addresses a Pilot, now more than a flier, representing human daring to further penetrate matter and spirit. Thus, though we cannot create matter, we can "get control . . . of at least some part" and thereby gain "Wholeness in a sense" – that is, the understanding of the relationship between matter and spirit. Here Frost makes an equivalence between scientific invention and poetry, or art, implying that their grasp of organizing principles gives us both insight and a sense of wholeness. Our "becoming fear," the fear that is most attractive, is our fear of not "getting thought expressed" – that is, of not formulating our deepest insights. "Expressed" also means "pressed out" into reality, another metaphor for the overlap of material and spiritual.

The final section of Part Two of "Kitty Hawk," entitled "The Mixture Mechanic," returns to a description of powered flight as a metaphor for humanity's thrusting from its smallness into the limits of the universe. Our approving of the sun and moon on the move means that we are adjusting our spirits and accomplishments to the energy and meaning of cosmic things. Our approval of evolution outside ourselves links us to it. Frost suggests that Nature will perceive its evolutionary success only if it sees us "in flight," represented by "We two," which seems to be a flying machine, now become a spaceship, guided by a human. This accomplishment will allow us to give to the stars that meaning which we sometimes think we just derive from them. Frost is working in the romantic tradition of cooperation between the universe and the human mind to produce meaning. Now Frost moves to a kind of prayer, but though it is offered to the "God of the machine"–still mistakenly seen by some as Satanic–surely it is also offered to the God who creates everything, including the author's poem, which as verbal artifact is a "token flight," just as the Wright brothers' flight was a token of further accomplishment. The poem concludes by drawing up into tight-mouthed praise of the daring of everyday Americans by comparing the Wright brothers to Darius Green, whom Joan St. C. Crane (184:242) identifies as the fictional aviator-hero of John Townsend Trowbridge's poem "Darius Green and His Flying Machine," first published in 1867 and alluded to by Frost in a talk he gave in 1917, two years after he had met the poem's aging author.

The poem "Auspex," its title Latin for auspice, meaning a prophetic sign, is a brief tale of a flight not taken in the flesh but still taken in the spirit by the poet. The terrifying eagle that swept down and "measured" him but did not carry him off is typically American, but the poem proceeds with a classical allusion in the strained notion that his parents thought the royal bird found him unworthy to be like the handsome Trojan prince who became a cupbearer to Jove. Frost playfully expresses disbelief that Jove would not find him worthy to be his "barkeep," and indeed, "to this day," he resents anyone but himself who "presume[s] to say / That there [is] anything [he] couldn't be." Thus he implies that he went on to conquer celestial regions, if only through writing poems.

Many of the poems following "Auspex" are probably placed here to show struggles leading to a variety of spiritual successes and failures. "The Draft Horse" is an allegory about a couple starting out in life and running into incomprehensible difficulties that only persuade them to forge on, though perhaps differently than they had originally. "Draft" puns on the word's meanings of "pulling a heavy load" and "an unsuccessful model of what is needed," and after the horse is killed, the "draft" breathed by the night is a gust of air, suggesting a frightening emptiness. The poem resembles "On a Tree Fallen Across the Road" in its refusal to admit defeat, but the plot is more personal, and the relentless movement, rather than mocking outside forces, revels in the mutual strength with which the two people face a challenge. They seem to be a married couple looking back at their most difficult passages and thus resemble Robert and Elinor Frost. Each of the first four lines insists on difficulties of situation and equipment, and as if that were not enough to stop them, forces of unreason burst out in the sinister figure who stabs their horse to death. Donald J. Greiner suggests that "We are not quite sure whether the night is resentful about the killing or about the human presence in the forest," which connects to his view that the poem is "tempered by the almost humorous, matter-of-fact expression of their blind fatalism" (88:387). After this terrible event, they go on as determinedly as ever, and without anger, for if they were angry they could not go on. Their acceptance of fate and their refusal to see themselves as special objects of evil shows that from the first they had been determined to face evil. The last stanza sees the destruction represented by the man who killed the horse as illustrating the inscrutable nature of existence and of the problem of evil. The couple's having to "get down / And walk the rest of the way" shows humility wedded to determination and suggests that they kept going indefinitely. A long analysis of the poem by Frederick L. Gwynn offers conclusions like these but in more elaborate terms. Gwynn finds that the poem's central action parallels ritual animal sacrifices as described in Frazer's *The Golden Bough* and describes the atmosphere as demonic. The primary theme, he declares, is "the ironic acceptance of superhuman power. . . . [as] the protagonists witness a primitive religious ritual attesting to power, in which their horse is sacrificed instead of them" (168:225). Paul Burrell proposes a more down-to-earth interpretation: that the ineffective lamp, "frail" buggy, and clumsy horse represent "makeshifts to which man learns to resign himself as he goes through this world of compromises and disappointments" (167).

"Ends," a strangely Robinsonian lyric narrative for Frost, portrays a couple whose marriage has failed. The second-person speakers may seem to be supposing all the actions inside the house they pass, but they are familiar with the bitterness inside and are capable of recognizing the end of a doomed relationship. As the shouts from the house shock them into stumbling, they realize that the worst is happening. They have heard the husband's complaints and know that he has not denied his wife's youth and appeal. Still, they are well aware of the bitterness that leads people to end a relationship completely rather than to discard or fight those things in it that hurt. They are familiar with how lovers fling wild accusations, but in this case they know that the man has determined to end things, and they seem almost grimly satisfied with their perception or prediction.

"Peril of Hope," slightly reminiscent of "There Are Roughly Zones," is about pervasive danger to blossoming things, which may represent the kinds of human situations shown in "Ends." Here the space "between / The orchard bare / And the orchard green" is the turn toward spring, a time of beautiful flowering and great risk. The last stanza presents as a certainty what is only a possibility—that climate is always determined to take such moments to bring a night of killing frosts. The tone here is one of poignant regret, but the theme incorporates something of the hopeless fatality of the conflict between the couple in "Ends" and of the way grim fatality brings fresh impetus for struggle to the couple in "The Draft Horse."

"Questioning Faces," a concise parable, also deals with matters of fate, though more indirectly. The owl that saves itself from smashing into a window presents a picture not of spilled blood but of radiant sunset to the children who watch from their safe indoor haven. They have been spared the sight and the threat of a painful wreck, but they do not seem to understand the risk that the bird ran to create such a picture and to present such a potential lesson. Its being glassed out seems a better fate than theirs, for it controls its risks, whereas they are passively subject to risk.

The next six poems and, to a degree, the remainder of the collection make somewhat cranky political statements that qualify Frost's optimism about America as expressed in "Kitty Hawk" and in his poem for the Kennedy inauguration. "Does No One at All Ever Feel This Way in the Least?" is an apologetic title for a complaint about the narrowing of boundaries between America and other nations, particularly ancestral England. Addressing the Atlantic Ocean, the speaker tells the sea that its vast physical separation of the Old World from the New World would finally be a disappointment if that separation did not make us in the New World different in even one trait from the people of the Old. He notes that we in the New World have changed one thing by substituting the English word "corn," which in England meant "wheat," for the Indian name for maize. But this is just one of many examples of the homesickness that has led us to abort our newness. He angrily tells the sea it is of no value and deserves to be blamed. Now the airplane and faster boats make the sea's physical separation of the continents meaningless. Even "the savor of . . . salt" is diluted and rendered innocuous by all the fresh water flowing into the ocean. The narrator holds up "a dead shell" and challenges the sea to "do work for women" by grinding it "into a lady's finger ring or thimble," since it is incapable of doing anything else worthwhile. He goes on to say that if the ocean won't pay attention to him, he knows a place where he can go to escape it–so far inland that no one mentions it except in "baby-school," where the teacher knows so little about it that she can only say it is "a pool" and talk about Sinbad, the sailor in the Arabian Nights.

"The Bad Island–Easter (Perhaps so called because it may have risen once)" puns on the volcanic origin of Easter Island and on its providing an example of spiritual failure rather than resurrection. Easter Island lies in the Pacific Ocean, 2,200 miles from Chile. Its name comes from its discovery on Easter Day in 1722 by a Dutch explorer. The island suffered plagues and economic disasters under Dutch and Spanish rule and is the site of huge, inexplicable stone statues, the construction of which must have required enormous labor. Samples of them have never been transported overseas; Frost's misconception on this score is probably based on his having seen photographic studies of them.

The narrator is talking to someone about the head of one of the massive statues. He treats it phrenologically, saying that it is easy to understand its character from its configuration, which shows "the woes of the past." The key to it is the "scornfully curled" lip that has led others to cart the head from Easter Island. The narrator says that the carving and setting up of the head as "a throne" was an enormous labor. He thinks its creators gave it that face to reflect their own scorn at themselves "for having been born" and then letting themselves be conned into having rulers. He wonders how they could have been free and yet also have been persuaded that they would profit from having rulers. He says they floundered for a while under the "fraud and . . . force" of such rule until too much was asked of their strength and resources and they began to diminish. The only ones left were "vile" and talkative. These people were "punished and bribed" to no avail; somewhere a "mistake had been made,"–something had been done that had looked like a gain but was not. But one thing we can know: whatever culture they paraded, whatever utopian thought they aspired to achieve, has left no trace except the doctrine of sharing with one's fellows–and even that has degenerated into a belief in thievery and a persistence in it "with cynical daring." The poem seems to be an allegory of the United States' adoption of the welfare state system, which turns out to be a mask for everyone grabbing from others.

After what appears to be an attack on make-work projects as a form of charity and cheating, Frost places "Our Doom to Bloom," apparently an attack on a state that is eroding because its main principle is to give things away. The epigraph "Shine, perishing republic" is the title of a Robinson Jeffers poem that sees America hastening to its end through the pursuit of materialism and imperial power. Frost borrows the metaphor of nation as flower, but his flower is becoming overblown by giving everything, "coats, oats, votes, to all mankind." Frost addresses the Cumaean Sibyl, a famous prophetess of ancient Cumae who was a "charming Ogress" because she lost her great beauty to withering age after Apollo gave her eternal life but denied her eternal youth because she withheld her favors. The Sibyl, a successful prophet, bids Americans see how their lot resembles ancient Rome's. She tells the narrator that progress may be an illusion and that if not, it is a spreading around of power, food, and money to everyone. The sole function of any government "is to give." Her attitude toward this process is shown in the comparison of the state and its history to the flower bud that must bloom until it is overblown and its petals fall. She concludes by saying that this fate is inevitable unless the state would prefer to lose all life at once rather than gradually.

Political satire continues, but more obliquely, in "The Objection to Being Stepped On," which provides a brief parable of the dangers of letting others step on oneself or one's nation and on trying to beat swords into ploughshares. The speaker has had the painful and not uncommon experience of hitting himself in the head with a hoe's handle by stepping on its blade. Its turning his head into "the seat of my sense" implies that his brains have stupidly become his butt. He curses himself for his carelessness and then generalizes on the danger of following the biblical injunction about weapons. He tried something like that advice by stepping on a tool, but it became a weapon, paralleling the danger of trying to turn weapons into tools. He (and his nation) ought to be well prepared militarily, he seems to suggest.

In "A-Wishing Well," whose curiously hyphenated title suggests people going a-wishing. Frost turns from criticizing liberals for their too-trusting willingness to disarm, and ridicules their general wishfulness that things were just made better. Most of the poem pretends to share this wishful attitude. Looking longingly at planets lucky enough to have more than one moon, the speaker childishly wishes that our earth would acquire an additional moon by means like the creation of the first. Frost jokes with stupid inquirers about the sources of his own poems, and instead of describing the hard work that produces them, suggests that they are delivered by stork. He makes fun of Arcadians – people from the Pan-haunted woodlands of ancient Greece – who claim to remember the moon's creation. Then he describes their version of earth's birth agony as the moon was "torn from her Pacific side." "Enormous Caf" probably refers to "carriage and freight." He ridicules his fantasy Arcadians by imagining them clinging to a plant, the silphion; "some of them gave way at the wrist / before they gave way at the fist," and the skeletons of their hands remain attached to the plant. The silphion seems to be Frost's own invention, but its name may be a corruption of sylphium, a resin-bearing plant of the Mediterranean region. Toward his conclusion, the speaker jokes that his opponents, the liberals, will object to the destruction of human life involved in his proposal that we get another moon, this time from the Atlantic. But he is willing to subject the Demiurge – the godlike creator of the physical universe – to such a task, and he does not worry too much about predictions of an end to mankind (another thing liberals worry about) because the story of Noah shows that we can always start over again. Claude Simpson, who thinks this poem relates to early space probes, sees in it not political allegory but a celebration of humanity's will to prevail, as shown by the courage of invention (128:135).

Political satire continues in the fantasy flights of the narrative parable "How Hard It Is to Keep from Being King When It's in You and in the Situation." The poem's many sources, mostly in medieval legend, have been traced by Sister Mary Jeremy Finnegan in an article that also illuminates much of the poem's meaning (180). The ancient stories from which Frost works provide the motifs of a king who learns, usually from another royal person, of a worm inside a precious jewel, offers a reward in the form of food, and learns that he is illegitimate. Frost adds to the story a son for the first king and various subtle thematic elaborations, especially the combined concerns with poetry and society. Frost ranges widely, fantastically, and achronologically through numerous historical and literary allusions. The poem's protagonist is the king who resigns his throne and goes off voluntarily with his son to be sold into slavery for funds to sustain the son's undertakings, especially as a poet. The antagonist is Darius – perhaps Darius the Great, conquering king of ancient Persia, or a conflation of that king and the two less successful Dariuses who followed his reign. The main points of the poem come from Frost's Darius turning out not to be a king – as demonstrated by his preferring food to character, a mistake that the ex-king swiftly realizes and lectures Darius about. The ex-king's insight shows that he is the proper king, and as the poem concludes, he is about to assume Darius's throne. The ex-king's knowledge that character is more important than food is Frost's answer to liberals who emphasize charity more than aspiration and who would unknowingly corrupt people by supporting them instead of having them sustain themselves. Frost develops this theme as the ex-king tells Darius that a good king should make his subjects "as happy as is good for them" and "not without consultation with their wishes," which is a slap at dictatorships like the Soviet Union and expresses Frost's apprehension that liberals introduce too many social compulsions.

The point of "pliant permanence" that Frost and the ex-king praise is attributed to a faith like that of James Madison, a president who fought for the Constitution and the Bill of Rights but then drew back from the power of Federalism. As the poem concludes, the ex-king's son explains that his father is mistaken about the son's being a free-verse poet. Like Frost, he writes blank verse, not free verse, though he does so with a certain freedom. In denouncing his son's supposed free verse, the ex-king had rung satirical changes on the Four Freedoms as proposed by Franklin Roosevelt, but the son, it turns out, is no proponent of careless freedoms. Rather, he approves of the freedom of departure that his father showed by resigning his kingship and that Frost cherishes as the freedom to steer clear of entanglements unsuitable to one's soul. As a poet he wants not free verse but the freedom of his own material: "It's what my father must mean by departure, / Freedom to flash off into wild connections." He foresees that Darius will be executed and his father will replace Darius, which seems to be what Darius wanted and what his father was fated for, despite his fleeing it. Royal attributes triumph, with the king in his proper place and the poet in his, though Frost's joking that this "is half the trouble with the world," implies that no problems are easily solved.

The three poems that follow these political satires show a playfully annoyed reaction to the earliest years of unmanned space travel. Only the first two stanzas of "Lines Written in Dejection on the Eve of Great Success" were published in 1959. The remaining five stanzas first appear in *In the Clearing*. In January 1959 the Russians sent a space probe that missed the moon by some 4,000 miles, and in March of that year an American space probe missed the moon by some 37,000 miles. Frost's title parodies the names of such romantic poems as Shelley's "Stanzas Written in Dejection . . ." and Coleridge's "Dejection: An Ode," though the parodying adds little to Frost's poem. The first two stanzas, echoing the Mother Goose rhyme "Hey diddle diddle, the cat and the fiddle," suggest that poetic imagination jumped over the moon long ago but that humans, with their mineral-powered rockets, have not quite caught up with this kind of accomplishment, though they seem close to it. In the "Postscript" to the poem, Frost somewhat inconsistently maintains that he would not have succeeded had he tried to let the cow carry him over the moon, for it would have revolted. The legendary man who punished a cow for rebelling against such an attempt seems to represent rage at not having succeeded in space travel, no matter how powered, and his testy question of how the trouble began reminds Frost of how people always ask who began rather than who won a war, which suggests frustration over competition about space travel. Thus, the "dejection" of the title seems to apply to Frost's feelings about the competitive element of space exploration. This contradicts the national pride that Frost shows in "Kitty Hawk" and elsewhere, but the Russians' early lead in space travel may have induced Frost's frustration over the competition. Possibly he is dejected by the circumstances of the coming success and annoyed that science seems to be replacing imagination.

"The Milky Way is a Cowpath" also begins with frustration over the initial failure of moon probes and joins to it a slightly confusing annoyance at humanity's challenging the heavens. The speaker reports a dialogue with his wife, who thinks it was the cow who overshot the moon and who may join the speaker in imagining that the cow will make valuable discoveries out there. Once more, Frost may be playing with the idea of imagination's powers. That the cow seems in danger of being cut by the "razor edge" of the universe (a stab at Einstein's theory of space) does not concern anyone except the speaker – perhaps because others do not care enough about the imagination. However, the poem's coherence seems strained as Frost suggests that he also does not care about the cow's failures. Presumably only the successes of imagination and of science, too, really count for him, which might help explain the dejection in the preceding poem.

"Some Science Fiction," first published in 1955, probably predates the other poems about space travel. It reveals an explicit antipathy to the pace of modern life. Frost anticipates that those who are enthralled with space travel will look down at his slow, philosophic pace, and he worries that their fanaticism may lead them to send him up to colonize the moon. At first he suggests that he might tolerate giving such help to "a noble experiment," but on second thought he suggests that he is too good for the venture, which should be thrust on a "wastrel." After the end of the poem, in the verse addressing his friend Hyde Cox, who lives on Crow Island (off the coast of

Maine), he implies that his defensive position may entertain a man who, like himself, prefers his old-fashioned privacy.

"Quandary" begins what was initially a section called *Quandary*, extending to this collection's conclusion. This philosophical poem approaches the problem of evil lightheartedly, implying criticism of liberals who find evil intolerable and who refuse to make various kinds of discriminations. As for Frost, he accepts the necessity of evil if good is also to exist, and he prefers over the gentler Christian idea the Delphic wisdom that one should love one's friends and hate one's enemies. To hate one's neighbor as one hates oneself, his personal variation on the Delphic formula, implies the usefulness of self-criticism, though such self-criticism also puts one in a quandary. But the overall quandary chiefly concerns the problem of how there can be good without evil and relates to the idea that humanity's fall was into a useful state of knowledge – or using our brains. The forbidden fruit taught us that we need brains to understand the problems that the fall got us into. Frost then replies to someone who tries to put down his praise of brains by suggesting that "sweetbreads" would do as well, a joke based on the similarity in appearance between sweetbreads (the pancreas or thymus of animals) and brains. Sweetbreads are popularly held to increase sexual virility, an idea alluded to in Frost's "With innuendo I detest," which shows his disgust with the joke that he needs sexual potency rather than brains. Still, the joke reminds him that he had once mistaken sweetbreads for brains until he had learned the truth from experts on the subject. He tries to have the last word by suggesting that eating those sweetbreads did the work of brains: by eating them, he gained not sexual power but intelligence.

Just having boasted about the power of intelligence, Frost takes some of it back in "A Reflex," in which he ridicules scientific attempts to get at the essence of life. Probing for the nature of vitality, science almost got bitten. The ferocity of this response makes science consider that perhaps there is a God, a creative force, which resists human attempts to grasp the inexplicable.

"In a Glass of Cider," a parable about ways of knowing, is probably positioned here to balance "A Reflex." Frost sees himself as less dogmatic than scientists in his pursuit of knowledge. As "a mite of sediment," he rises on a bubble from a ferment of ideas or imagination – but a bubble cannot sustain him long. Nevertheless, his descent is not very troublesome because he understands the tentative nature of knowledge, and he took pleasure in the elation of his rise. Thus, Frost defends knowledge as imaginative experimentation whose best satisfactions are emotional.

"From Iron," subtitled "Tools and Weapons," is dedicated to an assistant secretary of the United Nations. The title refers to a piece of iron ore placed in a meditation room at the United Nations. The subtitle shows that iron can be made into such contrasting things as tools for work and cooperation, and weapons for war and division. Frost expresses wariness at the unifications called for by this international body and suggests that to maintain their integrity, nations must stand up for themselves—perhaps to the extent of using, as well as having, weapons. When the poem was misquoted to Frost during an interview, he corrected the word "decides" to "divides" and, after explaining the source of the poem, remarked on his own belief in the separateness of nations "even if it means a risk of fighting with each other" (15:196).

"Four-Room Shack" glances briefly at how television is coming to dominate the landscape. An antenna on a shack tries to overcome its isolation and lowly condition by drawing down the visions from television waves into its viewing screen. They go past without intelligence, significance, or meaningful direction. The concluding two lines offer Frost's own signing-off from the phenomenon and imply that the shoddy fare offered by television is what the audience wants. The last lines satirically suggest that the shack will be pleased to subsist on a kind of nothingness.

"But Outer Space . . ." returns briefly to criticism of space exploration. People seem very excited over space exploration, but that it is "more popular / Than populous" suggests both that its successes are severely limited and that those of us gazing up at its potential accomplishments are not very happy at the thought of being among the space travelers.

"On Being Chosen Poet of Vermont" is an occasional piece. Frost asserts his patriotism and congratulates his neighbors on their acceptance of his not always easily understood poems. He is happy to find that his people understand and somewhat approve of his work, implying that this is not the most common occurrence. The lines parody the famous passage from Sir Walter Scott's "Lay of the Last Minstrel" that begin: "Breathes there a man with soul so dead / Who never to himself has said: / This is my own my native land." Possibly Frost is simultaneously praising his neighbors and putting himself down through an allusion that has become a cliché. He may also be alluding to Jesus' comment that a prophet is without honor in his own country.

In "We Vainly Wrestle . . ." Frost directs skepticism toward the human race and probably reflects back on his own excessive self-assurances. Thinking, perhaps, of his own affirmations and of the human accomplishments he has just been criticizing, he declares that we all have some awareness that what we value will pass away, but that we struggle against the idea that our deaths will bring an end to the things we most value.

The epigram "It Takes All Sorts . . ." achieves wit through the clash of formal terms such as "schooling" and "adapted" with the informality of "sorts" and "fooling." The fooling is the jokes—the outer and inner-directed satire—of his poems. One requires a knowledge of the outdoors to see how Frost uses his natural material for symbols and a knowledge of indoor things to see the intellectual twist that he gives to common things. Frost also suggests that it takes learning from all kinds of experience to get involved in his kind of imaginative playing with experience.

"In Winter in the Woods . . ." makes a farewell reminiscent of "Closed for Good," though here the speaker seems to leave only his spirit and not proxies behind him. Laurence Perrine, in describing this poem as Frost's "Crossing the Bar," suggests that as the poet retreats into death, he anticipates some kind of a return to strike a blow for life (120:96). A more down-to-earth interpretation, however, seems likelier. The speaker acts in opposition to nature, representing material forces that must be subdued and understood. Having chosen a tree, he cuts it down with perfect assurance. In this northern winter afternoon with its early twilight, he leaves behind him "a line of shadowy tracks," standing for his poems as well as for the force of his presence, which in "Closed for Good" he could see in the animals that would survive him. But he concludes with a stanza symbolizing the eternal conflict between humans and nature. The one tree he has defeated may represent an artistic or intellectual success, and he seems pleased that he has not defeated Nature – that it remains as imposing, vast, and unconquerable as ever. But he also refuses to see any defeat for himself – or, presumably, for humanity – for he regathers his forces and continues toward additional struggles. With calm understatement, the poem asserts a limitless persistence, implying that toward the end of his life Frost, serving as a model for those who follow him, will not give up his exploratory stance.

# CHAPTER 13

---

*A Masque of Reason*
(1945)
*A Masque of Mercy*
(1947)

---

Although his two blank-verse closet dramas were not Frost's final publications, he wished them placed at the end of his collected poems, surely viewing them as summary comment on his life and work. These works continue to receive very different evaluations and interpretations. Perhaps a majority of the early reviewers saw them as shallow, frivolous, generally misguided, and unworthy of their author. Other reviewers and some subsequent critics have argued that their comic method is appropriate to their serious subjects and have praised them either for a deliberate openness of judgment or a profound working-through toward traditional faith. Frost termed these poetic dramas *masques* after the form of stately processional-verse dramas of the renaissance, in which decor and song were as important as the speeches of typically allegorical and not very individualized characters. In England the masque was widely practiced by Ben Jonson, and also by Milton in *Comus* and by Shakespeare in scenes within plays (as in the act 4 of *The Tempest*).

Comprehension of both dramas requires a basic knowledge of those Bible stories for which they provide continuations. *Reason* consists of "Chapter Forty-three of Job," as Frost puts it in the last line, and *Mercy* is a continuation of Jonah, in which the protagonist appears in modern-day New York City, once more fleeing God's commandment that he preach to the wicked and again angry that God will not exact just punishment on sinners. Frost reportedly worked on these dramas simultaneously and knew that he often could not resist letting the material run away from him. Each drama centers on the theme of its title. *Reason* pursues a reason for God's injustice to Job, whose manifold woes illustrate an incomprehensible world in which the good may suffer and the wicked prosper, not one in which justice is uniformly meted out according to deserts. *Mercy* turns the problem around and asks both why the wicked often escape justice and how humanity is to learn and to live by the proper relation between mercy and justice. Both dramas play ideas off against one another in a dialectic that reaches only tentative conclusions, insofar as the characters' arguments often balance one another out, and core questions remain unanswered.

A seemingly infinite pattern of interpretation is possible for both plays because the tone, nuance, context, and interrelations of their central statements can be perceived in various ways. The great abundance of literary, religious, and historical allusions – material very lightly used elsewhere in Frost – complicates the problem of explanation and annotation of these works, as do Frost's frequent and sometimes outrageous puns, which often provide more fun than ideas. Laurence Perrine has written a nine-page article, "A Set of Notes for Frost's Two Masques" (196), citing and partly explaining most of the allusions, some of which are deeply buried. The most frequent and important allusions are to the Bible. Among the poets and writers Frost cites or alludes to are Shakespeare, Yeats, Waller, Kipling, Emerson, Browning, Milton, Herrick, Francis Thompson, Robinson, O'Neill, Bunyan, the Southern Agrarians, and William Blake as artist. Other allusions are to Marx, Luther, St. Thomas, and Aesop, and to some abstruse details of anthropology and geography.

The Book of Job, the most artistically celebrated portion of the Old Testament, tells the story of a completely just and enormously wealthy man who is subjected by God first to loss of his family and worldly goods and then to many bodily afflictions in order to test his fidelity to the Lord. In an introductory passage widely regarded as an addition to the original text, God is shown tormenting Job because Satan taunts God about his claims to the utter fidelity of Job, which God then wishes to prove. During his sufferings, Job undergoes extensive interviews with three of his friends, who variously try to persuade him that he must be guilty of something to merit such punishment. Though he never accepts their judgment and calls out to God for explanation, he remains faithful to God. In the end God answers him by declaring himself the inexplicable Lord of creation, whose ways are not to be understood by humans. After this, in a passage also regarded as of later composition, Job has his goods restored and acquires a new family.

*A Masque of Reason* features four characters: Job; his wife, who is named Thyatira, after a city mentioned in Revelations, whose church was criticized for allowing women prophets to teach; a very humanized God; and a vaguely characterized Satan. The action occurs in a desert that seems to be a version of Heaven, as shown by God's pitching his throne there. The time is perhaps a thousand years after the original Bible story, but the dialogue is larded with modern references. Despite the reference to a Christmas tree, whose glitter is described in a parody of W. B. Yeats's poem "Sailing to Byzantium," Christian allusions are absent, unless the description of someone caught in the branches of the Christmas tree (lines 15-16) alludes to the crucifixion. After God arrives for a conversation with Job and his wife, Job thinks it is Judgment Day—apparently for the judgment not only of whatever qualities Job maintains but also, more importantly, of God's actions toward Job and humanity. Job questions God both directly and indirectly and receives answers sometimes serious and sometimes comically elusive. God, who comments on himself as variously human, thanks Job for helping him rescind the Old Testament promise (the word of the Deuteronomist) that the good shall prosper and the wicked suffer, for only thus can life become a trial, as it was for Job. Job's wife interrupts with various protests about the treatment of women, but her questions mostly reinforce Job's.

Thyatira differs from Job in that she lacks interest in philosophy (she goes to sleep when the subject is discussed), but she recognizes more quickly than Job that "There isn't any universal reason." God and Job continue to discuss the reasons for the world being as it is—a place where there's no clear relationship between merit and reward. God credits Job for demonstrating this situation but defends himself as the creator of permanent truths that science can never replace. Thyatira interrupts by asking God who invented earth, but his replies stick to the central subject—the nature of existence. The Devil, God maintains, helped him make the earth, just as Job helped God show that man must learn submission to unreason. This implies that the texture of good and evil is necessary in order that life and choice have meaning. But Job persists by questioning why it was he who was chosen for the demonstration, declaring "The artist in me cries out for design," which voices Frost's desire to perceive order.

Frightened by God's hesitation in replying, Job despairs of there being any meaning in things or any immortal soul. Thyatira, who had asked about earth's invention, interrupts to reiterate the Frostian view that earth is a place for trial (as already suggested by God) and otherwise would be Heaven at once. God declares that he tortured Job just to show off to the devil, as chapters 1 and 2 of The Book of Job state. Job finds this reply "almost less than I can understand," implying that it has no bearing on rational processes, but he offers some justification for reality's being as it is by citing the myth of the serpent that swallows itself (an image of self-renewing eternity) and by quoting from Emerson's poem "Uriel" ("the greatest Western poem yet"), which sees good as somehow dependent on evil. At the end of this speech, however, Job's "I hold rays deteriorate to nothing" replaces such affirmations with a stab of nihilism. God proceeds to defend his mysterious ordering of things, assures Job that he helped God demonstrate the mystery of good and evil, and seems pleased that the Devil is everywhere. Although it is Thyatira who says "The Devil's ... God's best inspiration," both Frost and God presumably approve of this. To please Thyatira, God summons up the Devil, much reduced by church neglect, and Thyatira has the three male figures pose for a photograph, which suggests that they form a symbolic portrait of an intractable and inexplicable condition.

Most critics of this poetic drama think that it offers little conclusion to the problem of reason, but they differ about the meaning of this inconclusiveness. D. Bradley Sullivan (197), for instance, declares that the play shows man trying to believe into existence a God who makes sense and holds this shows man's better sense overcome by his making God follow man's rules. Thus, Job's reason will not allow for any improved understanding or personal growth, and Job remains unchanged, unlike Jonah in *Mercy*. From a slightly different viewpoint, John T. Gage (193) maintains that Frost is treating the question of whether reason is adequate to answer the dilemmas of knowledge and shows Job being put off by a God who pursues rhetorical effect rather than an explanation of truth. Thus, Job's comment that God's admission that he was showing off to the Devil is "almost less than I can understand" demonstrates that reason presents only rationalizations, not explanations, of truth. Gage concludes that the atmosphere is deliberately absurd, as in Samuel Beckett's plays, and that Frost is mocking the notion of explaining an absurd universe. In simpler fashion, Lawrance Thompson declared in a book review that Frost makes fun of shallow answers to profound questions and sees no final answers in "the dogma of religious dualism or of philosophic monism" (57:201).

These views suggest that Frost perceives God as a creation of the human mind, but otherwise they are not very different from those of critics who see Frost as traditionally theistic, though not sectarian. For them, Frost also plays with ideas of God but does not thereby deny his reality. Thus, W. R. Irwin (194:302-12) maintains that *Reason* reviews the original issues of the Book of Job and reaches similar conclusions—that nothing can really be clarified and that salvation remains by grace alone—though he maintains that *Mercy* is designed to reach a firmer conclusion. From a more orthodox standpoint, Heyward Brock (191) maintains that the play makes God ridiculously human in order to satirize man's absurd questioning of God. Thus, God's statement that he was showing off to the devil shows the absurdity of pursuing reasons in God, and the photograph at the play's end gives God, the devil, and humans a similar status and thereby reinforces the play's inconclusiveness (191:143).

Peter J. Stanlis (198) makes a similar claim that the play satirizes modern man's Faustian confidence in human reason, but Stanlis sees God's excuse that he was showing off to the Devil not as a sign of an absurd view of God but rather as an expression of the notion that the Devil is God's best inspiration—a notion made explicit by Thyatira and one that presumably assumes the necessity of a world of both good and evil whose principles remain hard to understand. More mutedly, Reuben Brower declares that God must teach Job to accept the Devil as real (27:217). Brower also points out that in the Bible story, Job knew nothing of God's bargain with the Devil, and that as God's best inspiration the Devil is neglected by Protestant modernism, which Brower identifies as "that tendency" which Thyatira says the Devil needs to "come off."

Compared with the Book of Job, the tale of Jonah is very brief, and though it is philosophically less sophisticated, many of its nuances are hard to follow. Jonah was a Hebrew prophet whom the Lord bade go to preach in the sinful city of Nineveh. Not wanting to save the city from destruction, Jonah tried to flee aboard a ship headed to Tarshish, but when this ship was almost overwhelmed by a storm, its sailors detected Jonah as the cause of their trouble and cast him overboard. He was swallowed by a huge fish that God had called forth, and three days later he was cast up on the shore near Nineveh. Still loath to preach to the city, Jonah sheltered himself beneath a vine, which the Lord destroyed to demonstrate to Jonah both his power and the greater value of human life. Then Jonah preached to the sinners of Nineveh, the Lord mercifully spared them, and Jonah presumably remained resentful at God's showing mercy rather than justice. Some commentators think Jonah did not want to help save Nineveh because it was a foreign nation.

*A Masque of Mercy* is set in modern-day New York City, and its four characters are a strange combination of biblical and modern people. The protagonist is Jonah, here sometimes called Jonas Dove (for Jonah means "dove" in Hebrew). He is in flight from the Lord, who has again told him to preach to sinners lest they be destroyed. Jonah takes refuge in a bookstore that has just closed for the night, and within it he converses with the other three characters: Keeper (short for My Brother's Keeper), the bookstore owner, whose name reveals his attachment to mildly socialistic or at least very liberal principles like those of Roosevelt's New Deal; Jesse Bel, his neurotic and perhaps alcoholic wife, whose skepticism about faith and life in general makes her antagonistic to most of the serious views that are proposed and whose name associates her with the idolatrous wife of Ahab (a typically abandoned woman whose story is told in books 1 and 2 of Kings); and Paul, Jesse Bel's doctor or psychoanalyst, though he remains a pretty consistent spokesman for the views of the biblical Saint Paul, whom the other characters take him to represent or be.

The action, or rather argument, moves more slowly than that in *Reason*. Jonah indicates that he doesn't wish to preach against the "city evil," and Keeper twits him as if Jonah were an agrarian. Jesse Bel announces a major theme by regretting that Jonah's failure shows that "the saddest thing in life / Is that the best thing in it should be courage," a courage whose lack she shows in taking another drink. Jonah then announces his basic principle: "I can't trust God to be unmerciful." Paul points out that as a liberal and a Unitarian, Keeper sees God only as a symbol of human brotherhood, whereas he, Paul, pities Jonah and wants him to confront God's "mercy-justice contradiction," the solution to which he begins to describe by saying that justice matters little, a point he will later expand on. After some joking about Paul's being Jesse Bel's psychoanalyst (Frost ridicules the idea of love transference in the patient-psychoanalyst relationship), Jonah, Paul, and Keeper begin to debate the application of justice and mercy to politics, social relationships, and religious faith.

Paul prepares to explain to Jonah that perception of God's refusing to be unmerciful is the beginning of wisdom. Rather than comment on this, Keeper mocks Jonah by demanding how he wants to see New York punished. Jonah, denouncing New York for its hedonism (it has an underlying "Funday Fault"), looks forward if not to earthquakes at least to destructive economic confusions. The bookstore itself begins to shake, but just from passing trucks that knock books from the shelves, providing for jokes about studying St. Thomas. At this point, Jonah expresses views that oppose Keeper's faith in social amelioration and strongly parallel Frost's own conservatism. Jonah is worried that God's mercy will "take the punishment out of all failure / To be strong, careful, thrifty, diligent," all virtues that Frost's antiliberalism fears will be undermined by New Dealish measures. Keeper jokingly replies that "this modern lenience" began with fire insurance, which helped people spread their losses around, and this joking approach suggests that Frost is not wholly opposed to such strategies.

Beginning with this drama's most difficult pun, Paul offers a tentative reply to Keeper by alluding to the biblical Daniel, here called Dana Lyle, who reconciled science and prophecy and was skilled in interpreting dreams. Jonah begins looking at the Book of Daniel and, paralleling the writing on the wall at Belshazzar's feast, both improvises and interprets a dream that he seems to be reading. The gist of this dream is that the city's pretensions will destroy it, whereas more fundamental thoughts might have preserved it. But Jonah's continued anger seems to be answered by more falling books, by which God is trying to flush Jonah from his hiding place. Again, Jonah and Paul debate the merits of justice and mercy, and Paul declares that Jonah should be proud that his book of the Bible taught the necessity of mercy as a great prelude to the Gospels.

The subject shifts toward politics: Jonah fears that a racket in the streets is the beginning of a revolution. Jesse Bel points out that Paul's argument for mercy may force Keeper to admit that his liberal politics parallel Christianity and so demand that he accept it. Expressing Frost's conservatism in a humorously qualified fashion, Paul declares that a revolution that will take things from the rich is a form of injustice but perhaps a partly necessary one:

it is "intentional injustice. / It [is] their justice being mercy-crossed." But Keeper's views, Paul fears, will bring "an outbreak of mass mercy," which might homogenize mankind and thereby lower its level of accomplishment. Not quite certain how extreme are Keeper's views, Paul warns against outrage and violence promoting mercy (which looks like a version of communism). Paul agrees that justice must be crossed, but in asking if it should be "evil-crossed or mercy-crossed," he argues (along with Frost's now-moderating conservatism) that extremities must be avoided.

However, Keeper offers yet another alternative—that mercy be "star-crossed" (an allusion to the lovers of *Romeo and Juliet*). Jonah poignantly admits that he feared mercy-crossed would really be evil-crossed, a reminiscence of Paul's worries about homogenization. Keeper responds with almost vicious jokes, ridiculing Jonah by referring to cruel sacrifices of Mayan Indians, who thought their acts were holy, and implying both that lack of mercy is brutal and that modern people know better—but Keeper goes on to praise the perhaps moderate and pragmatic liberalism of Andrew Jackson. This passage makes a tangle of political oppositions and probably shows the formerly very conservative Frost coming to terms with the necessity of some liberal distributivism, as illustrated in his late-life declaration that he was getting used to the idea of more socialism for America and hopeful of the development of more democracy in Russia. Careful examination of speeches by Keeper, Jonah, and Paul shows a variety of ideas that Frost can approve of even as he remains aware and skeptical of the struggle to balance them.

But Paul will not abandon his religious position. Criticizing W. B. Yeats's stand against Christianity and praise of Greek ideals (hardly the equivalent of Keeper's views, however), Paul declares that "Christ came to introduce a break with logic" and was merciful to those who could not live up to the injunctions of the Sermon on the Mount. Keeper takes this as an attack on humanity's trying to solve its own problems (religion and humanism here become antagonists, paralleling conservatism and liberalism). But when all the characters have a quick look at the Sermon, Jesse Bel finds it "the same old nothing" (showing cynicism), Keeper sees it as "a beautiful impossibility" (implying the need for social rather than individual controls), and Paul finds it the only source of hope, for it shows that "mercy is only to the undeserving," which we all are. Paul's core idea here is that "failure is failure, but success is failure," implying that the best we can do is so little that we all need God's mercy. Keeper's reply that he would "rather be lost in the woods / Than found in church" strongly parallels Frost's nonsectarianism and open-mindedness about faith, but Keeper grows more serious in declaring that Paul approaches Christ through Rome—that is, through the rules of the church—whereas he approaches more through Palestine, or the vision of the prophets, who pursued both justice and mercy. Keeper refuses to see failure and success as of equal value, which goes along with Frost's conservative stance (he always favored discrimination between the accomplished and the unaccomplished).

Jonah has been holding back from this debate, and at this point both Paul and Keeper bid him exit not by the outer but by the cellar door, which Heyward Brock says represents complete faith and rejection of the self; the allusion to Martin Luther (made by Keeper) refers to Luther's discovery that "the just shall live by faith alone" in Hebrews 10.38 (191:147). Suggestion for this descent is followed by a variety of jokes. Jesse Bel sees the cellar as an empty place for pretense. Keeper jokes about Marx as a substitute savior, then about Old Testament martyrs, and then about the psychological pessimism of Jeffers and O'Neill, for whom the cellar would represent the dark unconscious. More seriously, Paul proposes the cellar as a place for Christian abnegation, where Jonah must lie before the crucifix. Jonah hesitates to enter and protests that if the always-erring or guilty human must depend on God's mercy, it is hard to tell why one should make efforts. As Jonah tries the door, it slams in his face and he falls to the floor. His last words indicate that by giving up his sense of justice he is losing his very identity, though in the end he asks for mercy for himself. The remaining characters all declare their fondness for Jonah, suggesting that he has acted out their dilemmas. Jesse Bel's "He was rejected for his reservations" suggests that she too would like to embrace the ideal of mercy. But Keeper has been affected by Jonah's sacrifice. He declares that if he had Jonah's prophetic ability, Jesse Bel would be forgiven, and in agreeing with her earlier judgment that courage is great, he suggests that Jonah perished because he lacked the courage to trust in mercy. The door swings threateningly again, suggesting some peril to Keeper, but Keeper maintains that he is not afraid of punishment for his sins. The fear he admits to is that he does not know if he has taken the right position about justice and mercy—that is, whether he has been "fighting on the angels' side"—and he admits that his uncertainty about his various choices has been so painful that it requires mercy from God.

In the play's last two speeches, Paul and Keeper strive for a full reconciliation. Paul agrees with Keeper's apprehensions about how God will judge his decisions, perceives Jonah's death as a sacrifice to this dilemma, and prays that his (and everyone's) "sacrifice / Be found acceptable in Heaven's sight." Keeper has the last words. He compares himself to Jonah in lacking the courage to overcome fear of judgment and so "go ahead to any accomplishment." He asks from "fellow feeling" to lay Jonah's body before the cross and, standing at Jonah's feet, concludes that "nothing can make injustice just but mercy." Thus, both Paul and Keeper end their final speeches with a prayer that their best efforts be accepted as making up for their deficiencies and that God's mercy ultimately balance out any injustice they have suffered. However, Paul's desire that the best we have to offer be found acceptable by Heaven stresses God's relation to the individual, whereas Keeper's plea that mercy make injustice just incorporates a plea for mutual responsibility among mankind.

Most but not all critics who compare these two dramas find *Mercy* more serious than *Reason*. An exception is Peter Stanlis, who finds a strong continuity through *Reason*'s discarding man's reason as a means to explain life's moral mystery and then *Mercy*'s affirming that God's love is the basis for hope and faith. Thus, for Stanlis, both plays stress the limitations of man's knowledge and the necessity of faith (198:465). Other critics differ in describing the central conflict in *Mercy*. Noam Flinker (195) thinks that the play centers on conflicts between Jonah's demand for justice and the contrasting and variant views of mercy by Paul and Keeper (Paul arguing for Christianity and Keeper for secular socialism), but with the arguments set up so that each reader must work out an individual position. Peter Stanlis finds Frost's views about equally divided between Keeper and Paul, but he regards Keeper's opting for a justice that is "star-crossed" rather than having to choose between one "mercy-crossed" or "evil-crossed" to be merely flippant (198:463), whereas D. Bradley Sullivan takes "star-crossed" to refer to a reality that cannot be reduced to black-and-white choices (197:319). Another interpretation might be that "star-crossed" refers to the necessity of accepting the immediate cruelties and kindnesses of fate.

Other critical differences center on the reason for, and significance of, Jonah's death. Taking a traditional stance, W. R. Irwin claims that Jonah dies contemplating the light of truth and that Jonah's willing death leads Keeper to acknowledge the fear of God and throw himself on God's mercy (194:310-11). This view is paralleled by Noam Flinker's that Jonah's contact with the cellar door shows that courage to overcome fear is impossible and thus that man's fear can only be eased by God's mercy (195:67). Reuben Brower identifies the cellar as "the Pauline catacomb of salvation" (27:222), which Jonah cannot enter because he understands too late the necessity to choose between justice "mercy-crossed" or "evil-crossed." But D. Bradley Sullivan argues that Jonah "dies because he fails to commit himself to either unforgiving extreme and because he cannot accept the fundamental uncertainty of Keeper's vision," which uncertainty persists to the play's end (197:320).

A conflation of these varying views lends strong credence to Frost's having played his own ideas out against one another throughout this drama, as they relate to his life-long conflict between feeling that on the one hand, it is bad to help other people too much (as liberals wish to do) and to feel guilty about not being constantly conscious of their sufferings, and feeling that on the other hand, it is bad not to take as charitable a view of others' suffering as one would want for oneself. Frost is also torn with conflicts about the meaning of his own deserts, as manifested in his own early lack of recognition as a writer and the terrible tragedies that had affected his family. He wondered not only what all these meant but how they were to be made up for by himself and God, and whether his accomplishments as a poet and a person would bring him mercy. Surely the final statements of both Paul and Keeper – "May my sacrifice / Be found acceptable in Heaven's sight," and "Nothing can make injustice just but mercy" – are Frost's prayer for his work and his life, as well as summary comment on those evils he saw as creative even while he suffered from them, such as the long-ago death in war of his dear friend Edward Thomas.

# Bibliography

## Bibliographies

1. Greiner, Donald J. *Robert Frost: The Poet and His Critics*. Chicago: American Library Association, 1974.
2. Lentricchia, Frank, and M. L. Lentricchia. *Robert Frost: A Bibliography, 1913-1974*. Metuchen, N.J.: Scarecrow Press, 1976.
3. Van Egmond, Peter. *The Critical Reception of Robert Frost*. Boston: G. K. Hall & Co., 1974.

## Poetry Collections by Frost

4. *Complete Poems of Robert Frost*. New York: Henry Holt, 1949.
5. *In the Clearing*. New York: Holt, Rinehart and Winston, 1962.
6. *The Poetry of Robert Frost*. Ed. Edward Connery Lathem. New York: Holt, Rinehart and Winston, 1969.
7. *Robert Frost: Poetry and Prose*. Ed. Edward C. Lathem and Lawrance Thompson. New York: Holt, Rinehart and Winston, 1972.
8. *Robert Frost's Poems*. Ed. Louis Untermeyer. New York: Washington Square Press, 1982.
9. *Selected Poems*. Introduction by Robert Graves. Holt, Rinehart and Winston, 1961.

## Letters, Interviews, and Prose

10. Cook, Reginald. *Robert Frost: A Living Voice*. Amherst: University of Massachusetts Press, 1974.
11. Frost, Robert. *Robert Frost on Writing*. Ed. Elaine Barry. New Brunswick, N.J.: Rutgers University Press, 1973.

12. ____. *Selected Letters.* Ed. Lawrance Thompson. New York: Holt, Rinehart and Winston, 1964.

13. ____. *Selected Prose.* Ed. Hyde Cox and Edward Connery Lathem. New York: Holt, Rinehart and Winston, 1966.

14. ____. *The Letters of Robert Frost to Louis Untermeyer.* Ed. Louis Untermeyer. New York: Holt, Rinehart and Winston, 1963.

15. Lathem, Edward Connery, Ed. *Interviews with Robert Frost.* New York: Holt, Rinehart and Winston, 1963.

## Biographies

16. Burnshaw, Stanley. *Robert Frost Himself.* New York: George Braziller, 1986.

17. Mertins, Louis. *Robert Frost: Life and Talks Walking.* Norman: University of Oklahoma Press, 1965.

18. Pritchard, William. *Frost: A Literary Life Reconsidered.* New York: Oxford University Press, 1984.

19. Sergeant, Elizabeth Shepley. *Robert Frost: The Trial By Existence.* New York: Holt, Rinehart and Winston, 1960.

20. Thompson, Lawrance. *Robert Frost: The Early Years, 1874-1915.* New York: Holt, Rinehart and Winston, 1966.

21. ____. *Robert Frost: The Years of Triumph, 1915-1938.* New York: Holt, Rinehart and Winston, 1970.

22. ____ and R. H. Winnick. *Robert Frost: The Later Years, 1938-1963.* New York: Holt, Rinehart and Winston, 1976.

23. ____. *Robert Frost: A Biography.* New York: Holt, Rinehart and Winston, 1981.

24. Walsh, John Evangelist. *Into My Own: The English Years of Robert Frost, 1912-1915.* New York: Grove Press, 1988.

## Critical Books

25. Barry, Elaine. *Robert Frost.* New York: Frederick Ungar, 1973.

26. Borroff, Marie. *Language and the Poet: Verbal Artistry in Frost, Stevens, and Moore.* Chicago: University of Chicago Press, 1979.

27. Brower, Reuben. *The Poetry of Robert Frost: Constellations of Intention.* New York: Oxford University Press, 1963.

28. Cook, Reginald. *The Dimensions of Robert Frost.* New York: Henry Holt, 1958.

29. Doyle, John R., Jr. *The Poetry of Robert Frost.* New York: Hafner, 1962.

30. Gerber, Philip L. *Robert Frost,* Rev. ed. Boston: Twayne Publishers, 1982.

31. Hadas, Rachel. *Form, Cycle, Infinity: Landscape Imagery in the Poetry of Robert Frost and George Seferis.* Lewisburg, Pa.: Bucknell University Press, 1985.

32. Hall, Dorothy Judd. *Robert Frost: Contours of Belief.* Athens: Ohio University Press, 1984.

33. Holland, Norman N. *The Brain of Robert Frost.* New York and London: Routledge, Chapman & Hall, 1988.

34. Isaacs, Elizabeth. *An Introduction to Robert Frost.* Denver: Alan Swallow, 1962.

35. Jennings, Elizabeth. *Frost.* Edinburgh and London: Oliver and Boyd, 1964.

36. Kemp, John C. *Robert Frost and New England.* Princeton, N.J.: Princeton University Press, 1979.

37. Lentricchia, Frank. *Robert Frost: Modern Poetics and the Landscape of Self.* Durham, N.C.: Duke University Press, 1975.

38. Lynen, John F. *The Pastoral Art of Robert Frost.* New Haven, Conn.: Yale University Press, 1960.

39. Monteiro, George. *Robert Frost and the New England Renaissance.* Lexington: The University Press of Kentucky, 1988.

40. Munson, Gorham B. *Robert Frost: A Study in Sensibility and Good Sense.* New York: George H. Doran, 1927.

41. Nitchie, George W. *Human Values in the Poetry of Robert Frost.* Durham, N.C.: Duke University Press, 1960.

42. Poirier, Richard. *Robert Frost: The Work of Knowing.* New York: Oxford University Press, 1977.

43. Potter, James L. *Robert Frost Handbook.* University Park: Pennsylvania State University Press, 1980.

44. Sharma, T. R. S. *Robert Frost's Poetic Style.* Atlantic Highlands, N.J.: Humanities Press, 1981.

45. Squires, Radcliffe. *The Major Themes of Robert Frost.* Ann Arbor: University of Michigan Press, 1963.

46. Thompson, Lawrance. *Fire and Ice: The Art and Thought of Robert Frost.* New York: Henry Holt, 1942.

47. _____. *Robert Frost.* Minneapolis: University of Minnesota Press, 1959.

## Collections of Critical Essays

48. Cox, James M., ed. *Robert Frost: A Collection of Critical Essays.* Englewood Cliffs, N.J.: Prentice Hall, 1962.

49. Gerber, Philip L., ed. *Critical Essays on Robert Frost.* Boston: G. K. Hall & Co., 1982.

50. Greenberg, Robert A., and James G. Hepburn, eds. *Robert Frost: An Introduction.* New York: Holt, Rinehart and Winston, 1961.

51. Harris, Kathryn Gibbs, ed. *Robert Frost: Studies in the Poetry.* Boston: G. K. Hall & Co., 1979.

52. Kuzma, Greg, ed. *Gone Into if Not Explained: Essays on Poems by Robert Frost.* Crete, Nebraska: The Best Cellar Press, 1976.

53. Tharpe, Jac L., ed. *Frost: Centennial Essays.* Jackson: University Press of Mississippi, 1974.

54. _____. *Frost: Centennial Essays II.* Jackson: University Press of Mississippi, 1976.

55. _____. *Frost: Centennial Essays III.* Jackson: University Press of Mississippi, 1978.

56. Thornton, Richard, ed. *Recognition of Robert Frost.* New York: Henry Holt, 1937.

57. Wagner, Linda W., ed. *Robert Frost: The Critical Reception.* New York: Burt Franklin, 1977.

58. Wilcox, Earl J., ed. *Robert Frost: The Man and the Poet.* Rock Hill, S.C.: Winthrop Studies on Major Modern Writers, 1981.

## General Critical Articles and Chapters in Books

59. Abel, Darrel. "'Unfriendly Nature' in the Poetry of Robert Frost." *Colby Library Quarterly* 17 (1981): 201-10.

60. Auden, W. H. "Robert Frost." In *The Dyer's Hand,* 337-53. New York: Random House, 1962.

61. Bacon, Helen. "In- and Outdoor Schooling: Robert Frost and the Classics." *American Scholar* 43 (1974): 640-47.

62. Bartini, Arnold G. "Robert Frost and Moral Neutrality." *CEA Critic* 38 (1976): 22-24.

63. Bass, Eben. "Frost's Poetry of Fear." *American Literature* 63 (1972): 603-15.

64. Baym, Nina. "An Approach to Robert Frost's Nature Poetry." *American Quarterly* 17 (1965): 713-23.

65. Berger, Harry, Jr. "Poetry as Revision: Interpreting Robert Frost." *Criticism* 10 (1968): 1-22.

66. Berkelman, Robert G. "Robert Frost and the Middle Way." *College English* 3 (1942): 347-53.

67. Bogan, Louise. "Robert Frost." In *Major Writers of America,* Vol. 2., ed. Perry Miller, 643-53. New York: Harcourt, Brace & World, 1962.

68. Carlson, Eric W. "Robert Frost on 'Vocal Imagination, the Merger of Form and Content." *American Literature* 33 (1962): 519-22.

69. Chabot, C. Barry. "The 'Melancholy Dualism' of Robert Frost." *Review of Existential Psychology and Psychiatry* 13 (1974): 42-56.

70. Childs, Kenneth W. "Reality in Some of the Writings of Robert Frost and Williams James." *Utah Academy of Sciences, Arts and Letters* 44 (1967): 150-58.

71. Cook, Marjorie E. "Dilemmas of Interpretation: Ambiguities and Practicalities." See no. 58, 125-41.

72. _____. "The Serious Play of Interpretation." *South Carolina Review* 15 (1973): 77-87.

73. _____. "Acceptance in Frost's Poetry: Conflict as Play." See no. 54, 223-35.

74. Cook, Reginald L. "Emerson and Frost: A Parallel of Seers." *New England Quarterly* 31 (1958): 200-217.

75. _____. "Frost as Parablist." *Accent* (1949): 33-41.

76. _____. "Frost on Frost: The Making of Poems." *American Literature* 28 (1956): 62-72.

77. _____. "Robert Frost: An Equilibrist's Field of Vision." *Massachusetts Review* 15 (1974): 385-401.

78. _____. "Robert Frost's Constellated Sky." *Western Humanities Review* 22 (1968): 189-98.

79. Cox, James M. "Robert Frost and the Edge of the Clearing." *Virginia Quarterly Review* 35 (1959): 73-88.

80. Dabbs, J. McBride. "Robert Frost and the Dark Woods." *Yale Review* 23 (1934): 514-20.

81. Donoghue, Denis. "A Mode of Communication: Frost and the 'Middle' Style." *Yale Review* 52 (1963): 205-19.

82. Dendinger, Lloyd N. "The Irrational Appeal of Frost's Dark Deep Woods." *Southern Review,* n.s., 2 (1966): 822-29.

83. _____. "Robert Frost: The Popular and the Central Poetic Images." *American Quarterly* 21 (1969): 792-804.

84. Eberhart, Richard. "Robert Frost: His Personality." *Southern Review,* n.s., 2 (1966): 762-88.

85. Fleissner, Robert F. "Like 'Pythagoras' Comparison of the Universe with Number': A Frost-Tennyson Comparison." See no. 53, 205-19.

86. Foster, Richard. "Leaves Compared with Flowers: A Reading of Robert Frost's Poems." *New England Quarterly* 46 (1973): 402-23.

87. Gelpi, Albert. "Robert Frost and John Crowe Ransom: Diptych of Ironists, the Woodsman and the Chevalier." In *A Coherent Splendor: The American Poetic Renaissance, 1910-1950,* 8-33. Berkeley: University of California Press, 1987.

88. Greiner, Donald J. "Robert Frost's Dark Woods and the Function of Metaphor." See no. 53: 373-88.

89. Griffith, Clark. "Frost and the American View of Nature." *American Quarterly* 20 (1968): 21-37.

90. Hart, Jeffrey. "Frost and Eliot." *Sewanee Review* 84 (1976): 417-47.

91. Hartsock, Mildred E. "Robert Frost: Poet of Risk." *Personalist* 45 (1964): 157-75.

92. Haymes, Donald T. "The Narrative Unity of *A Boy's Will.*" *PMLA* 87 (1972): 452-64.

93. Hopkins, Vivian. "Robert Frost: Out Far and In Deep." *Western Humanities Review* 14 (1960): 247-63.

94. Howarth, Herbert. "Frost in a Period Setting." *Southern Review,* n.s., 2 (1966): 789-99.

95. Huston, J. Dennis. "'The Wonder of Unexpected Supply': Robert Frost and a Poetry Beyond Confusion." *Centennial Review* 13 (1969): 317-29.

96. Irwin, W. R. "Robert Frost and the Comic Spirit." *American Literature* 35 (1963): 299-310.

97. Jarrell, Randall. "The Other Frost." *Poetry and the Age.* New York: Farrar, Straus & Giroux, 1953, 28-36.

98. ____. "To the Laodiceans." *Poetry and the Age.* New York: Farrar, Straus & Giroux, 1953, 37-69.

99. Juhnke, Anna K. "Religion in Robert Frost's Poetry: The Play for Self-Possession." *American Literature* 36 (1964): 153-64.

100. Kantak, V. Y. "Poetic Ambiguity in Frost." *Western Humanities Review* 28 (1974): 31-46.

101. Lasser, Michael L. "The Loneliness of Robert Frost." *Literary Review* 3 (1959-1960): 287-97.

102. Lentricchia, Frank. "Robert Frost: The Aesthetics of Voice and the Theory of Poetry." *Criticism* 15 (1973): 28-47.

103. Lieber, Todd M. "Robert Frost and Wallace Stevens: 'What to Make of a Diminished Thing.'" *American Literature* 47 (1975): 64-83.

104. Lindner, Carl M. "Robert Frost: Dark Romantic." *Arizona Quarterly* 29 (1973): 235-45.

105. McPhillips, Robert T. "Diverging and Converging Paths: Horizontal and Vertical Movement in Robert Frost's *Mountain Interval.*" *American Literature* 58 (1986): 82-98.

106. Miller, Lewis H., Jr. "The Poet as Swinger: Fact and Fancy in Robert Frost." *Criticism* 16 (1974): 58-72.

107. Monteiro, George. "Redemption through Nature: A Recurring Theme in Thoreau, Frost, and Richard Wilbur." *American Quarterly* 20 (1968): 795-809.

108. ____. "The Facts on Frost." *South Carolina Review* 22 (1989): 87-96.

109. Montgomery, Marion. "Robert Frost and His Use of Barriers: Man vs. Nature toward God" *South Atlantic Quarterly* 57 (1958): 339-53.

110. Morris, John. "The Poet as Philosopher: Robert Frost." *Michigan Quarterly Review* 11 (1972): 127-34.

111. Morrison, Theodore. "Frost: Country Poet and Cosmopolitan Poet." *Yale Review* 59 (1970): 179-96.

112. Mulder, William. "Freedom and Form: Robert Frost's Double Discipline." *South Atlantic Quarterly* 54 (1955): 386-93.

113. Munson, Gorham. "The Classicism of Robert Frost." *Modern Age* 7 (1964): 291-305.

114. Napier, John T. "'A Momentary Stay Against Confusion.'" *Virginia Quarterly Review* 33 (1957): 378-94.

115. Newdick, Robert S. "Robert Frost and the Sound of Sense." *American Literature* 9 (1937): 289-300.

116. O'Donnell, W. G. "Robert Frost and New England: A Revaluation." *Yale Review* 37 (1948): 698-712.

117. Oster, Judith. "The Figure a Marriage Makes." *South Carolina Review* 22 (1989): 109-19.

118. Perkins, David. "Robert Frost." In *A History of Modern Poetry: From the 1890's to the High Modernist Mode,* 227-51. Cambridge: Belknap Press of Harvard University Press, 1976.

119. ____. "Robert Frost and Romantic Irony." *South Carolina Review* 22 (1989): 33-37.

120. Perrine, Laurence. "Robert Frost and the Idea of Immortality." See no. 54, 85-98.

121. Pratt, Linda Ray. "Robert Frost and the Limits of Thought." *Arizona Quarterly* 36 (1980): 240-60.

122. Robson, W. W. "The Achievement of Robert Frost." *Southern Review,* n.s., 2 (1966): 735-61.

123. Ryan, Alvin S. "Frost and Emerson: Voice and Vision." *Massachusetts Review* 1 (1959): 5-23.

124. Sampley, Arthur M. "The Myth and the Quest: The Stature of Robert Frost." *South Atlantic Quarterly* 70 (1971): 287-98.

125. ____. "The Tensions of Robert Frost." *South Atlantic Quarterly* 65 (1966): 431-37.

126. Sasso, Laurence J., Jr. "Robert Frost: Love's Question." *New England Quarterly* 42 (1969): 95-107.

127. Sears, John F. "William James, Henry Bergson, and the Poetics of Robert Frost." *New England Quarterly* 48 (1975): 341-61.

128. Simpson, Claude M. "Robert Frost and Man's 'Royal Road.'" In *Aspects of American Poetry,* ed. Richard M. Ludwig, 121-47. Columbus: Ohio State University Press, 1962.

129. Swennes, Robert H. "Man and Wife: The Dialogue of Contraries in Robert Frost's Poetry." *American Literature* 42 (1970): 363-72.

130. Traschen, Isadore. "Robert Frost: Some Divisions in a Whole Man." *Yale Review* 55 (1965): 57-70.

131. Vander Ven, Tom. "Robert Frost's Dramatic Principle of 'Oversound.'" *American Literature* 45 (1973): 238-51.

132. Van Doren, Mark. "The Permanence of Robert Frost." *American Scholar* 2 (1936): 190-98.

133. Vinson, Robert S. "The Roads of Robert Frost." *Connecticut Review* 3 (April): 102-7.

134. Watkins, Floyd. "The Poetry of the Unsaid – Robert Frost's Narrative and Dramatic Poems." *Texas Quarterly* 15 (1972): 85-98.

135. ____. "Going and Coming Back: Robert Frost's Religious Poetry." *South Atlantic Quarterly* 73 (1974): 445-59.

136. Willige, Eckhart. "Formal Devices in Robert Frost's Short Poems." *Georgia Review* 15 (1961): 324-30.

137. Winters, Yvor. "Robert Frost: Or, The Spiritual Drifter as Poet." *Sewanee Review* 56 (1948): 564-96.

## Discussions of Individual Poems

"Acquainted with the Night"

138. Martin, Wallace. "Frost's 'Acquainted with the Night.'" *Explicator* 26 (1968): 64.

139. Perrine, Laurence. "Frost's 'Acquainted with the Night.'" *Explicator* 25 (1967): 50.

"After Apple-Picking"

140. Conder, John. "'After Apple-Picking': Frost's Troubled Sleep." See no. 53, 171-81.

141. Ferguson, Joe. "Frost's 'After Apple-Picking.'" *Explicator* 22 (1964): 53.

142. Fleissner, Robert F. "Frost as Ironist: 'After Apple-Picking' and the Pre-Autumnal Fall." *South Carolina Review* 21 (1988): 50-57.

143. Monteiro, George. "Frost's 'After Apple-Picking.'" *Explicator* 30 (1972): 62.

144. Scheele, Roy. "The Laborious Dream: Frost's 'After Apple-Picking.'" See no. 52, 147-53.

145. Stein, William B. "'After Apple-Picking': Echoic Parody." *University Review* 35 (1969): 301-5.

"Away"

146. Kau, Joseph. "Frost's 'Away!': Illusions and Allusions." *Notes on Modern American Literature* 7 (1983): 17.

"The Black Cottage"

147. Allen, Margaret V. "'The Black Cottage': Robert Frost and the Jeffersonian Ideal of Equality." See no. 53, 221-29.

"Blueberries"

148. Goede, William. "The 'Code Hero' in Frost's 'Blueberries.'" *Discourse* 11 (1968): 33-41.

"Bond and Free"

149. Marcus, Mordecai. "Robert Frost's 'Bond and Free': Structure and Meaning." *Concerning Poetry* 8 (1975): 61-63.

"Build Soil"

150. Classen, Jo-Marie. "Robert Frost's 'Build Soil': A Modern Text Based on an Ancient Mode, the Pastoral." *Theoria* (South Africa) 65 (1985): 1-13.

151. Perrine, Laurence. "The Meaning of Frost's 'Build Soil.'" See no. 53, 230-35.

"Come In"

152. Ornstein, Robert. "Frost's 'Come In.'" *Explicator* 15 (1957): 61.

"The Death of the Hired Man"

153. French, Warren. "'The Death of the Hired Man': Modernism and Transcendence." See no. 55, 382-401.

154. Marcus, Mordecai. "Motivation of Frost's Hired Man." *College Literature* 3 (1976): 63-68.

155. Vogel, Nancy. "Post Mortem on 'The Death of the Hired Man.'" See no. 53, 201-6.

156. Vogt, Victor E. "Narrative and Drama in the Lyric: Robert Frost's Strategic Withdrawal." *Critical Inquiry* 5 (1979): 529-51.

"Design"

157. Hiatt, David. "Frost's 'In White' and 'Design.'" *Explicator* 28 (1970): 41.

"Directive"

158. Blum, Margaret. "Robert Frost's 'Directive': A Theological Reading." *Modern Language Notes* 76 (1961): 524-25.

159. Briggs, Pearlanna. "Frost's 'Directive.'" *Explicator* 21 (1963): 71.

160. Clark, David. "An Excursus on the Criticism of Robert Frost's 'Directive.'" *Costerus* 8 (1972): 37-56.

161. ____. "'The Thatch' and 'Directive.'" In *Lyric Resonance,* 105-33. Amherst: University of Massachusetts Press, 1972.

162. Doyle, John Robert, "A Reading of Robert Frost's 'Directive.'" *Georgia Review* 22 (1968): 501-8.

163. Dougherty, James P. "Robert Frost's 'Directive' to the Wilderness." *American Quarterly* 18 (1966): 208-19.

164. Duvall, S. P. C. "Robert Frost's 'Directive' out of *Walden*." *American Literature* 31 (1960): 480-88.

165. Hartsock, Mildred. "Frost's 'Directive.'" *Explicator* 16 (1958): 42.

166. Peters, Robert. "The Truth of Frost's 'Directive.'" *Modern Language Notes* 75 (1960): 29-32.

"The Draft Horse"

167. Burrell, Paul. "Frost's 'The Draft Horse.'" *Explicator* 25 (1967): 60.

168. Gwynn, Frederick L. "Analysis and Synthesis of Frost's 'The Draft Horse.'" *College English* 26 (1964): 223-25.

169. Perrine, Laurence, and Margaret M. Blum. "Frost's 'The Draft Horse.'" *Explicator* 24 (1966): 79.

"Dust of Snow"

170. Knapp, Edgar H. "Frost's 'Dust of Snow.'" *Explicator* 28 (1969): 9.

171. Perrine, Laurence. "Frost's 'Dust of Snow.'" *Explicator* 29 (1971): 61.

"An Empty Threat"

172. Perrine, Laurence. "Frost's 'An Empty Threat.'" *Explicator* 30 (1972): 63.

"The Fear"

173. Perrine, Laurence. "Frost's 'The Fear': Unfinished Sentences, Unanswered Questions." *College Literature* 15 (1988): 199-207.

"For Once, Then, Something"

174. Hoffman, Dan G. "Frost's 'For Once, Then, Something.'" *Explicator* 9 (1950): 17.

"The Gift Outright"

175. Von Frank, Alfred J. "Frost's 'The Gift Outright.'" *Explicator* 38 (1979): 13.

"Ghost House"

176. Vail, Dennis. "Frost's 'Ghost House.'" *Explicator* 30 (1971): 11.

"The Gum-Gatherer"

177. Wilbur, Richard. "On Robert Frost's 'The Gum-Gatherer.'" See no. 52, 141-43.

"The Hill Wife"

178. Pratt, Linda Ray. "Prosody as Meaning in Frost's 'The Hill Wife.'" See no. 52, 97-109.

"Home Burial"

179. Jarrell, Randall. "Frost's 'Home Burial.'" In *The Third Book of Criticism*, 191-231. New York: Farrar, Straus & Giroux, 1965.

"How Hard It Is to Keep from Being King When It's in You and in the Situation"

180. Finnegan, Sister Mary Jeremy. "Frost Remakes an Ancient Story." See no. 53, 389-97.

"Iota Subscript"

181. Allen, Ward. "Robert Frost's 'Iota Subscript.'" *English Language Notes* 6 (1969): 285-87.

"Iris By Night"

182. Perrine, Laurence. "Frost's 'Iris By Night.'" *Concerning Poetry* 12 (1979): 35-43.

"I Will Sing You One-O"

183. Lynen, John F. "'I Will Sing You One-O.'" See no. 52, 163-70.

"Kitty Hawk"

184. Crane, Joan St. C. "Robert Frost's 'Kitty Hawk.'" *Studies in Bibliography* 30 (1977): 241-49.

185. Goldstein, Laurence. "'Kitty Hawk' and the Question of American Destiny." *Iowa Review* 9 (1978): 41-49.

"The Last Mowing"

186. Gierasch, Walter. "Frost's 'The Last Mowing'" *Explicator* 10 (1952): 25.

"The Lesson for Today"

187. Sutton, Betty S. "Form as Argument: Frost's 'Lesson for Today.'" *Fu Jen Studies* 18 (1985): 81-96.

"The Literate Farmer and the Planet Venus"

188. Schutz, Fred C. "Frost's 'The Literate Farmer and the Planet Venus': Why 1926?" *Notes on Contemporary Literature* 4 (1974): 8-10.

"The Lovely Shall Be Choosers"

189. Nitchie, Elizabeth. "Frost's 'The Lovely Shall Be Choosers.'" *Explicator* 13 (1955): 39.

190. Schwartz, Edward G. "Frost's 'The Lovely Shall Be Choosers.'" *Explicator* 13 (1954): 3.

*A Masque of Reason* and *A Masque of Mercy*

191. Brock, Heyward. "Robert Frost's Masques Reconsidered." *Renascence* 3 (1978): 137-51.

192. Finnegan, Sister Mary Jeremy. "Frost's *Masque of Mercy*." *Catholic World* 186 (1958): 357-61.

193. Gage, John T. "Rhetoric and Dialectic in Robert Frost's *A Masque of Reason*." *Pacific Coast Philology* 17 (1982): 82-91.

194. Irwin, W. R. "The Unity of Frost's Masques." *American Literature* 32 (1960): 302-12.

195. Flinker, Noam. "Robert Frost's Masques: The Genre and the Poems." *Papers on Language and Literature* 15 (1979): 59-72.

196. Perrine, Laurence. "A Set of Notes for Frost's Two Masques." *Resources for American Literary Study* 7 (1977): 125-33.

197. Sullivan, D. Bradley. "'Education by Poetry' in Robert Frost's Masques." *Papers on Language and Literature* 22 (1986): 312-21.

198. Stanlis, Peter J. "Robert Frost's Masques and the Classic American Tradition." See no. 53, 441-68.

"Mending Wall"

199. Broderick, John G. "Frost's 'Mending Wall.'" *Explicator* 14 (1956): 24.

200. Cunningham, Donald. "'Mending Wall.'" See no. 52, 67-73.

201. Dragland, S. L. "Frost's 'Mending Wall.'" *Explicator* (1967): 39.

202. Holland, Norman H. "The Unconscious of Literature: The Psychoanalytic Approach." *Contemporary Criticism* (London) *Stratford-Upon-Avon Studies in Literature* 12 (1970): 130-53.

203. Hunting, Robert. "Who Needs Mending?" *Western Humanities Review* 17 (1963): 88-89.

204. Jayne, Edward. "Up Against the Mending Wall: The Psychoanalysis of a Poem by Frost." *College English* 34 (1973): 934-51.

205. Marcus, Mordecai. "Psychoanalytic Approaches to 'Mending Wall.'" See no. 51, 179-90.

206. Monteiro, George. "Unlinked Myth in Frost's 'Mending Wall.'" *Concerning Poetry* 7 (1974): 10-12.

207. Watson, Charles N. "Frost's Wall: The View from the Other Side." *New England Quarterly* 44 (1971): 653-56.

"A Missive Missile"

208. Hancher, Michael. "Sermons in Stones." *Centrum* (Minnesota Center of Advanced Study) 2 (1974): 79-86.

"The Mountain"

209. Perrine, Laurence. "Frost's 'The Mountain': Concerning Poetry." *Concerning Poetry* 4 (1971): 5-11.

"Neither Out Far nor In Deep"

210. Lepore, D. J. "Robert Frost–The Middle-Ground: An Analysis of 'Neither Out Far Nor in Deep.'" *English Journal* 13 (1964): 215-16.

211. Pearlman, Daniel. "A Political Satire Unveiled: Frost's 'Neither Out Far nor In Deep.'" *Agenda* 17 (1979): 41-63.

212. Perrine, Laurence. "Frost's 'Neither Out Far nor In Deep.'" *Explicator* 7 (1949): 46.

"Never Against Would Birds' Song Be the Same"

213. Hollander, John. *Vision and Resonance.* 2d ed., New Haven, Conn.: Yale University Press, 1985, 41-43.

"New Hampshire"

214. Gaylord, Alan T. "The Imaginary State of 'New Hampshire.'" See no. 52, 7-52.

"Not All There"

215. Fleissner, Robert F. "Frost's 'Not All There.'" *Explicator* 31 (1973): 33.

"Nothing Gold Can Stay"

216. Anderson, Charles R. "Frost's 'Nothing Gold Can Stay.'" *Explicator* 22 (1964): 63.

217. Quinn, Sister M. Bernetta. "Symbolic Landscape in Frost's 'Nothing Gold Can Stay.'" *English Journal* 55 (1966): 621-24.

218. Rea, John A. "Language and Form in 'Nothing Gold Can Stay.'" See no. 51, 17-25.

"Once By the Pacific"

219. Van Doren, Mark. *Introduction to Poetry.* New York: William Sloane, 1951, 77-80.

"One More Brevity"

220. Bacon, Helen H. "The Contemporary Reader and Robert Frost: The Heavenly Guest of 'One More Brevity' and *Aeneid* 8.'" *St. Johns Review* 32 (1981): 3-10.

"Our Doom to Bloom'"

221. Rosen, Kenneth. "Visions and Revisions: An Early Version of Robert Frost's 'Our Doom to Bloom.'" See no. 53, 369-72.

"'Out, Out –'"

222. Doxey, Williams S. "Frost's 'Out, Out.'" *Explicator* 29 (April 1971): 70.

223. Henderson, Archibald. "Robert Frost's 'Out, Out.'" *American Imago* 34 (1977): 12-27.

224. Thornton, Weldon. "Frost's 'Out, Out.'" *Explicator* 25 (May 1967): 71.

"The Oven Bird"

225. Bock, Martin. "Frost's 'The Oven Bird' and the Modern Poetic Idiom." *Texas Review* 7 (1986): 28-31.

226. Herndon, Jerry A. "Frost's 'The Oven Bird.'" *Explicator* 28 (1970): 64.

227. Monteiro, George. "Robert Frost's Solitary Singer." *The New England Quarterly* 44 (1971): 134-40.

228. Osborne, William. "Frost's 'The Oven Bird.'" *Explicator* 26 (1968): 47.

229. Rotella, Guy. "Metaphor in Frost's 'Oven Bird.'" See no. 58, 19-27.

230. Van Doren, Mark. *Introduction to Poetry.* New York: William Sloane, 1951, 73-77.

"An Old Man's Winter Night"

231. Davis, Charles G. "Frost's 'An Old Man's Winter Night.'" *Explicator* 27 (1968): 19.

"The Pasture"

232. Freedman, William. "Frost's 'The Pasture.'" *Explicator* 29 (1971): 80.

233. Oehlschlaeger, Fritz. "Robert Frost's 'The Pasture': A Reconsideration." *Concerning Poetry* 16 (1983): 1-9.

234. Rosenthal, M. L. *Poetry and the Common Life.* New York: Oxford University Press, 1974, 11.

"Paul's Wife"

235. Benoit, Raymond. "Folklore by Frost: 'Paul's Wife.'" *Notes on Modern American Literature* 5 (1981): 22.

236. DeFalco, Joseph M. "Frost's 'Paul's Wife': The Death of an Ideal." *Southern Folklore Quarterly* 29 (1965): 259-65.

"The Pauper Witch of Grafton" (*see* "Two Witches")

"The Peaceful Shepherd"

237. Vail, Dennis. "Point of View in Frost's 'The Peaceful Shepherd.'" *Notes on Contemporary Literature* 5 (1974): 2-4.

"Pod of the Milkweed"

238. Perrine, Laurence. "Frost's 'Pod of the Milkweed.'" *Notes on Modern American Literature* 5 (1980): 5.

"Provide, Provide"

239. Kumin, Maxine. "A Note on 'Provide, Provide.'" See no. 52, 63-64.

240. Perrine, Laurence. "Robert Frost's 'Provide, Provide.'" *Notes on Modern American Literature* 8 (1981): 5.

"Putting in the Seed"

241. Barnes, Daniel R. "Frost's 'Putting in the Seed.'" *Explicator* 31 (1973): 59.

"Range-Finding"

242. Mansell, Darrel Jr. "Frost's 'Range Finding.'" *Explicator* 24 (1966): 63.

"The Road Not Taken"

243. Fleissner, Robert F. "A Road Taken: The Romantically Different *Ruelle*." See no. 51, 117-31.

244. Griffiths, Ben W. "Frost's 'The Road Not Taken.'" *Explicator* 12 (1954): 55.

245. Hall, Ted. "A Note on 'The Road Not Taken.'" See no. 52, 137-38.

246. Malbone, R. G. "Frost's 'The Road Not Taken.'" *Explicator* 24 (1965): 27.

247. Mood, John J. L. "Frost's Dark Road—A Pedagogical Inquiry." *Rendezvous* 10 (1975): 11-14.

248. Perrine, Laurence, and Eleanor M. Sickels. "Frost's 'The Road Not Taken.'" *Explicator* 19 (1961): 28.

"The Rose Family"

249. Fleissner, Robert F. "Sub Rosa: Frost's 'Five-Petaled' Flower." *Colby Library Quarterly* 20 (1984): 207-11.

250. Perrine, Laurence. "Frost's 'The Rose Family.'" *Explicator* 26 (1968): 43.

"Sand Dunes"

251. Perrine, Laurence. "Frost's 'Sand Dunes.'" *Explicator* 14 (1956): 38.

"The Self-Seeker"

252. Perrine, Laurence. "The Sense of Frost's 'The Self-Seeker.'" *Concerning Poetry* 7 (1974): 5-8.

"A Servant to Servants"

253. Jones, Donald. "Kindred Entanglements in Frost's 'A Servant to Servants.'" *Papers on Language and Literature* 2 (1966): 150-61.

254. James, Stuart B. "The Home's Tyranny: Robert Frost's 'A Servant to Servants' and Andrew Wyeth's 'Christina's World.'" *South Dakota Review* 1 (1964): 3-15.

255. Rooke, Constance. "The Elusive/Allusive Voice: An Interpretation of Frost's 'A Servant to Servants.'" *Cimmaron Review* No. 38 (1977): 13-23.

"The Silken Tent"

256. Gierasch, Walter. "Frost's 'The Silken Tent.'" *Explicator* 30 (1971): 10.

"Skeptic"

257. Sanders, Charles. "Frost's 'Skeptic.'" *Explicator* 40 (1982): 47-48.

"Spring Pools"

258. Combellack, C. R. B. 'Frost's 'Spring Pools.'" *Explicator* 30 (1971): 27.

259. Coxe, Louis O. "Frost's 'Spring Pools.'" See no. 52, 157-59.

260. Scheele, Roy. "Source and Resource: A Stylistic Note on Frost's 'Spring Pools.'" *Papers on Language and Literature* 15 (1979): 316-19.

261. Toor, David. "Frost's 'Spring Pools.'" *Explicator* 28 (1969): 28.

"The Star-Splitter"

262. Waddell, William S., Jr. "By Precept and Example: Aphorism in 'The Star-Splitter.'" See no. 58, 115-24.

"Stopping by Woods on a Snowy Evening"

263. Armstrong, James. "The 'Death Wish' in 'Stopping by Woods.'" *College English* 25 (1964): 440-45.

264. Ciardi, John. "Robert Frost: The Way to the Poem." *Saturday Review of Literature* 41 (1958): 13-15, 65.

265. Elkins, Bill J. "The Spiritual Crisis in 'Stopping by Woods.'" *Cresset* 35 (1972): 6-8.

266. Shurr, William. "Once More to the Woods: A New Point of Entry into Frost's Most Famous Poem." *New England Quarterly* 47 (1974): 584-94.

267. Wilcox, Earl. "Frost's 'Stopping by Woods.'" *Explicator* 27 (1968): 7.

"The Subverted Flower"

268. Munford, Howard. "Frost's 'The Subverted Flower.'" *Explicator* 17 (1959): 31.

269. Morse, Stearns. "'The Subverted Flower': An Exercise in Triangulation." See no. 55, 170-76.

270. Scheele, Roy. "Sensible Confusion in Frost's 'The Subverted Flower.'" *South Carolina Review* 10 (1977): 89-98.

271. Stauffer, Donald B. "Frost's 'The Subverted Flower.'" *Explicator* 15 (1957): 38.

272. Storch, Margaret. "Robert Frost's 'The Subverted Flower.'" *American Imago* 43 (1986): 297-305.

273. Weltman, Sharon Aronofsky. "The Least of It: Metaphor, Metamorphosis, and Synechdoche in Frost's 'The Subverted Flower.'" *South Carolina Review* 22 (1989): 71-78.

"The Thatch" (*see* note 161).

"To Earthward"

274. Scott, Wilbur S. "Frost's 'To Earthward.'" *Explicator* 16 (1958): 23.

"To the Thawing Wind"

275. Stillians, Bruce. "Frost's 'To the Thawing Wind.'" *Explicator* 31 (1972): 31.

"Two Tramps in Mud Time"

276. Braverman, Albert and Bernard Einbond. "Frost's 'Two Tramps in Mud Time.'" *Explicator* 29 (1970): 25.

277. Kaplan, Charles. "Frost's 'Two Tramps in Mud Time.'" *Explicator* 12 (1954): 51.

278. Narveson, Robert. "'Two Tramps in Mud Time': Thoreau versus 'Poor Richard.'" See no. 52, 83-94.

279. Perrine, Laurence. "'Two Tramps in Mud Time' and the Critics." *American Literature* 44 (1973): 671-76.

"Two Witches"

280. Briggs, Christine. "The Dramatic Monologue in Robert Frost's 'The Pauper Witch of Grafton.'" *Ball State University Forum* 21 (1980): 48-53.

281. Marcus, Mordecai. "The Whole Pattern of Robert Frost's 'Two Witches': Contrasting Psycho-Sexual Modes." *Literature and Psychology* 26 (1976): 69-78.

282. Slights, Camille, and William Slights. "Frost's 'The Witch of Coös.'" *Explicator* 27 (1969): 40.

"The Vanishing Red"

283. Meredith, William. "A Fratricide: Robert Frost's 'The Vanishing Red.'" See no. 52, 77-80.

"The Vindictives"

284. Linebarger, J. M. "Sources of Frost's 'The Vindictives.'" *American Notes and Queries* 12 (1974): 150-54.

"West-Running Brook"

285. Doyle, John Robert. *Sources of "West-Running Brook."* Charleston, South Carolina: The Citadel Monograph Series, 1974.

286. Morrow, Patrick. "The Greek Nexus in Robert Frost's 'West-Running Brook.'" *Personalist* 49 (1968): 24-33.

287. Webster, H. T. "Frost's 'West-Running Brook.'" *Explicator* 8 (1950): 32.

"The White-Tailed Hornet"

288. Perrine, Laurence. "A House for Frost's 'White-Tailed Hornet.'" *Notes on Contemporary Literature* 10 (1980): 3.

"Wild Grapes"

289. Bacon, Helen. "For Girls: from 'Birches' to 'Wild Grapes.'" *Yale Review* 67 (1977): 13-29.

"The Wind and the Rain"

290. Pritchard, William. "Bearing Witness: 'The Wind and the Rain.'" See no. 52, 129-34.

"The Witch of Coös" (*see* "Two Witches")

"A Witness Tree"

291. Ryan, Alvin S. "Frost's 'A Witness Tree.'" *Explicator* 7 (1949): 34.

"The Wood-Pile"

292. Bishop, Ferman. "Frost's 'The Wood-Pile.'" *Explicator* 18 (1960): 58.

293. Narveson, Robert. "On Frost's 'The Wood-Pile.'" *English Journal* 57 (1968): 39-40.

# Index to Poems

References to main explications are in italics.

# Index of Critics

## The Author

Mordecai Marcus, professor of English at the University of Nebraska-Lincoln, holds degrees from Brooklyn College, New York University, and the University of Kansas. He has taught at Rutgers, Kansas, and Purdue Universities and has been at Nebraska since 1965. His critical articles on a wide range of writers have appeared in many scholarly journals, and a number of these have been reprinted in anthologies. His poems have also been widely published and have been collected in five chapbooks.